CONTEMPORARIES *of*
MARCO POLO

IN THE POWER OF THE ETERNAL
HEAVEN, THE ORDER OF THE
OCEANIC KHAN OF THE PEOPLE OF
THE GREAT MONGOLS. THE CON-
QUERED PEOPLE MUST RESPECT
IT AND FEAR THEM

CONTEMPORARIES OF MARCO POLO

Consisting of the Travel Records to the Eastern Parts of the World of William of Rubruck [1253-1255]; *The Journey of* John of Pian de Carpini [1245-1247]; *The Journal of* Friar Odoric [1318-1330] *& The Oriental Travels of* Rabbi Benjamin *of* Tudela [1160-1173]

Edited by MANUEL KOMROFF

DORSET PRESS • NEW YORK

This edition published by Dorset Press
a division of Marlboro Books Corporation.
1989 Dorset Press

ISBN 0-88029-438-8

Printed in the United States of America

M 9 8 7 6 5 4 3 2 1

THE TEXTS

The text of Friar John of Pian de Carpini was edited by a comparison of the old English text of Richard Hakluyt (first printed in London, 1589) with the various texts edited by Beazley and printed for the Hakluyt Society, London, 1903, as well as the translation by William Rockhill printed for the Hakluyt Society in 1900.

The first part of The Journey of Friar William of Rubruck was done from *Hakluyt's Voyages* and the volume by Beazley entitled *The Texts and Versions of John de Plano Carpini and William de Rubruquis*, printed for the Hakluyt Society, 1903. But neither of these is complete. The second half of Rubruck was translated from *Guillaume de Rubrouck* by Louis de Backer and the entire text compared with that of William Rockhill: *The Journey of William of Rubruck to the Eastern Parts of the World;* Hakluyt Society, 1900.

The Journal of Friar Odoric was edited from the text first published in *Hakluyt's Voyages* and compared with the text translated by Sir Henry Yule and edited by Henri Cordier, as printed in *Cathay and the Way Thither*, Vol. II, Hakluyt Society, 1913-6.

The Travels of Rabbi Benjamin of Tudela were prepared from the text edited by Thomas Wright and published in *Early Travels in Palestine*, Bohn Library, 1848.

Other volumes used for reference are listed in the bibliography printed at the end of this volume.

ACKNOWLEDGMENTS

The works and notes of the distinguished American scholar and diplomat, William W. Rockhill, have contributed much to make this volume possible. Mr. Rockhill was born in 1854. He undertook two long journeys in the years 1888-1892 through China, Mongolia and Tibet. These he accomplished while disguised as a native. He also served the Department of State as Minister to Greece, Roumania, Servia, and in 1900 Minister to China. He was later Ambassador to Russia and Turkey. He died in 1914 while on his way to serve as adviser to the President of China and with his death America lost one of its most distinguished Oriental scholars. Some of his books are listed in the bibliography attached to this volume.

Special thanks are due to the officials of the Vatican for permission to work in their library, consult the archives and photograph documents. To Professor Gino Borghezio, of the Vatican Library, for his many kindnesses and also for his translations from original documents. To Hiram K. Moderwell and the office of the Chicago *Daily News* in Rome for their good services, and to Albert D. Lippman and Miss R. Seeman for aid with translations.

It was at the suggestion of Dr. Dawson Johnston, of the Library of Congress, that I prepared the bibliography contained in this volume. To this Harold Lamb suggested several additions. I have also to thank Miss Julie M. Eidesheim for the very serious task of proofreading and the preparation of a full index. And finally Herschel Brickell for his friendly encouragement.

M. K.

MARCO POLO was not the only traveller to journey to China. He was preceded by several travellers who visited the Mongol Courts and brought back to Mediæval Europe vivid records and detailed pictures of that strange Eastern civilization.

The conquering Mongols had already lost a good deal of their vitality when Marco Polo visited their last Great Khan, Kublai; the empire was already breaking up, degeneracy had set in and the silken lap of luxury had softened the warriors who descended directly from the great Chinghis Khan.

Between Chinghis and Kublai were three other Great Khans: Ogotay, Kuyuk and Mangu. It was the courts of these last two that Friar Carpini and Friar Rubruck visited. In their records they have left us an intimate and striking picture of this spectacular civilization which sprung from the steppes of Mongolia and was destined to conquer almost the whole of Asia and to sweep across a good part of Europe.

China went to Europe and opened the roads through which these travellers journeyed. But when the invading armies returned home and the western lands fell under the rule of Mongol princes, those roads were soon neglected and ever since that time have been closed. These roads, however, established by the invading forces, brought to Europe the first true accounts of the East.

How China Came to Europe

Chinghis Khan was already master of the greater part of Asia, the great empire of Turkey, its mosques, palaces, libraries and storehouses were plundered, its cities laid waste and ruined, the inhabitants slaughtered and the proud emperor Muhammad Shah a fugitive. The savage Mongol army sent out flying flanks with orders to follow Muhammad wherever he went and bring him back dead or alive. In disguise he fled to the shores of the Caspian and was about to take refuge on a small island but paused at a mosque long enough to read the prayers and reveal his identity. The Mongols were soon close behind, but Muhammad escaped in a boat and took refuge on an island, in the Caspian, where soon after he died in wretchedness and poverty.

The invading hordes marched north and around the Caspian in their search for the Emperor of the Turks. They carried fire and slaughter throughout entire Persia and at length came through the gorges of the Caucasus. In these campaigns Chinghis was aided by his sons, Ogotay, Tuluy and Chagatai.

The year following, Chinghis decided to return to his home lands in Mongolia by way of India and Tibet. This was in 1223. He reached his native land two years later after an absence of seven years.

But while Chinghis himself returned home, a greater part of his armies, under the leadership of his sons, remained in Persia and the Caucasus. At the foot of the hills they found a vast army of Kipchaks and Russians already assembled for defence. The Mongols at once retreated and allowed themselves to be pursued for twelve days. This stratagem scattered the attacking forces, who then soon fell victims to the ambushed Mongols. After a desperate battle lasting two days the Mongols defeated the Russian forces and entered European Russia.

Now the Russian princes assembled at Kiev and agreed to join forces against the common enemy. While the armies gathered on the shores of the Dnieper, the Mongols sent ten ambassadors to the Russian princes to open peaceful relations. The ten ambassadors were killed by the Russians, who at once opened their attack. The Mongols suffered several slight defeats but when their main army was brought into action they swept through the entire Russian forces, completely destroyed them, and followed those who escaped as far as the Dnieper. Here some of the Russian princes were captured and tied to planks upon which the Mongols sat to eat and drink and celebrate their victory. Fire, famine and slaughter followed.

Then for a time the war-like activities of the Mongols in the west subsided. Chinghis was occupied with the conquest of the Kin empire in Northern China and died in 1227. His son, Ogotay, succeeded him.

Ogotay Khan

The Kin dynasty was not fully overthrown until about ten years later and it was not until then that Ogotay Khan took up the conquests in the western countries begun by his father. Russian records tell us that the fierce Prince Batu, grandson of Chinghis and nephew of Ogotay, wintered with his army near the Volga in 1236-7, not far from the capital of the Bulgars, which he destroyed in the following autumn.

At the same time the Mongol troops were harried by bands of robbers on the banks of the river and Mangu, son of Tuluy, the brother of Ogotay, was ordered to build two hundred boats, each capable of holding a hundred men, and attack the river robbers. The opposite bank of the river and its adjacent forests were searched. The Mongols returned with much loot as well as the leader of the bands, who asked as a favour that he be killed by Mangu's own hand. Mangu, however, ordered his brother to cut the robber chief through the middle.

The frontiers of Russia, then bounded on the east by Bulgaria, were in turn attacked. Cities were plundered and destroyed. The Mongols cut roads through the forests wide enough to allow three carts to pass abreast and the walled cities were attacked with stone-throwing engines. We learn from Persian records that in order to count the dead resulting from one of these sieges, instructions were given to cut off the right ear from all corpses. The number thus found slain amounted to two hundred and seventy thousand. And still the Mongol horde pushed on, and at length attacked the ancient city of Kiev.

"Like dense clouds the Tartars (Mongols) pushed themselves forward towards Kiev, investing the city on all sides. The rattling of their innumerable carts, the bellowing of camels and cattle, the neighing of horses, and the wild battle-cry, were so overwhelming as to render inaudible the conversation of the people inside the city." [1] In spite of the resistance of the Russians, Kiev was captured and almost the entire population massacred. Prince Dmitry was taken prisoner but his life was spared by Batu. It is also recorded that Dmitry managed to persuade Batu to leave Russia and invade the rich country of Hungary.

The Mongols first appeared in Poland in the year 1240. The Polish army marched against them in the following year but were defeated. They plundered Galicia, the city

[1] From the Russian annals of Woskressensk. *History of Russia,* by Karamsin. Vol. IV.

of Krakow, they entered Silesia and crossed the river Oder.
It was during this time that a serious quarrel was said
to have occurred between the Mongol chiefs. Batu sent
an envoy to the emperor Ogotay Khan with the following
letter: "By the favour of Heaven and an auspicious fate,
O emperor, my uncle! the eleven nations have been subdued.
When the army had returned, a banquet was arranged, at
which all the (Mongol) princes were present. Being the
eldest, I drank one or two cups of wine before the others.
Buri and Kuyuk were incensed, left the banquet and mounted
their horses, at the same time abusing me. Buri said, 'Batu
is not superior to me; why did he drink before I drank?
He is an old woman with a beard. By a single kick I could
knock him down and crush him.' Kuyuk said, 'He is an old
woman with bow and arrows. I shall order him to be
thrashed with a stick.' Another proposed to fasten a wooden
tail to my body. Such is the language that was used by the
prince when, after the war with the different nations, we
had assembled to deliberate on important matters, and we
were obliged to break up without discussing the affairs.
Such is what I have to report, O emperor, my uncle." [2]

Ogotay Khan severely rebuked his son Kuyuk for his
conduct and gave orders that Buri should present himself to
his grandfather, who would hear his case and render judgment. For a short time this quarrel delayed attacks on
European cities. During the summer and autumn of 1241
the Mongols remaining in the plain of Hungary collected
their forces and prepared for a more extensive attack. In
the winter following, they sent troops over the frozen
Danube and destroyed the city of Gran. But a thaw set

[2] The account of this quarrel, as well as more detailed descriptions of the expeditions of
the Mongols to the West, will be found in *Mediæval Researches*, by E. Bretschneider.

in and the troops returned to the main army while the ice could still hold them.

But now the main army was retreating and the reason for this was that a courier had arrived bringing the news of the death of Ogotay Khan. The Mongol princes hurried home to Mongolia, leaving the western armies in charge of Batu.

The Popes and Kings of Europe

But in the meantime what was happening in Europe?

News of the invasion of Russia by the Mongols did not reach western Europe for many years. It was not until the second Mongol expedition in 1238 had carried slaughter and ruin over a good part of eastern Europe that Christendom suddenly awakened to the serious danger.

A mission from eastern Europe to the Kings of France and England asking for aid was entirely disregarded. The Bishop of Winchester standing beside Henry III of England, on hearing this mission exclaimed: "Let those dogs devour each other and be utterly wiped out, and then we shall see, founded on their ruins, the universal Catholic Church, and there shall truly be one shepherd and one flock."

But this mission brought to western Europe a terrible picture of the Mongols, whom they named "the Tartars." In these words were they described: "That the joys of mortal men be not enduring, nor worldly happiness long lasting without lamentations, in this same year (1240) a detestable nation of Satan, to wit, the countless army of the Tartars, broke loose from its mountain-environed home, and piercing the solid rocks (of the Caucasus), poured forth like devils from the Tartarus, so that they are rightly called

Tartari or Tartarians. Swarming like locusts over the face of the earth, they have brought terrible devastation to the eastern parts (of Europe), laying it waste with fire and carnage. After having passed through the land of the Saracens, they have razed cities, cut down forests, killed townspeople and peasants. If, perchance, they have spared any suppliants, they have forced them, reduced to the lowest condition of slavery, to fight in the foremost ranks against their own neighbours. Those who have feigned to fight, or have hidden in the hope of escaping, have been followed up by the Tartars and butchered. . . . For they are inhuman and beastly, rather monsters than men, thirsting for and drinking blood, tearing and devouring the flesh of dogs and men, dressed in ox-hides, armed with plates of iron, short and stout, thickset, strong, invincible, indefatigable, their backs unprotected (to prevent retreat), their breasts covered with ʾrmour; drinking with delight the pure blood of their flocks, with big, strong horses, which eat branches and even trees. . . . They are without human laws, know no comforts, are more ferocious than lions or bears, have boats made of ox-hides. . . . They have one-edged swords and daggers, are wonderful archers, spare neither age, nor sex, nor condition. . . . They wander about with their flocks, and their wives who are taught to fight like men." [3] This was the first real news that western Europe had of the Mongols.

So great was the fear of the Mongols at this time that people of Gothland and Friesland did not dare come to Yarmouth for the herring fishery, and because of this, it is recorded,[4] "the herrings were so cheap that forty or fifty sold for a piece of silver."

[3] Matthew Paris—*Chronica Majora*.
[4] William Rockhill—*The Journey of William of Rubruck*. Introduction.

Meanwhile the great Mongol general, Batu, entered Hungary and swept away the last barrier against an invasion of central and western Europe. The princes of European countries and the Pope were at this time bound up in petty wars, jealousies and intrigues. The many years of crusades had left Europe feeble and indifferent. And now when the Pope and Church and the princes attempted to unite against a common foe, they found themselves unable to organize an effective resistance. The Mongol horde was already encamped on European soil and it was too late to raise an opposing army.

Moreover, the Pope was more absorbed in his own quarrels involving Jerusalem and Constantinople than he was in the invasion of Russia and Hungary. But he did write a letter to the Queen of Georgia, sympathising with her misfortune and promising that those who took up the cross against the Mongols would have the same indulgences as if they had gone on a pilgrimage to the Holy Land. This was all that Pope Gregory IX ever did to check the Mongol invasion. He died in 1241. But in the same year Ogotay Khan, son of Chinghis, also died and the leaders of the Mongol forces returned to Mongolia to sit in council and elect their new ruler.

The death of Ogotay suddenly put an end to the invasion of Europe. What the outcome would have been if Ogotay had lived another year or two is a subject for speculation. Certainly Paris and Rome could, at this time, offer little defence. The religion of Christ and the Christian name might still have survived and not suffered complete extinction but it would certainly have been submerged for several centuries.

Innocent IV was elected Pope two years later and he at

once took steps to check the invasion already halted by the death of Ogotay. He sent missions to the pagan tribes of north-eastern Europe as well as to the Mongols to preach to them the fear of Divine wrath, as well as other aspects of Christianity, and at the same time he hoped to learn through these missionaries what the Mongols intended to do in Europe.

Encouraged by the results and under the belief that the enemy halted for fear of Divine wrath, for he knew nothing of the death of Ogotay Khan, he organized two missions to go direct to the Mongols. Friar John of Pian de Carpini, who at that time was in the monastery at Cologne, was sent on one of these missions. His narrative, recorded in this volume, gives a first-hand account of the manners and customs of this strange race of people. With letters from the Pope to the Emperor of the Mongols, he left Lyons several months before the sitting of the General Council, which was opened in June, 1245.

The Council was called to deliberate on the conflict between Emperor Frederick II and the Pope, as well as to find measures against heresy and the invading horde. It decided that, "whereas the Tartars are the most bitter enemies of the Christian name, and the Christians are still exposed to their attacks—for, not having conquered them all yet, as they in their desire to extinguish the religion of Christ wish to do, they will surely come back, and the horrors seen in Poland, Russia, Hungary, and other countries will be renewed." All Christian people were advised to block every road or passage by which the enemy could enter. The Church promised to contribute to the expense of these defences.

Kuyuk Khan

The Mongolian prince, Batu, sent Carpini with his letter from the Pope, across Persia, Tibet and China. By the time Carpini and his companion, Friar Benedict, arrived in Mongolia the Eastern princes were already assembled. Here the friars waited several months and were present at the enthroning of Kuyuk, the son of Ogotay. They presented their letter to Kuyuk Khan and received from him a reply which they brought back with them.

After a journey lasting about two years Carpini returned to Lyons and related the amazing events and hardships of his journey.

The letter to the Pope, written in Persian and to which was affixed the Mongol seal of the Khan Emperor, has recently been found in the Vatican Archives.[5] Many of the Oriental documents had been destroyed when the Vatican moved to Avignon (1309) but this one had fortunately been spared. It begins: "By the power of the eternal Heavens, we the oceanic Khan of the entire great people of the earth; our order. This is an order sent to the great Pope so that he may know it and understand it. . . . The petition of submission that you sent to us we have received through your ambassadors. If you act according to your own words, you who are the great Pope, with the kings, will come all together in person to render us homage and we will then have you learn our orders."

The letter then refers to the Pope's wish that Kuyuk be baptized and to the invasion of territories in Europe. Kuyuk states that he does not understand how things can be made right by his being baptized and, regarding the lands, they

---

[5] This seal, found on a separate page at the front of this volume, is reproduced by permission of the Vatican Library, who also allowed me to photograph the letter.

were invaded because the princes showed "themselves arrogant and have killed our envoy-ambassadors." The letter asks how by the order of God can a person use the force of God to kill and plunder.

This amazing document concludes with the following: "And if you say:—I am a Christian; I adore God; I scorn and (hate) the others,—then how shall you know whom God absolves and in whose favour He grants mercy, how know you when you speak such words? In the face of God, since the rising of the sun until its setting, all the territories have been granted us. Except by God's order how shall any one act? To-day you ought to say with all your heart: 'We will be (your) subjects; we will give you of our strength.' You in person, at the head of kings, all together, without exception, come and offer us service and homage. Then shall we recognise your submission. And if you do not observe the order of God and disobey our orders, we will know you as our enemies. That is what we make known to you. If you disobey, how should we know? God will know it. In the last days of jumada, the second of the year 644 (3-11 November, 1246)." [6]

Such was the nature of the reply of Kuyuk Khan to the Pope.

Friar Carpini, who visited the court of Kuyuk Khan, gives us a first-hand description of this Mongol ruler. His record is accurate and trustworthy. Kuyuk Khan ruled but a few years and was succeeded by his cousin, Mangu Khan, a son of Tuluy and grandson of the Great Chinghis.

Mangu Khan

The Mongol chiefs, descendants of the family of Chin-

[6] The letter was translated by the distinguished French scholar, Paul Pelliot, in collaboration with Professors Berghezio, Masse and Tisserant. It is reproduced, with comments, in *Revue de L'Orient Chrétien*, Vol. III, 1922-3, Nos. 1 and 2.

ghis, in western Asia were by this time practically independent of the Great Khan. They governed their states with complete sovereignty and made wars without the consent or support of the ruler of Mongolia. This is the first indication of the decline of the Mongol dynasty.

Shortly after the return of Friar Carpini, King Louis IX of France, known as Saint Louis, set out upon a crusade against the Saracens. Landing on the island of Cyprus, he received an envoy from Persia who gave him very pleasing news, to the effect that the name of the Pope was famous among the Mongols and that the mother of the Great Khan was a Christian and that the Khan himself was friendly to all Christians. Louis soon after determined to send a mission to the Great Khan for the purpose of advising the Mongol lord regarding the performance of Christian duties.

Friar William of Rubruck, who accompanied the king on his crusade, was, therefore, sent to the Court of Mangu Khan. The king provided him with a small amount of money, letters to the Mongol Khan, as well as a Bible. He had also as a present from Queen Margaret a beautifully illuminated Book of Psalms and some church vestments. These, besides his breviary and a valuable Arabic manuscript, made up the greater portion of his simple outfit. He took with him a travelling companion named Bartholomew of Cremona.

His narrative, which forms the most important section of this volume, is quite unique. It is full of colour and presents the most intimate picture of the Mongols that has come down to us. For acuteness of observation and historical importance, it ranks next to Marco Polo as a travel record. Rubruck and his companions endured great hardships and after many annoying delays finally returned in 1255.

While the results of his mission were rather doubtful and Mangu Khan did not become a Christian,—in fact he suggested that Louis of France and the Pope would do well to become his subjects,—still Friar William's careful observations greatly extended the horizon of knowledge. His main contributions were the indication of the sources and directions of the rivers Don and Volga, the fact that the Caspian was a lake—not a gulf, the mention of Korea and the identity of many tribes of Asia. He was the first to give us an accurate description of Chinese writing as well as of the scripts of the other eastern races. He was also the first to tell about the various Christian communities that he found in the Mongol empire as well as the Lamas and their temples. The distinguished scholar, William Rockhill, says of him: "No one traveller since his day has done half so much to give a correct knowledge of this part of Asia." And Sir Henry Yule has said of his character: "These paint for us an honest, pious, stouthearted, acute and most intelligent observer, keen in acquisition of knowledge; the author, in fact, of one of the best narratives of travel in existence."

With the western armies in the hands of Batu and the princes, Mangu Khan felt free to give his whole attention to the final overthrow of the Sung rulers, who had now taken refuge in southern China. In these campaigns Mangu received the full support of his younger, but more gifted brother, Kublai, who was entrusted with the full charge of all operations designed to complete the conquest of China.

Two years after Friar Rubruck had returned to his home land, Mangu Khan died and Kublai became the Great Khan of the Mongols, with domains that stretched from eastern Europe to the shores of the Pacific.

Kublai Khan

Kublai Khan, the fifth and last of the Great Khans, was interested in Christianity, for he was quite willing to employ any forces that could hold together so vast an empire. It was during his rule that an embassy of sixteen Mongols arrived in Lyons as delegates from Abaga Khan, nephew of Kublai and ruler of western Asia. They arrived in time to attend the second Council of Lyons, held in the summer of 1274. From the unreliable records written by some one in England signing himself "Matthew of Westminster," we learn that the sixteen Tartars came forward after the delegation from Greece had left the stage and presented their papers from their king to the Council. Then they declaimed in a most pompous manner and told of the great importance of the Mongols. Latin texts of their speech have, in recent times, been discovered and a careful examination shows that the object of the mission was to seek an alliance with the Christian world.[7] They also reported that their king was ready to unite forces against the enemies of Christ and recover Jerusalem. Also they presented letters to the Pope but there remains no record to show that the Council took any notice of this proposal.

A similar idea to this was entertained by Kublai Khan when he wrote to the Pope to send him a hundred learned men. This message was delivered by Marco Polo's father and uncle but again it met with the same fate of the other tentatives. There were also rumours that some of the wives of the Khan rulers were Christians and would, no doubt, help friendly relations.[8] But Christianity had spent its

[7] Discovered by Professor G. Borghezio and privately published in Latin by the Vatican Press, Rome, 1923.

[8] Mangu and Kublai had a Christian mother; Halagu, a Christian wife. Abaga married a bastard daughter of Michael VIII, Palæologos, and his son, King Arghun, also took to himself a Christian. See *The History of Yaballaha III*, by James A. Montgomery.

force, lost its vitality through years of Crusades and now lay sick and enfeebled, worried by dissenting kings, scheming cardinals and a wave of heresy.

In the meantime the Mongols had attached to their courts certain groups of Christians, selected from some of the Asiatic communities described by Friar Rubruck. They took part in the services, and the idea of Christ had considerable fascination for the Mongols. For a short period trade relations with the Mongol Empire, along the well-established highways, proceeded in a friendly manner. Natural products of the east came to Europe. Missionaries, travellers, merchants and ambassadors all journeyed safely across vast stretches of land with comparative safety.

The Mongols were at this time confronted with four first-class religions:—Buddhism, Christianity, Confucianism and Islam. The last was not regarded with very much favour because it was the religion of their enemy, the Turk. Still it had some consideration. They were willing to try each.

It seems strange that conquering countries usually assume many of the outstanding characteristics of those whom they have vanquished. The more smashing the victory the more do the victors seem to absorb from the conquered. In the end they become like their enemies.

Fascinated and lured by the religion of the enemy, at the earliest opportunity the victors are tempted to see if it can be transplanted and made to work,—if it will do more for them than the religion they have been practising with doubtful results. The lower civilization usually has the vitality to overpower the higher, but that power is at once lost when the religion of the higher civilization is embraced. The kiss of Christianity has weakened more than one race. And so while the death of Ogotay no doubt saved Rome and Paris from the fate of Kiev and Moscow, still the Mongols under the spiritual influence of Christianity would not have endured long as an arrogant, warring nation.

But it was luxury and sudden riches rather than Christianity that weakened and finally ruined the Mongol Dynasty. An excellent picture of these last years may be gathered from Marco Polo's accounts of the Court of Kublai Khan. The fierce fire and slaughter of the early Mongol tribes were now spent. They became soft and effeminate. They built palaces in Peking of gold, jade and lacquer. And Kublai, with the hundred most beautiful maidens that were annually selected for his personal use, grew lazy and fat with the overabundance and richness of living. Silks, perfumes, concubines and imported religions soon left the Mongol Dynasty an easy victim and paved the way for the return of the Chinese to power in eastern Asia.

This amazing rise and decline is all within the space of a single century, and the fruit of conquest turned out, as it often does, to resemble the mango of the Chinese magician.

Friar Odoric and Rabbi Benjamin

About twenty years after Marco Polo returned from the Court of Kublai Khan, a Franciscan friar was sent to the east as part of an extended missionary movement. His record of India, Sumatra, Java and China, where he spent three years, is faithful and intelligent. He returned overland through Tibet and Persia, and was the first traveller after Marco Polo to describe these parts. He saw the shrine of St. Thomas and described many things that Marco Polo failed to mention. Soon after his death, in 1331, his fame as a Saint and traveller spread over the whole of Europe.

Rabbi Benjamin of Tudela may be said to have been the

first of the mediæval travellers, for he journeyed farther into the eastern countries than any of his predecessors. While he travelled many years before Carpini and Rubruck, they are, nevertheless, important for they give us a picture of western Asia before the Mongols swept through leaving their wake of slaughter and ruin. We gain through his record an idea of the eastern civilizations which were almost entirely extinguished by the Mongol invasions. We learn something of a culture which studied and preserved many of the Greek and Latin classics while Europe was going through its Dark Ages.

Rabbi Benjamin was a Jew from Spain. His descriptions are quite accurate and his love of the marvellous lends romance and colour to his record. He names the principal Jews of the congregation in each city that he visited and makes note of trade and commerce. He tells about the Hebrew Prince of the Captivity as well as the ruins of the Tower of Babel. He was much interested in the stories he heard of the discovery of the Tomb of David, locates the spot where Lot's wife was changed into a pillar of salt. Many other legends he records.

The information he collected agrees in the main with the writings of contemporary Arabian geographers and through him we know the fact that Jews in the east were famous for the arts of dyeing and glass-making. His travel narrative, unlike the others contained in this volume, is one of mediæval peace and culture rather than of primitive force and ignorance.

This record completes a picture of these amazing times.

MANUEL KOMROFF.

How the Great and Lesser Khans Are Related

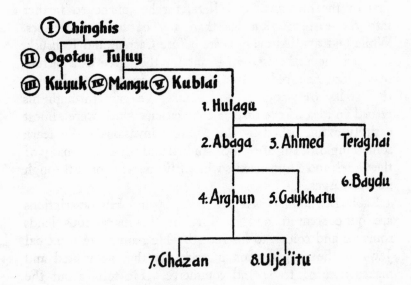

Great Khans

	died
Chinghis	1227
Ogotay	1241
Kuyuk	1248
Mangu	1257
Kublai	1294
(Yuen Dynasty)	

Lesser Khans

	died
Halagu	1265
Abaga	1281
Ahmad	1284
Arghun	1291
Gaykhatu	1295
Baydu	1295
Ghazan	1304
Ulja'itu	1316

NOTE:—The above tables, except for the death of Ogotay, which I have placed at 1241, are taken from Lane-Poole, *Mohammedan Dynasties*, based on Howorth's *History of the Mongols*. They have also been reprinted by James Montgomery in his introduction to *The History of Yaballaha III*.

CONTENTS

THE JOURNEY OF
FRIAR JOHN OF PIAN DE CARPINI
1245-1247

FRIAR JOHN OF PIAN DE CARPINI

Carpini was born in about the year 1182 and at an early age entered the order of the Franciscan Friars. He soon gained a high repute in the order and took an active part in its teachings throughout Northern Europe. He held offices in Saxony, Germany, Spain and Cologne.

Four years after the disastrous battle of Liegnitz in 1241, in which the Tartars broke loose from the east and seriously threatened the whole of Christian civilization, Pope Innocent IV dispatched his first mission to the Mongols in order to protest against the invasion of Christian lands and also to find out the extent of their power. In spite of his age, for Carpini was then about sixty-five, he was placed at the head of this mission and set out from Lyons on Easter day, 1245, on a journey of untold hardships, the first noteworthy journey of a European into the vast Mongol empire.

Ogotay Khan, the son of Chinghis, died at this time and Carpini reached the East in time to witness, at first hand, the formal enthronement of Kuyuk the eldest son of Ogotay. His description of the coronation of a Tartar emperor at the very height of Mongol power is one of the most unique records in all medieval travel literature.

Carpini asked Kuyuk Khan to become a Christian, but the emperor replied by dictating a letter to the Pope which closed with asking the Pope to come to the East and give homage to them;— "And if you do not observe the order of God and disobey our orders, then we will know you as our enemy." The original of this letter has recently been found in the archives of the Vatican.

Carpini delivered this document to the Pope at Lyons in 1247, after a journey of great deprivation. Often they slept on the bare snow and had little or nothing to eat. But Carpini was once a companion and disciple of St. Francis of Assisi, and his account of the journey contains no personal complaint. Moreover he was a very heavy man, and so fat that he walked with difficulty and required to have a donkey carry him over some of the stretches. His record is the first to reveal the Eastern empires and Tartar manners to the Western world. He did not long survive his hard journey but died in August, 1252, soon after he had been made an archbishop.

THE JOURNEY OF
FRIAR JOHN OF PIAN DE CARPINI
TO THE
COURT OF KUYUK KHAN

1245-1247
AS NARRATED BY HIMSELF

Chapter 1

OF THE SITUATION ❧ CLIMATE ❧ EMPEROR ❧ AND NATURE OF THE TARTAR'S LAND

THERE IS TOWARDS THE EAST a land which is called Mongol, or Tartary, lying in that part of the world which is thought to be most north-easterly. On the east part it has the country of Cathay: on the south part the country of the Saracens: on the south-east the land of the Huins: and on the west the province of Naimans: but on the north side it is bounded by the ocean sea. In some parts it is full of mountains, and in other places plain and smooth ground, but everywhere sandy and barren, neither is the hundredth part of it fruitful. For it cannot bear fruit unless it be moistened with river waters, which are very

3

rare in this country. Therefore they have neither villages nor cities among them, except one which is called Cara-carum [the Karakorum of Marco Polo] and is said to be a proper town. We ourselves did not see this town, but were almost within half a day's journey, when we remained at *Syra orda,* which is the great court of their emperor, Kuyuk Khan.

Though this land is unfruitful, yet it is very commodious for the raising of cattle. In certain places there are some small groves of trees growing, but otherwise it is altogether destitute of woods. Therefore the emperor, and his noble men and all others warm themselves, and cook their meat, with fires made of the dung of oxen and horses. The air also in this country is very intemperate; in the midst of summer there are great thunders and lightnings, by the which many men are slain, and at the same time there falls a great abundance of snow. There are also such mighty tempests of cold winds, that sometimes men are not able to sit on horseback. So great is the great wind that we were often constrained to lie grovelling on the earth, and could not see by reason of the dust.

There is never any rain in winter, but only in summer, and so little that sometimes it is scarcely sufficient to down the dust, or to moisten the roots of the grass. There is often times great quantities of hail also. When the emperor-elect was to be placed on his imperial throne, myself being then present, there fell such abundance of hail, that, upon its sudden melting, more than one hundred and sixty persons were drowned. Many tents and other things were also carried away. In the summer season there are sudden waves of extreme heat, and suddenly again waves of intolerable cold.

Chapter 2

OF THEIR FORM ❧ HABIT ❧ AND MANNER OF LIVING

THE Mongols or Tartars, in outward shape, are unlike to all other people. For they are broader between the eyes, and the balls of their cheeks, than men of other nations. They have flat and small noses, little eyes, and eyelids standing straight upright; they are shaven on the crowns like priests. They wear their hair somewhat longer about their ears, than upon their foreheads; but behind they let it grow long like woman's hair, which they braid into two locks, binding each of them behind either ear. They have short feet also.

The garments, of their men as well as of their women, are all of one fashion. They use neither cloaks, hats, nor capes. But they wear jackets framed after a strange manner, of buckram, scarlet, or brocade. Their gowns are hairy on the outside, and open behind, with tails hanging down to their hams. They do not wash their garments, neither will they allow them to be washed, especially at the time of thundering.

Their habitations are round and cunningly made with wickers and staves in manner of a tent. But in the middle of the tops, they have an opening to convey the light in and the smoke out. For their fire is always in the midst. Their walls are covered with felt. Their doors are made of felt also. Some of these tabernacles may quickly be taken apart, and set together again, and are carried upon beasts' backs. Others cannot be taken apart, but are moved upon carts. And wherever they go, be it either to war or to any other place, they transport their tabernacles with them.

They are very rich in cattle, such as camels, oxen, sheep, and goats. And I think they have more horses and mares than all the rest of the world. But they have no cows nor other beasts. Their emperors, chiefs, and other of their nobles have much silk, gold, silver, and precious stones.

Their victuals are all things that may be eaten; for we even saw some of them eat lice. They drink milk in great quantity, but especially mares' milk, if they have it. They cook a flour in water, making it so thin, that they may drink thereof. Every one of them drinks off a cupful, or two, in the morning, and sometimes they eat nothing else all the day long. But in the evening each man hath a little flesh given him to eat, and they drink the broth of the meat. In summertime, when they have mares' milk enough, they seldom eat flesh, unless perhaps it be given them, or they take some beast or bird in hunting.

Chapter 3

OF THEIR MANNERS ❧ BOTH GOOD AND BAD

THEIR manners are partly praiseworthy, and partly detestable; for they are more obedient to their lords and masters, than any other either clergy or lay-people in the whole world. They highly reverence them, and will deceive them neither in words nor deeds. They seldom or never fall out among themselves, and, as for fightings or brawlings, wounds or manslaughters, they never happen among them. Neither thieves nor robbers of great riches are to be found, and therefore the tabernacles and carts that have any treasures are not secured with locks or bars.

If any beast should go astray, the finder either lets it go, or drives it to those who are put in office for the purpose, at whose hands the owner of the beast may demand it, and without any difficulty receive it again. They honour one another greatly, and bestow banquets very liberally, notwithstanding that good victuals are dainty and scarce among them. They are also very hardy, and when they have fasted a day or two, they sing and are merry as if they had eaten their bellies full. In riding, they endure much cold and extreme heat. There are, in a manner, no disputes among them, and although they often are drunk, yet they do not quarrel in their drunkenness. No one of them despises another but helps him as much as he conveniently can.

Their women are chaste, neither is there so much as a word uttered concerning dishonesty. Some of them will, however, speak filthy and immodest words. But towards other people, the Tartars are most insolent, and they scorn other persons, noble and ignoble. We saw in the emperor's court the great Duke of Russia, the king's son of Georgia, and many great sultans receiving no due honour. Even the very Tartars assigned to serve them, would always go before them, and take the upper hand of them, and sometimes would even compel them to sit behind their backs. Moreover they are angry and of a disdainful nature unto other people, and beyond all measure deceitful, and treacherous towards them. While they speak fair in the beginning, in conclusion, they sting like scorpions. For crafty they are, and full of falsehood, circumventing all men whom they are able, by their sleights. Whatsoever mischief they intend to practise against a man, they keep it wonderfully secret, so that he may by no means provide for himself, nor find a remedy against their conspiracies.

They are unmannerly also and unclean in taking their meat and their drink, and in other actions. Drunkenness is honourable among them, and when any of them has taken more drink than his stomach can well bear, he calls it up and falls to drinking again. They are most intolerable exactors, most covetous possessors, and most niggardly givers.

The slaughter of other people is accounted a matter of nothing with them.

Chapter 4

OF THEIR LAWS ❧ AND CUSTOMS

MOREOVER, they have this law or custom, that whatever man and woman are taken in adultery, they are punished with death. A virgin likewise who has committed carnal sin, they slay together with her mate. Whosoever is taken in robbery or theft, is put to death without pity. Also, if any man disclose their secrets, especially in time of war, he receives an hundred blows on the back with a bastinado, laid on by a tall fellow. In like sort when any inferiors offend, they find no favour at their superiors' hands, but are punished with grievous stripes.

They join in matrimony to all in general, even to their near kinsfolks except their mother, daughter and sister by the mother's side. They marry their sister by the father's side only, and also the wife of their father after his decease. The younger brother also, or some other of his kindred, is bound to marry the wife of his elder brother deceased. At the time of our abode in this country, a certain duke of Russia, named Andreas, was accused before Chief Batu for conveying the Tartars' horses out of the land, and for selling them to others; and although it could not be proved, yet he was put to death. His younger brother and the wife of the party deceased, hearing this, came and made their petition to the chief, that the dukedom of Russia might not be taken from them. But he commanded the youth to marry his deceased brother's wife, and the woman also to take him as her husband, according to the custom of the Tartars. She answered that she had rather die, than to so transgress the law. However, he delivered her unto him, although they both refused as much as they could. Carrying them to bed, they compelled the youth, who was lamenting and weeping, to lie down and commit incest with his brother's wife. To be short, after the death of their husbands, the Tartars' wives very seldom marry the second time, unless perhaps some man takes his brother's wife, or his step-mother, in marriage.

They make no difference between the son of their wife and of their concubine, but the father gives what he pleases unto each one. The late king of Georgia having two sons— one lawfully begotten called Melich; but the other, David, born in adultery—at his death left part of his land to his unlawful son. Hereupon Melich, unto whom the kingdom fell by right of his mother because it was governed before-time by women, went unto the Emperor of the Tartars, David also having taken his journey unto him. Now both of them came to the court and brought large gifts. The son of the harlot made suit, that he might have justice, according to the custom of the Tartars. Well, sentence passed against Melich, that David, being his elder brother, should have superiority over him, and should quietly and peaceably possess the portion of land granted unto him by his father.

Whensoever a Tartar has many wives, each one of them has her family and dwelling-place by herself. And some-time the Tartar eats, drinks and lies with one, and sometime with another. One is accounted chief among the rest, with whom he is oftener conversant than with the other. Though they are many, yet do they seldom fall out among themselves.

Chapter 5

OF THEIR SUPERSTITIOUS TRADITIONS

By reason of certain traditions, which either they or their predecessors have devised, they believe some things to be faults. One is to thrust a knife into the fire, or any way to touch the fire with a knife, or with their knife to take flesh out of the boiling vessel, or to hew with a hatchet near the fire. For they think by these means one takes away the head or force from the fire. Another is to lean upon a whip with which they beat their horses: for they ride not with spurs. Also to touch arrows with a whip, to take or kill young birds, to strike a horse with the rein of their bridle, and to break one bone against another. Also to pour out milk, meat, or any kind of drink upon the ground or to make water within their tabernacle: which whosoever does willingly, he is slain, but otherwise he must pay a great sum of money to the enchanter to be purified. Who likewise must cause the tabernacle, with all things therein, to pass between two fires. Before it is in this way purified no man dare enter into it, nor take out anything.

Besides this, if any man has a morsel given him, which he is not able to swallow, and for that cause casts it out of his mouth, there is an hole made under his tabernacle, by which he is drawn forth and slain without compassion. Likewise, whosoever treads upon the threshold of any of their chief's tabernacles, is put to death.

Many other things there are like these, which they take for heinous offences. But to slay men, to invade the dominions of other people, and to rifle their goods, to transgress the commandments and prohibitions of God, are with them no offences at all. They know nothing concerning eternal life and everlasting damnation, and yet they think that after death they shall live in another world; that they shall multiply their cattle, that they shall eat and drink and do other things which living men perform here upon earth.

At a new moon, or a full moon, they begin all new enterprises and they call the moon the Great Emperor, and worship it upon their knees. All men that abide in their tabernacles must be purified with fire: which purification is done in this way. They kindle two fires, and pitch two javelins into the ground near the fires, tying a cord to the tops of the javelins. About the cord they tie certain bits of buckram. Then under the cord, and between the fires, men, beasts, and tabernacles do pass. There stand two women also, one on the right side, and another on the left, casting water, and repeating certain charms. If any man be slain by lightning, all that dwell in the same tabernacle with him must pass by fire in the manner described. Their tabernacles, beds, and carts, they themselves and their garments, and whatever things they have, are touched by no man, but are abandoned by all men as things unclean. In short, they think that all things are to be purged by fire. Therefore, when any ambassadors, princes, or other personages whatsoever come to them, they and their gifts must pass between two fires to be purified, lest they have practised some witchcraft, or have brought some poison or other mischief with them.

Chapter 6

OF THE BEGINNING ◆ THEIR EMPIRE ◆ AND GOVERNMENT

THE east country, which is called Mongol, is reported to have had of old time four forces of people. One of them was called Yeka Mongol, that is, the Great Mongols. The second was called Sumongol, that is, the Water-Mongols, who called themselves Tartars, from a certain river running through their country named Tartar. The third was called Merkit, and the fourth Metrit. All these people had the same attire of body and language, but they were divided by princes and provinces.

In the province of Yeka Mongol, there was a certain man called Chinghis. This man became a mighty hunter. He learned to steal men, and to take them for prey. He ranged into other countries taking as many captives as he could, and joining them unto himself. Also he allured the men of his own country unto him, who followed him as their captain and ringleader to do mischief. Then began he to make war upon the Sumongols, or Tartars, and slew their captain, and after many conflicts, subdued them and brought them all into bondage. Afterward he used their help to fight against the Merkits, dwelling by the Tartars, whom also he vanquished in battle. Proceeding from thence, he fought against the Metrits, and conquered them also.

He was a mighty and puissant emperor, unto whom all these nations paid tribute. Whose sons, when he was dead, succeeded him in his empire. But being young and foolish, they knew not how to govern the people, but were divided, and fell at variance among themselves. Now Chinghis being exalted, they nevertheless invaded the fore-named countries, put the inhabitants to the sword, and carried away their goods. Which Chinghis having heard of, he gathered all his subjects together. The Naimans also and the people called Kara-Cathay assembled and banded themselves at a certain strait valley, where, after a battle fought, they were vanquished by the Mongols. And being thus vanquished, they were, the greater part of them, slain; and others, which could not escape, were carried into captivity.

In the land of the city of Caracarum, Ogotay Khan, the

son of Chinghis Khan, after he was created emperor, built a
certain city, which he called Chanyl. Near this city, on the
south side, there is a huge desert, which wild men are certainly reported to inhabit, who cannot speak at all and are
destitute of joints in their legs, so that if they fall they
cannot rise alone by themselves. But they are prudent and
make felts of camel's hair, with which they clothe themselves, and which they hold against the wind. If at any
time the Tartars, pursuing them, chance to wound them with
their arrows, they put herbs into their wounds, and fly
strongly before them.

Chapter 7

OF THE MANY VICTORIES BETWEEN THEM ❦ AND THE PEOPLE OF CATHAY

But the Mongols, returning home to their own country,
prepared themselves to battle against the Cathayans: which
their emperor hearing, set forward against them with his
army, and they fought a cruel battle, wherein the Mongols
were overcome, and all their nobles in the army, except
seven, were slain. And for this cause, when they, purposing
to invade any region, are threatened by the inhabitants
thereof, they do to this day answer: "In old time also our
whole number besides being slain, we remained but seven of
us alive, and yet we have grown to a great multitude; think
not therefore to daunt us with such threats." But Chinghis
and the residue that remained alive fled home into their
country.

And having rested a little, he prepared himself to war,
and went forth against the people called Huyri. These men
were Christians of the sect of Nestorians. And these also
the Mongols overcame, and received letters or learning from

them; for before that time they had not the art of writing, and now they call it the hand or letters of the Mongols.

Immediately after, he marched against the country of Saruyur, and of the Karanites, and against the land of Hudirat: all of which he vanquished. Then he returned home to his own country. Afterward, assembling his warlike troops, they marched with one accord against the Cathayans, and waging war with them a long time, they conquered a great part of their land, and shut up their emperor in his greatest city; which city they so long besieged that they began to want necessary provision for their army. And when they had no victuals to feed upon, Chinghis Khan commanded his soldiers, that they should eat every tenth man of the company. They of the city fought manfully against them, with engines, darts, and arrows, and when stones wanted they threw silver, and especially melted silver: for the city abounded with great riches. Also, when the Mongols had fought a long time and could not prevail by war, they made a great trench underneath the ground from the army unto the midst of the city, and there issuing forth they fought against the citizens, and the soldiers without the walls also fought. At last, breaking open the gates of the city, they entered, and putting the emperor with many others to the sword, they took possession and carried away the gold, silver, and all the riches therein. And having appointed certain deputies over the country, they returned home into their own land. When the emperor of the Cathayans was vanquished, Chinghis Khan obtained the empire. But some part of the country, because it lies within the sea, they could by no means conquer until this day.

The men of Cathay are pagans, having a special kind of writing by themselves, and, as it is reported, the Scriptures of the Old and New Testaments. They have also recorded in histories the lives of their forefathers: and they have monks, and certain houses made after the manner of our churches. They say that they have many saints also, and they worship one God. They adore and reverence Christ Jesus our Lord, and believe the article of eternal life, but are not baptized. They do also honourably esteem and reverence our Scriptures. They love Christians, and bestow much alms, and are a very courteous and gentle people. They have no beards, and they agree partly with the Mongols in the disposition of their countenance. In all occupations which men practise, there are not better craftsmen in the whole world. Their country is exceeding rich, in corn, wine, gold, silk, and other commodities.

Chapter 8

OF THEIR WAR AGAINST INDIA MAJOR ❧ AND MINOR

AND when the Mongols with their emperor, Chinghis Khan, had rested themselves after their victory, they divided their armies. For the emperor sent one of his sons, named Tuluy, whom also they call Khan, that is to say, emperor, with an army against the people of Comania, whom he vanquished with much war, and afterward returned to his own country. He sent his other son [Ogotay] with an army against the Indians, who also subdued India Minor.

These Indians are the black Saracens, which are also called Ethiopians. But here the army marched forward to fight against Christians dwelling in India Major. When the king of the country, who is commonly called Prester John, heard this, he gathered his soldiers together and came forth against them. And making men's images of copper, he set each of them upon a saddle on horseback, and put fire within them, and placed a man with a pair of bellows on

the horseback behind every image.   And so with many
horses and images in such sort furnished, they marched on
to fight against the Mongols, or Tartars.

Coming near to the place of the battle, they first of all
sent those horses one after another.   But the men that sat
behind laid a good deal upon the fire within the images,
and blew strongly with their bellows.   Then it came to
pass, that the men and the horses were burnt with wild fire,
and the air was darkened with smoke.   Then the Indians
cast darts at the Tartars, of whom many were wounded and
slain.   And so they expelled them out of their dominions
with great confusion, neither did we hear that ever they
returned.

Chapter 9

HOW BEING REPELLED BY MONSTROUS MEN SHAPED LIKE DOGS ◄ THEY OVERCAME THE PEOPLE OF BURITHABETH

RETURNING through the deserts, they came to a certain
country, wherein—as it was reported to us in the emperor's
court, by certain clergymen of Russia, and others, who were
long time among them—they found certain monsters resembling women.   Being asked by interpreters, where the men
of that land were, they answered that whatsoever women
were born there, resembled the shape of mankind, but the
males were like dogs.   And after a time, in that country
they met with the dogs on the other side of the river.   And
in the midst of sharp winter, these cast themselves into the
water; afterward they wallowed in the dust upon the main
land, and so the dust, being mingled with water, was frozen
to their backs, and having oftentimes repeated this, the ice
became strongly frozen upon them.   Then with great fury
they came to fight against the Tartars.

When the Tartars threw their darts, or shot their arrows

among them, they rebounded back again, as if they had lighted upon stones. And the rest of their weapons could by no means hurt them. However, the dogs made an assault upon the Tartars, and wounding some of them with their teeth, and flaying others, at length they drove them out of their countries. And because of this they have a proverb still current among them, and they say in jesting one to another: "My father or my brother was slain by dogs."

The women whom they captured they brought into their own country, and they remained there till their dying day. And in travelling homewards, the army of the Mongols came to the land of Burithabeth, the inhabitants whereof are pagans, and conquered the people in battle. These people have a strange or rather a miserable kind of custom. For when any man's father dies, he assembles all his kindred, and they eat him. These men have no beards at all. We saw them carry a certain iron instrument in their hands, with which they pluck out any hairs that grow upon their chin. They are also very deformed. From here the Tartar army returned to their own home.

Chapter 10

HOW THEY HAD BEEN REPULSED AT THE CASPIAN MOUNTAINS AND WERE DRIVEN BACK BY MEN DWELLING IN CAVES

MOREOVER, Chinghis Khan, at the time when he sent other armies against the east, himself marched with a force into the land of Kerkis, but he did not conquer in that expedition, and as it was reported to us. He went forward even to the Caspian mountains. But the mountains where they camped were of lodestone, and therefore they drew into them their arrows, and weapons of iron. And certain men within these Caspian mountains, hearing, as it was thought, the noise of the army, made a breach through, so that when the Tartars returned to the same place ten years after, they found the mountain broken. Attempting to go through, they could not; for there stood a cloud before them, beyond which they were not able to pass, being deprived of their sight as soon as they approached. They on the other side, thinking that the Tartars dared not come near them, made the assault, and when they came to the cloud, they also could not proceed.

Also the Tartars, before they came to the mountains, passed for the space of a month and more through a vast wilderness, and departed towards the east. They were over a month travelling through another huge desert.

At length, they came into a land wherein they saw roads, but could not find any people. But at the last, diligently seeking, they found a man and his wife, whom they presented before Chinghis Khan. Demanding of them where the people of that country were, they answered, that the people lived under the ground in mountains. Then Chinghis Khan kept the woman, sent her husband to them, ordering them to come out at his command. Going to them, he declared all things that Chinghis Khan had commanded. But they answered, that they would upon such a day visit him, to satisfy his desire. And in the meantime, by blind and hidden passages under the earth assembling themselves, they came against the Tartars in warlike manner, and suddenly issuing forth, they slew a great number.

The Tartars were not able to endure the terrible noise, which the sun made in this place. At the time of the sunrising, they were forced to lay one ear upon the ground, and to stop the other close, lest they should hear that dreadful sound. Chinghis Khan, therefore, and his company, seeing that they could not conquer, but continually lost some of their number, fled and departed out of that land. But the man and his wife they carried along with them, who all their lifetime lived in the Tartars' country. On being asked why the men of their country live under the ground, they said, that at a certain time of the year, when the sun riseth, there is such a huge noise that the people cannot endure it. Moreover, they used to play upon cymbals, drums, and other musical instruments, so that they might not hear that sound.

Chapter 11

OF THE LAWS OF CHINGHIS KHAN ❧ OF HIS DEATH ❧ OF HIS SONS ❧ AND OF HIS CHIEFS

As Chinghis Khan came out of that country, his people wanted food, for they suffered extreme famine. Then by chance they found the fresh entrails of a beast; this they took, and casting away the dung thereof, caused it to be cooked and brought it before Chinghis Khan, who did eat thereof. And hereupon Chinghis Khan enacted, that neither the blood, nor the entrails, nor any other part of a beast which might be eaten, should be cast away, save only the dung.

When he returned into his own land, he ordained laws and statutes, which the Tartars do most strictly observe, of which we have before spoken. He was afterward slain by a thunderclap. Chinghis Khan had four sons; the first was called Ogotay, the second Tuluy Khan, the third Chagatai; the name of the fourth is unknown [Juji]. From these four descended all the chiefs of the Mongols. The first son of Ogotay is Kuyuk, who is now emperor; his brothers are Shiregi and Kashin. Batu [a son of Juji], next to the emperor, is richer and mightier than all the rest.

The mother of Mangu was named Serotan, and of all others was most honoured among the Tartars, except the emperor's mother, and mightier than any subject except Batu.

Chapter 12

OF THE AUTHORITY OF THE EMPEROR ❦ AND OF HIS CHIEFS

MOREOVER, the emperor of the Tartars has a wonderful control over all his subjects, for no man dare abide in any place, unless it has been assigned to him. Also he himself appoints where his chiefs should live. Likewise the chiefs assign places to every millenary, or conductor of a thousand soldiers, the millenaries to each captain of a hundred, the captains to every corporal of ten. Whatever is given them in charge, whenever, or wherever, be it to fight or to lose their lives, or however it be, they obey without any grumbling. For if he demands any man's daughter, or sister, even if a virgin, they presently deliver her to him without any contradiction. Yet, oftentimes he makes a collection of virgins throughout all the Tartars' dominions, and those whom he means to keep, he retains to himself, and the others he bestows unto his men.

Also, whenever he sends a messenger his subjects must without delay find them horses and other necessaries. Ambassadors who come to him, from lands that pay tribute, have horses, carriages, and expenses allowed them. But ambassadors coming from other places do suffer great misery, and are in much want both of food and of apparel; especially when they come to any of the chiefs, and there are obliged to make some stay. Then ten men are allowed so little sustenance that scarcely two could live upon it. Likewise, if any injuries are given them, they cannot without danger make complaint.

Many gifts also are demanded of them, both by chiefs and others, and if they do not bestow them, they are basely esteemed and set at nought. We were enforced to bestow in gifts a great part of those things which were given us by well-disposed people, to defray our charges. In short, all things are so in the power and possession of the emperor, that no man dare say, "This is mine, or this is my neighbour's." But all, goods, cattle and men, are his own. Concerning these matters he published a code of late. This same authority and jurisdiction the chiefs exercise upon their subjects.

Chapter 13

OF THE ELECTION OF EMPEROR OGOTAY ❦ AND OF THE EXPEDITION OF CHIEF BATU

AFTER the death of Chinghis Khan, the dukes, or chiefs, assembled and chose Ogotay, his son, to be their emperor. And he, entering into consultation with his nobles, divided his armies, and sent Chief Batu, his nephew, against the country of the Great Sultan, and also against the people called Bisermins, who were Saracens, but spake the language of Comania.

The Tartars invaded their country, fought with them, and subdued them in battle. But a certain city called Barchin resisted them a long time. The citizens had cast up many ditches and trenches about their city, and because of this the Tartars could not take it, till they had filled these ditches. The citizens of Sarguit, hearing of this, came forth to meet · them, surrendering of their own accord. Whereupon their city was not destroyed, but many of them were slain and others carried away captive, and taking spoils, they filled the city with other inhabitants, and so marched forth against the city of Orna. This town was very populous and exceeding rich; for there were many Christians therein, Gazars, Russians, and Alans, with others, and Saracens also. The government was in the Saracens' hand. The city stands upon a mighty river [the Syr-daria] and is a kind of port town having a great market. And when the Tartars could not otherwise capture it, they diverted the river, running through the city, out of its channel, and so drowned the city with the inhabitants and their goods.

After this they set forth against Russia, and made foul havoc there, destroying cities and cattle and murdering the people. They laid siege a long while upon Kiev, the chief city of Russia, and at length they took it and slew the citizens. When we were travelling through this country, we found an innumerable multitude of dead men's skulls and bones lying upon the earth. It was once a very large and populous city, but it is now in a manner brought to nothing; for there do scarce remain two hundred houses, and the inhabitants of these are kept in extreme bondage.

Moreover, out of Russia and Comania, the Tartars proceeded against the Hungarians and the people of Poland, and there many were slain. Had the Hungarians been able to hold out against them, the Tartars would have been confounded and driven back. Returning, they invaded the country of the Mordunis, who are pagans, and conquered them in battle. Then they marched against the people called Bilers, or Great Bulgaria, and utterly wasted the country. From here they proceeded north against the people called Bascarts, or Great Hungary, and conquered them also. · And so going on further north, they came to the Parositæ, who having little stomachs and small mouths, eat not anything at all, but seeing flesh they stand or sit over the pot, and receiving the steam or smoke, are therewith nourished. And if they eat anything at all, it is very little. From here the Tartars came to the Samogetæ, who live on hunting, dwell in tabernacles, and wear garments made of beasts' skins. From here they proceeded to a country lying upon the ocean sea, where they found certain monsters, who in all things resembled the shape of men, saving that their feet were like the feet of an ox, and they had indeed men's heads but dogs' faces. These spoke, as it were, two words like men, but at the third they barked like dogs. From hence they retired into Comania, and there some of them remain to this day.

Chapter 14

OF THE EXPEDITION OF CHIEF CYRPODAN

AT the same time Ogotay Khan sent Chief Cyrpodan with an army against Kerkis, and subdued them in battle. These men are pagans, having no beards at all. They have a custom when any of their fathers die, for grief and in token of lamentation, to draw, as it were, a leather thong around their faces, from one ear to the other.

This nation being conquered, Chief Cyrpodan marched with his forces southward against the Armenians. And travelling through certain desert places, they found monsters in the shape of men, which had each of them but one arm and one hand growing out of the middle of their breast, and but one foot. Two of them used to shoot one bow, and they ran so swiftly that horses could not overtake them. They ran also upon that one foot by hopping and leaping, and when weary of such walking they went upon their hand and their foot, turning themselves round in a circle. Isidorus of Seville calls them cyclopedes. It was told us in court, by the clergymen of Russia who remain with the emperor, that many ambassadors were sent from these people to the emperor's court, to obtain peace.

From here the Tartars proceeded forth into Armenia, which they conquered in battle, and part also of Georgia. And the other part of Georgia is under their jurisdiction, paying every year a tribute of twenty thousand pieces of coin called *yperpera*. From this country they marched into the dominions of the mighty Sultan called Deurum, whom also they vanquished in fight. And to be short, they went on farther sacking and conquering, even as far as the dominions of the Sultan of Aleppo. And now they have subdued that land also, determining to invade other countries beyond it. Neither have they returned into their own land to this day.

Likewise the same army marched forward against the Calif of Bagdad and his country, which they subdued also, and exacted the daily tribute of four hundred *bezants*, besides baldakins [brocades] and other gifts. Also every year they send messengers to the calif inviting him to come to them. He however sends back great gifts together with his tribute and asks them to look favourably upon him. But the Tartar emperor receives all his gifts, and yet nevertheless sends for him.

Chapter 15

HOW THE TARTARS CONDUCT THEMSELVES IN WAR

CHINGHIS KHAN divided his Tartars by captains of ten, captains of a hundred, and captains of a thousand, and over ten millenaries, or captains of a thousand, he placed one colonel, and over one whole army he authorized two or three chiefs, but so that all should be under one of the said chiefs. When they join battle against any other nation, unless they do all consent to retreat, every man who deserts is put to death. And if one or two, or more, of ten proceed manfully to the battle, but the residue of those ten draw back and follow not the company, they are in like manner slain. Also, if one among ten or more be taken, their fellows, if they fail to rescue them, are punished with death.

Moreover they are required to have these weapons: two long bows or one good one at least, three quivers full of arrows, and one axe, and ropes to draw engines of war. But the richer have single-edged swords, with sharp points, and somewhat crooked. They have also armed horses, with their shoulders and breasts protected; they have helmets and coats of mail. Some of them have jackets for their horses, made of leather artificially doubled or trebled, shaped upon their bodies. The upper part of their helmet is of iron or steel, but that part which circles about the neck and the throat is of leather. Some of them have all their armour of iron made in the following manner: They beat out many thin plates a finger broad, and a hand long, and making in every one of them eight little holes, they lace through three strong and straight leather thongs. So they join the plates one to another, as it were, ascending by degrees. Then they tie the plates to the thongs, with other small and slender thongs, drawn through the holes, and in the upper part, on each side, they fasten one small doubled thong, that the plates may firmly be knit together. These they make, as well for their horses as for the armour of their men; and they scour them so bright that a man may behold his face in them. Some of them upon the neck of their lance have an hook, with which they attempt to pull men out of their saddles. The heads of their arrows are exceedingly sharp, cutting both ways like a two-edged sword, and they always carry a file in their quivers to sharpen their arrowheads.

They are most efficient in wars, having been in conflict with other nations for the space of these forty-two years. When they come to any rivers, the chief men of the company have a round and light piece of leather. They put a rope through the many loops on the edge of this, draw it together like a purse, and so bring it into the round form of a ball, which leather they fill with their garments and other necessaries, trussing it up most strongly. But upon the midst of the upper part thereof, they lay their saddles and other hard things; there also do the men themselves sit. This, their boat, they tie to a horse's tail, causing a man to swim before, to guide over the horse, or sometimes they have two oars to row themselves over. The first horse, therefore, being driven into the water, all the others' horses of the company follow him, and so they pass through the river. But the common soldiers have each his leather bag or satchel well sewn together, wherein he packs up all his trinkets, and strongly trussing it up hangs it at his horse's tail, and so he crosses the river.

Chapter 16
OF THEIR SPIES ❧ AND HOW THEY MAY BE RESISTED

No one kingdom or province is able to resist the Tartars; because they use soldiers out of every country of their dominions. If the neighbouring province to that which they invade will not aid them, they waste it, and with the inhabitants, whom they take with them, they proceed to fight against the other province. They place their captives in the front of the battle, and if they fight not courageously they put them to the sword. Therefore, if Christians would resist them, it is expedient that the provinces and governors of countries should all agree, and so by a united force should meet their encounter.

Soldiers also must be furnished with strong hand-bows and cross-bows, which they greatly dread, with sufficient arrows, with maces also of strong iron, or an axe with a long handle. When they make their arrowheads, they must, according to the Tartars' custom, dip them red-hot into salt water, that they may be strong enough to pierce the enemies' armour. They that will may have swords also and lances with hooks at the ends, to pull them from their saddles, out of which they are easily removed. They must have helmets and other armour to defend themselves and their horses from the Tartars' weapons and arrows, and they that are unarmed, must, according to the Tartars' custom, march behind their fellows, and discharge at the enemy with long-bows and cross-bows. And, as it has already been said of the Tartars, they must dispose their bands and troops in an orderly manner, and ordain laws for their soldiers. Whosoever runs to the prey or spoil, before the victory is achieved, must undergo a most severe punishment. For such a fellow is put to death among the Tartars without pity or mercy.

The place of battle must be chosen, if it is possible, in a plain field, where they may see round about; neither must all troops be in one company, but in many, not very far distant one from another. They which give the first encounter must send one band before, and must have another in readiness to relieve and support the former in time. They must have spies, also, on every side, to give them notice when the rest of the enemy's bands approach. They ought always to send forth band against band and troop against troop, because the Tartar always attempts to get his enemy in the midst and so to surround him. Let our bands take this advice also; if the enemy retreats, not to make any long pursuit after him, lest according to his custom he might draw them into some secret ambush. For the Tartar fights more by cunning than by main force. And again, a long pursuit would tire our horses, for we are not so well supplied with horses as they. Those horses which the Tartars use one day, they do not ride upon for three or four days after. Moreover, if the Tartars draw homeward, our men must not therefore depart and break up their bands, or separate themselves; because they do this also upon policy, namely, to have our army divided, that they may more securely invade and waste the country. Indeed, our captains ought both day and night keep their army in readiness; and not to put off their armour, but at all time to be prepared for battle. The Tartars, like devils, are always watching and devising how to practise mischief. Furthermore, if in battle any of the Tartars be cast off their horses, they must be captured, for being on foot they shoot strongly, wounding and killing both horses and men.

Chapter 17

OF OUR JOURNEY TO THE FIRST LINE OF THE TARTARS

WE, therefore, by the commandment of the See Apostolic setting forth towards the nations of the East, chose first to travel to the Tartars, because we feared that there might be great danger imminent upon the Church of God, because of their invasions. Proceeding on, therefore, we came to the King of Bohemia [Wenceslaw I], who advised us to take our journey through Poland and Russia. We had kinsfolk in Poland, by whose assistance we might enter Russia. Having given us his letters, he caused our expenses also to be defrayed, in all his chief houses and cities, till we came to his nephew Boleslas, Duke of Silesia, who also was familiar and well known to us. The like favour he showed us also, till we came to Conrad, Duke of Lenczy, to whom then, by God's especial favour towards us, Lord Wasilko, Duke of Russia, had come, from whose mouth we heard more at large concerning the deeds of the Tartars; for he had sent ambassadors to them, and they had returned to him. Wherefore, it being given us to understand that we must bestow gifts upon them, we caused certain skins of beavers and other beasts to be bought with part of that money which was given for use on our journey. The Duke Conrad and the dukes of Cracow, and a bishop, and certain soldiers, hearing of this, gave us more of the same skins.

And, to be brief, Duke Wasilko being earnestly requested by the Duke of Cracow, and by the bishop and barons, on our behalf, conducted us with him, into his own land, and there for certain days entertained us at his own expense, to the end that we might refresh ourselves awhile. Then at our request he had caused his bishops to come to him, and we read before them the Pope's letters, admonishing them to return to the unity of the church. To the same purpose also, we ourselves admonished them, and to our ability persuaded the Duke as well as the bishops and others. However, because Duke Daniel, the brother of Wasilko, had at this time taken a journey to Batu and was absent, they could not give us a final answer.

After these things Duke Wasilko sent us forward with one of his servants as far as Kiev [captured by Batu in 1238], the chief city of Russia. We were always in danger of our lives on account of the Lithuanians, who did often invade the borders of Russia, even in those very places by which we were to pass. The greatest part of the Russians were either slain or carried into captivity by the Tartars. Moreover, at Danilon we were feeble even unto the death, notwithstanding we caused ourselves to be carried in a wagon through the snow and extreme cold. And having arrived at Kiev, we consulted with the millenary and other noble men there concerning our journey. They told us that if we carried those horses, which we then had, into Tartary, they would all die; because they knew not how to dig up the grass under the snow, as the Tartarian horses do, neither could there be aught found for them to eat, the Tartars having neither hay nor straw nor any other fodder. We determined, therefore, to leave them behind at Kiev with two servants appointed to keep them. And we were constrained to bestow gifts upon the millenary, that we might obtain his favour to allow us post horses and a guide. Wherefore beginning our journey the second day after the feast of the Purification of Our Lady [February 4, 1246], we arrived at the town of Kaniew, which was under the dominion of the Tartars. The governor allowed us horses and a guide to another town, wherein we found one Micheas to be governor, a man full of malice and spite, who extorted gifts from us in a deceitful manner before he consented to aid us and conduct us to the first guard of the Tartars.

Chapter 18

HOW OUR COMPANY WERE AT FIRST RECEIVED BY THE TARTARS ❧ AND OUR GIFTS

THE first Saturday next, after Ash Wednesday, having taken up our place of rest, at sundown, the armed Tartars came rushing upon us in uncivil and horrible manner, asking of us what manner of persons we were. We answered them that we were the Pope's envoys, and receiving some victuals at our hands, they immediately departed. Again in the morning, after rising and proceeding on our journey, the chief of their camp came to us, demanding why, or for what intent and purpose, we came; and what business we had with them. We answered, "We are the envoys of the Lord Pope, who is the father and lord of the Christians. He has sent us to your emperor, as well as to your princes, and all other Tartars for this purpose, because it is his pleasure, that all Christians should be friends with the Tartars, and should have peace with them. It is his desire also that they should be mighty with God in heaven; therefore, he advises them through us, as by his own letters, to become Christians, and to embrace the faith of our Lord Jesus Christ, because they could not otherwise be saved. Moreover, he gives them to understand that he is astonished at their monstrous slaughters and massacres of mankind, and especially of Christians, but most of all of Hungarians, Moravians, and Poles, who are all his subjects, and who have not injured them in aught, nor attempted to do them injury. And because the Lord God is grievously offended by this, he advises them from henceforth to beware of such dealing, and to repent of that which they had done. He requested, also, that they write an answer to him, what they purpose to do hereafter, and what their intention is." Having heard and understood, the Tartars said that they would give us post horses and a guide to Corenza. And immediately they demanded gifts at our hands, and obtained them.

Then receiving the same horses from which they dismounted, together with a guide, we took our journey into Corenza. But they rode a swift pace, and sent a messenger before to the chief Corenza, to tell him of the message which we had delivered to them. This chief is governor of all the Tartars who are encamped against the nations of the West, lest some enemy might on the sudden and at unawares break in upon them. And he is said to have sixty thousand men under him.

Chapter 19

HOW WE WERE RECEIVED AT THE COURT OF CORENZA

HAVING come to his court, he caused our tents to be placed far from him, and sent his agents to demand of us what we wanted to bow to him, that is to say, what gifts we would offer, in doing our obeisance to him. We answered, that our lord the Pope had not sent any gifts at all, because he was not certain that we should ever be able to come to them, for we passed through most dangerous places. Notwithstanding, to our ability, we will honour him with some part of those things which have been, by the goodness of God and the favour of the Pope, bestowed upon us for our sustenance.

Having received our gifts, they conducted us to the *orda*, or tent, of the chief, and we were instructed to bow thrice with our left knee before the door of the tent, and in any case to beware lest we set our foot upon the threshold of the said door. And that after we had entered, we should rehearse before the duke and all his nobles the same words which we had before said, kneeling upon our knees. Then we presented the letters of our lord the Pope; but our interpreter whom we had hired and brought with us from Kiev was not sufficiently able to interpret them, neither was there any other person competent to do so. Here certain post horses and three Tartars were appointed for us to conduct us with all speed to the Chief Batu. This Batu is the mightiest prince among them except the emperor, and they are bound to obey him before all other princes.

We began our journey towards his court the first Tuesday in Lent [February 26], and riding as fast as our horses could trot, for we had fresh horses almost thrice or four times a day, we posted from morning till night, yea, very often in the night also, and yet could we not come at him before Wednesday in Holy Week [April 4].

All this journey we went through the land of Comania, which is all plain ground, and has four mighty rivers running through it. The first is called Dnieper, on the side of which towards Russia, chief Corenza rules, but Mauchy of Abulghazi on the other side upon the plains is greater than he. The second river is called Don, upon the bank whereof rules a certain prince having in marriage the sister of Batu; his name is Catan. The third is called Volga, which is an exceeding great river, upon the banks whereof Batu marches. The fourth is called Jagac [Ural], upon which two millenaries do march, one on each side of the river. All these chiefs, in the wintertime, descend down to the sea, and in summer ascend back, by the banks of the rivers, up to the mountains. This sea is the Great Sea, out of which the arm of St. George goes towards Constantinople. These rivers do abound with plenty of fishes, but especially Volga, and they empty into the Grecian Sea, which is called Great Sea. Along the Dnieper we went many days upon the ice. Along the shore also of the Grecian Sea we went very dangerously upon the ice in many places, and that for many days together. About the shore the waters are frozen three leagues into the sea. But before we came to Batu, two of our Tartars rode ahead, to give him news of all we had said in the presence of Corenza.

Chapter 20

HOW WE WERE RECEIVED AT THE COURT OF THE GREAT PRINCE BATU

WHEN we came to Batu in the land of the Comans, we were made to camp a good league distant from his tabernacles. And before we were taken to his court, we were told that we must pass between two fires. But we could by no means be induced to do so. But they said to us: "You may pass through without danger; for we would have you do it for none other reason but only that if you intend any mischief against our lord, or bring any poison with you, the fire may take away all evil." We answered them, that to clear ourselves from all suspicion, we were contented to pass through. When we came to the *orda*, being questioned by his agent Eldegay regarding what present or gift we would bestow, we gave the same answer which we did at the court of Corenza.

The gifts being given and accepted, the reason of our journey also being heard, they brought us into the tabernacle of the prince, first bowing at the door, and being cautioned, as before, not to tread upon the threshold. Having entered, we spoke to him, kneeling upon our knees, and delivered our letters, and requested him to have interpreters translate them.

Accordingly on Good Friday translators were sent to us, and we together with them diligently translated our letters into the Russian, Tartar, and Saracen languages. This interpretation was presented to Batu, which he read, and attentively noted. At length we were conducted home again to our own lodging, but no food was given us, except once a little millet in a dish, the night of our arrival.

This Batu carries himself very stately and magnificently,

having porters and all officers after the manner of the emperor, and sits in a lofty seat or throne together with one of his wives. The rest, namely, his brethren and sons, as other great personages, sit underneath him in the center upon a bench, and others sit down upon the ground, behind him, but the men on the right hand and the women on the left. He has very fair and large tents of linen cloth also, which once belonged to the King of Hungary. Neither dare any man come into his tent, excepting his own family, unless he is called, be he ever so mighty and great, or unless he knows he is wanted. We sat on the left hand, for so do all ambassadors in going, but in returning from the emperor, we were always placed on the right hand. In the middle near the door of the tent stands a table upon which there is drink in golden and silver vessels. Neither does Batu at any time drink, nor do any of the Tartar princes, especially in public, without singing and music before them. And always, when he rides, there is a canopy or small tent carried over his head upon the point of a pole. And so do all the great princes of the Tartars, and their wives also. This Batu is courteous enough to his own men, and yet he is greatly feared by them. He is, however, most cruel in fight; he is exceedingly shrewd and crafty in war, because he has been a long time waging wars.

Chapter 21

HOW DEPARTING FROM BATU ❦ WE PASSED THROUGH THE LAND OF THE COMANS ❦ AND OF THE CANGLE

AT Easter eve we were called into the tent, and there came forth to meet us the agent of Batu, saying on his master's behalf, that we should go into their land, to the Emperor Kuyuk, detaining certain of our company with

the pretence that they might want to send them back to
the Pope. We gave them letters concerning all our affairs
to carry back and deliver to the Pope. But when they got
as far as Duke Mauchy, they were there kept until our
return.

Upon Easter day, having said our prayers, and taken a
slender breakfast, in the company of two Tartars which
were assigned to us, we departed with many tears, not knowing whether we went to death or to life. And we were so
feeble in body that we were scarce able to ride. For all
that Lent through, our food was only millet with a little
water and salt. And so likewise upon other fasting days.
Neither had we aught to drink, but snow melted in a kettle.

Passing through Comania we rode most earnestly, having
change of horses five times or oftener in a day, except when
we went through deserts, for then we were allowed better
and stronger horses, which could undergo the extra labour.
And thus far had we travelled from the beginning of Lent
until eight days after Easter.

The land of Comania on the north side immediately after
Russia hath the people called Mordunis; the Bilers, that is,
Great Bulgaria; the Bascarts, that is, Great Hungary. Next
to the Bascarts are the Parositæ and the Samogetæ. Next
to the Samogetæ are those people which are said to have
dogs' faces, inhabiting the desert shores of the ocean.

On the south side of Comania are the Alans, the Circassi,
the Gazars, Greece and Constantinople; also the land of
Ibers, the Cachs, the Brutaches (who are said to be Jews),
shaving their heads all over, the lands also of Scythia, of
Georgia, of Armenia, of Turkey. On the west side it has
Hungary and Russia. Also Comania is a most large and
long country. The inhabitants of this land the Tartars slew,
some notwithstanding fled from them, and the rest were

subdued under their bondage. Most of them that fled have returned again.

After we entered the land of the Cangle, which in many places suffers from great scarcity of waters, wherein there are but few inhabitants by reason of this lack of water. It happened that some of the servants of Jeroslav, Duke of Russia, as they were travelling towards him into the land of the Tartars, died for thirst in this desert. As before in Comania, so likewise in this country, we found many skulls and bones of dead men lying upon the ground like cattle-dung. Through this country we travelled from the eighth day after Easter until Ascension day [over thirty days]. The inhabitants are pagans, and neither they nor the Comans till the ground, but live only upon the produce of their cattle; neither do they build any houses but dwell in tents. These people also have the Tartars annihilated, and do possess and inhabit their country; those who remain are reduced to slavery.

Chapter 22

HOW WE CAME TO THE FIRST COURT OF THE NEW EMPEROR

LEAVING the land of the Cangle, we entered into the country of the Bisermins, who speak the language of Comania, but observe the religion of the Saracens. In this country we found innumerable cities with ruined castles, and many towns left desolate. The lord of this country was called the Great Sultan, who with all his progeny was destroyed by the Tartars.[1] This country has huge mountains. On the south side is Jerusalem and Bagdad, and the whole country of the Saracens. In the next territories adjoining are two brothers, chiefs of the Tartars, namely, Buri and

---

[1] Alayeddin Mohammed, according to Mohammedan writers, died in a little island in the Caspian, 1220, a hunted fugitive from the Mongols.

Kadan, the sons of Chagatai, who was the son of Chinghis Khan. On the north side thereof it has the land of the black Cathayans, and the ocean. In the same country is Sitan, the brother of Batu.

Through this country we were travelling from the Feast of the Ascension [May 17], until eight days before the Feast of St. John the Baptist [June 24].

Then we entered into the land of the black Cathayans, in which the emperor built a house, where we were called in to drink. Also the emperor's deputy in that place caused the chief men of the city and his two sons to dance before us. Departing from there, we found a certain small sea, upon the shore of which stands a little mountain. This mountain is reported to have a hole, from whence, in wintertime issue such violent tempests of winds that travellers can scarcely and with great danger pass by the same way. In summertime, the noise of the wind is heard there, but it comes gently out of the hole.

Along the shores of this sea we travelled for the space of many days, which, although it is not very great, yet has many islands, and we passed by, leaving it on our left hand. In this land dwells Ordu, who is older than any of the Tartar chiefs. And the *orda*, or court, is that of one of his wives who rules over it. For it is a custom among the Tartars, that the courts of princes or of noble men are not dissolved on their death, but always some women are appointed to keep and govern them, and the same amount of gifts are bestowed, as would be given to their lords. And so at length we arrived at the first court of the emperor, wherein one of his wives dwelt. But because we had not as yet seen the emperor, they would not invite us nor admit us into the *orda*, but gave us good attendance and entertainment, after

the Tartars' fashion, in our own tent. They caused us to
stay there, and refresh ourselves for a whole day.

Chapter 23

HOW WE CAME TO KUYUK HIMSELF ❧ WHO WAS SOON TO BE CHOSEN EMPEROR

DEPARTING from here on the eve of St. Peter and St.
Paul [June 28], we entered into the land of the Naimans,
who are pagans. But upon the very feast day of the said
apostles, there fell a mighty snow in that place, and we had
extreme cold weather. This land is full of mountains, and
cold beyond measure, and there is little plain ground to be
seen. These two nations did not till their ground, but, like
the Tartars, dwelt in tents, which the Tartars had destroyed.
Through this country we were travelling many days.

Then we came to the land of the Mongols, whom we call
Tartars. Through the Tartars' land we continued our travel
for the space of about three weeks, riding always hastily
and with speed, and upon the day of Mary Magdalene [July
22], we arrived at the court of Kuyuk the emperor-elect.[1]
But we made great haste all the way, because our guides
were commanded to bring us to the imperial court with all
speed, which court had been these many years ordained for
the election of the emperor. Therefore rising early, we
travelled until night without eating anything, and oftentimes we came so late to our lodging that we had no time to
eat the same night, but that which we should have eaten at
night was given us in the morning. Often changing our
mounts, for there was no lack of horses, we rode swiftly
and without intermission, as fast as our steeds could trot.

[1] While Ogotay Khan died in 1241, the council which elected Kuyuk only met in the
spring of 1246.

Chapter 24

HOW KUYUK ENTERTAINED US AT HIS COURT ❧ AND THE AMBASSADORS

WHEN we had arrived at the court of Kuyuk, he caused, after the Tartars' manner, a tent and all expenses necessary to be provided for us. And his people treated us with more regard and courtesy than they did any other ambassadors. However, we were not called before his presence, because he was not as yet elected, nor had they settled about the succession. The translations of the Pope's letters, and the message which we brought, were sent to him by Batu.

After five or six days, he sent us to his mother [the Regent Empress Turakina], under whom there was maintained a very solemn and royal court. When we came there we saw a huge tent of fine white cloth, which was, in our judgment, so great that more than two thousand men might stand within it, and round about it there was set up a wall of planks, painted with divers designs. We, therefore, with the Tartars assigned to attend upon us, went to this tent, and there were all the chiefs assembled, each one of them riding up and down with his train over the hills and dales. The first day they were all clad in white, but on the second they wore scarlet robes. Then came Kuyuk to the tent. On the third day they were all dressed in blue robes, and on the fourth in most rich robes of baldakin [brocade] cloth.

In the wall of boards about the tent were two great gates; by one of these, the emperor only was to enter, and at that gate there was no guard of men appointed to stand, although it stood continually open, because none dared go in or come out by it. All that were admitted, entered by another gate, at which there stood watchmen, with bows, swords, and arrows. And whosoever approached the tent beyond the bounds and limit assigned, and, being caught, was beaten, but if he fled, he was shot at with arrows. There were many who, in our judgment, had upon their bridles, trappings, saddles, and such like trimmings, to the value of twenty marks in pure gold.

The chiefs communed together within the tent, and consulted about the election of their emperor. But all the rest of the people were placed far away without the board walls, and in this manner they stayed almost till noon. Then they began to drink mares' milk, and so continued drinking till evening, and that in so great quantity that it was a rare sight. They called us inside the tent, and gave us mead, because we could not drink their mares' milk. And this they did unto us in token of great honour. But they compelled us to drink so much that, because of our customary diet, we could by no means endure it. Whereupon, giving them to understand that it was hurtful to us, they ceased to compel us to drink any more. Without the door stood Duke Jeroslav of Susdal, in Russia, and a great many dukes of the Cathayans, and of the Solangs. The two sons also of the King of Georgia, an ambassador of the Calif of Bagdad, who was a sultan and, we think, more than ten other sultans of the Saracens beside. And, as it was told us by the agents, there were more than four thousand ambassadors, partly of such as paid tribute and such as presented gifts, and other sultans and dukes, which came to present themselves, and such as the Tartars had sent for, and such as were governors of lands. All these were placed without the enclosure, and had drink given to them. But almost continually they all of them gave us and Duke Jeroslav a higher place, when we were in their company.

Chapter 25

HOW HE WAS MADE RULER OF HIS EMPIRE

To our remembrance, we remained there about the space of four weeks. The election was, we thought, there celebrated, but it was not published and proclaimed there. Kuyuk came forth out of the tent, he had a noise of music, and was bowed to, or honoured with inclined staffs, having red wool upon the tops of them, and that, so long as he remained, which service was performed to none of the other chiefs. This tent or court is called by them *Syra orda*.

Departing, we all with one accord rode three or four leagues to another place, where, in a fine plain by a river's side, between certain mountains, another tent was erected, which was called the *Golden orda*. Here Kuyuk was to be placed on the imperial throne upon the day of the Assumption of Our Lady [August 15]. But, because of the abundance of hail which fell at the same time, the matter was deferred. There was also a tent erected upon pillars, which were covered with plates of gold and joined to other timber with golden nails. It was covered inside with baldakin cloth, but there was other cloth spread over it on the outside. We remained there until the feast of St. Bartholomew [August 24], when there was assembled a huge multitude standing with their faces towards the south. And a certain number of them, a stone's cast distant from the rest, were making continual prayers, and kneeling upon their knees, went farther and farther towards the south. But we, not knowing whether they used enchantments, or whether they bowed their knees to God or to some other, would not kneel upon the ground with them. And having done so a long time, they returned to the tent, and placed Kuyuk on his imperial throne, and his chiefs bowed their knees before him. Afterward the whole multitude knelt down in like manner, except ourselves, for we were not his subjects.

Chapter 26

OF HIS AGE AND PERSON ❧ AND OF HIS SEAL

THIS emperor seemed to be about the age of forty or forty-five years. He was of a mean stature, very wise and politic, and passing serious and grave in all his demeanour. A rare thing it was for a man to see him laugh or behave himself lightly, as those Christians report which abode continually with him. Certain Christians of his family earnestly and strongly assured us that he himself was about to become a Christian. A token and argument of this was, that he received many clergymen of the Christians. He had likewise at all times a chapel of Christians, near his great tent, where the priests do sing publicly and openly, and ring bells at certain hours. Yet none of their chiefs do likewise.

It is the manner of the emperor never to talk himself with a stranger, though he be ever so great. He is spoken for by a speaker. And when any of his subjects are propounding any matter of importance to him, or hearing his answer, they continue kneeling to the end of their conference. Neither is it lawful for any man to speak of any affairs, until they have been made known to the emperor.

The emperor has in his affairs, both public and private, an official, and secretary of state, with scribes and all other officials, except advocates. Without the noise of pleading, or sentence giving, all things are done according to the emperor's will and pleasure.

But, be it known unto all men, that while we remained at the emperor's court, the Emperor Kuyuk, being emperor new elect, together with all his princes, erected a flag of defiance against the Church of God, and the Roman empire, and against all Christian kingdoms and nations of the West. Their intent and purpose is to subdue the whole world, as they had been commanded by Chinghis Khan. Hence it is that the emperor in his letters writes after this manner: "The power of God, and emperor of all men." Also upon his seal, there is engraved: "God in heaven, and Kuyuk Khan upon earth, the power of God: the seal of the emperor of all men."

Chapter 27

OF OUR ADMISSION TO THE COURT ❦ AND OF OTHER AMBASSADORS

In the same place where the emperor was established on his throne, we were summoned before him. And Chingay, his chief secretary, having written down our names, and the names of those who sent us, with the name of the Duke of Solangs, and of others, cried out with a loud voice, repeating the names before the emperor, and the assembly of his chiefs. When this was done, each one of us bowed his left knee four times, and they gave us warning not to touch the threshold. And after they had searched us most diligently for knives, and could not find any about us, we entered in at the door upon the east side; because no man dare presume to enter at the west door, but the emperor only. Every Tartar chief enters on the west side to his tent, but those of low rank do not greatly regard such ceremonies. This, therefore, was the first time we entered into the emperor's tent in his presence, after he was created emperor. Likewise all other ambassadors were there received by him, but very few were admitted into his tent.

There were presented to him such abundance of gifts by

the ambassadors, that they seemed to be infinite, namely, samites, robes of purple and of baldakin cloth, silk girdles wrought with gold, and costly skins, with other gifts also. Likewise there was a certain sun canopy, or small tent, which was to be carried over the emperor's head, presented to him, and this was set full of precious stones. A governor of one province brought to him a company of camels covered with baldakins. They had saddles also upon their backs, with certain other arrangements within which were places for men to sit. Also they brought many horses and mules to him furnished with trappings and armour, some being made of leather, and some of iron. They asked us whether we would bestow any gifts upon him or not: but we were not able to do so, having already spent all. There were also upon a hill standing a good distance from the tents, more than five hundred carts, which were all full of silver and of gold, and silk garments. And they were all divided between the emperor and his chiefs, and every chief bestowed upon his own followers what pleased him.

Chapter 28

OF THE PLACE WHERE THE EMPEROR ❧ AND HIS MOTHER PARTED

LEAVING this place, we came to another, where was pitched a wonderful tent, all of red purple, presented by the Cathayans. We were admitted into that also, and always when we entered there was given us ale and wine to drink, and cooked flesh when we desired to eat. There was also a lofty stage built of boards, where the emperor's throne was placed, being very curiously wrought out of ivory, wherein also there was gold and precious stones, and there were certain stairs to ascend to it. And it was round at the back.

Benches were placed about the throne, whereon the ladies sat toward the left hand of the emperor, but none sat on the right hand, and the chiefs sat upon benches below. Certain others sat behind the chiefs, and every day there resorted thither a great company of ladies.

The three tents we mentioned before were very large, but the emperor and his wives had other great tents made of white felt. This was the place where the emperor parted company with his mother; for she went to one part of the land, and the emperor to another to execute justice. For there was taken a certain aunt of this emperor, who had poisoned his father to death, at the time when the Tartar's army was in Hungary, and it was for this reason the army retreated. This aunt and many others were tried for this crime, and they were put to death.

At the same time Jeroslav the great Duke of Susdal, which is a part of Russia, died. Having been, as it were for honour's sake, invited to eat and drink with the emperor's mother, immediately after the banquet, on returning to his lodging, he fell sick, and within seven days he died. After his death, his body was of a strange blue colour, and it was commonly reported, that the duke was poisoned, to the end that the Tartars might freely and totally possess his dukedom.

Chapter 29

HOW WE CAME AT LENGTH TO THE EMPEROR WHO GAVE ❦ AND RECEIVED LETTERS

To be short, the Tartars brought us to their emperor, who, when he heard that we had come to him, commanded that we should return to his mother. For he was determined the next day, as it is above said, to set up a flag of defiance against all the countries of the West, which he wished us not to know. We stayed some few days with his mother, and so returned again to him. We remained with him for the space of one whole month in such extreme hunger and thirst that we could scarce hold body and soul together. The provisions allowed us for four days were scarcely sufficient for one day. Neither could we buy any sustenance, because the market was too far off. However, the Lord provided for us a Russian goldsmith, named Cosmas, who, being greatly in the emperor's favour, procured us some food. This man showed us the throne of the emperor, which he had made, before it was set in its proper place, and his seal, which he also had framed.

Afterwards the emperor sent for us, giving us to understand through Chingay, his chief secretary, that we should write down our messages and affairs, and should deliver them to him. This we performed accordingly. After many days he called for us again, demanding whether there were any with our lord the Pope, who understood the Russian, the Saracen, or the Tartar languages. We answered, that we used none of those letters or languages, but that there were certain Saracens in the land, but they were a great distance from our lord the Pope. And we said that we thought it most expedient, that when they had written their minds in the Tartar language, and had interpreted the meaning thereof to us, we should diligently translate it into our own tongue, and so deliver both the letter and the translation thereof to our lord the Pope. On this they departed and went to the emperor.

On the day of St. Martin [November 11], we were called for again. Then Kadac, principal secretary for the whole empire, and Chingay, and Bala, with divers other scribes, came to us, and interpreted the letter word for word.

And having written it in Latin, they made us interpret to them each sentence, to find out if we had erred in any word. And when both letters were written, they made us read them over twice more, lest we should have mistaken something. And they said to us: "Take heed that you understand all things thoroughly, for if you should not understand the whole matter, it might breed some inconvenience." They wrote the letters also in the Saracen tongue, that there might be found in our dominions some who could read and interpret them, if need should require.

Chapter 30

HOW WE WERE PERMITTED TO DEPART

OUR Tartars told us the emperor proposed sending ambassadors with us. However, he wanted that we ourselves should ask that favour at his hands. And when one of our Tartars, being an elderly man, advised us to make the petition, we thought it not good for us that the emperor should send his ambassadors. Therefore, we gave him our answer, that it was not for us to make any such petition, but if it pleased the emperor of his own accord to send them, we would diligently, by God's assistance, see them conducted in safety. We thought it expedient that they should not go, and that for different reasons. First, because we feared lest they, seeing the dissensions and wars which are among us, should be the more encouraged to make war against us. Secondly, we feared that they would be spies and informers in our dominions. Thirdly, we feared that they would be slain on the way; for our nations are arrogant and proud. For when those servants, who, at the request of the cardinal, attended upon us, returned unto him in the Tartar's attire, they were almost stoned on the way by the Germans and were compelled to put off those garments. And it is the Tartars' custom never to make peace with those who have slain their ambassadors, till they have revenged themselves. Fourthly, lest they should take us by main force and carry us off. Fifthly, because no good could come of their mission, for they were to have no other authority, but only to deliver their emperor's letter to the Pope, which very same letter we ourselves had, and we knew right well that much harm might come of it.

Therefore, the third day after this, namely, upon the feast of St. Brice, they gave us permission to leave and a letter sealed with the emperor's own seal, sending us to the emperor's mother, who gave to each of us a gown made of fox skins, with the fur on the outside, and a piece of purple. And our Tartars stole a yard out of every one of them. And out of that which was given to our servant, they stole the better half, which false dealing of theirs we knew well enough, but would make no words over it.

Chapter 31

HOW WE RETURNED HOMEWARD ◀ AND OF THE LETTERS TO THE POPE

THEN taking our journey to return, we travelled all winter long, lying in the deserts oftentimes upon the snow, except with our feet we made a piece of ground bare to lie upon. For there were no trees, and the plains were open. And oftentimes in the morning we found ourselves all covered with snow driven over us by the wind. And so travelling till the feast of our Lord's Ascension [May 9], we arrived at the court of Batu. When we had inquired, what answer he would send to our lord the Pope, he said that he had nothing to give us in charge, but only that we would diligently deliver that which the emperor had written. And, having received letters for our safe conduct, the thirteenth day after Pentecost [June 2], being Saturday, we reached Mauchy, where were our associates and servants, which had been withheld from us, and we caused them to be delivered to us.

From here we travelled to Corenza, to whom, requiring gifts the second time at our hands, we gave none. He gave us two Comans, who lived among the common people of the Tartars, to be our guides as far as the city of Kiev in Russia. One of our Tartars did not leave us, till we passed the last guard of the Tartars. But the other guides, namely the Comans, which were given us by Corenza, brought us from the last guard to the city of Kiev, in the space of six days. And there we arrived fifteen days before the feast of St. John the Baptist [June 9].

The citizens of Kiev hearing of our approach, they all came forth to meet us, with great joy. For they rejoiced over us, as over men that had risen from death to life. So likewise they did throughout all Russia, Poland, and Bohemia. Daniel and his brother Wasilko made us a royal feast, and entertained us against our wills for the space of eight days. In the meantime, they with their bishops, and other men of account, after a consultation on those matters of which we had spoken to them on our eastward journey towards the Tartars, answered us with common consent, saying that they would hold the Pope for their special lord and father, and the Church of Rome for their lady and mistress, confirming likewise all things which they had sent concerning this matter, before our coming, through their abbot. And after that they sent their ambassadors and letters with us, to our lord the Pope.

THE JOURNAL OF
FRIAR WILLIAM OF RUBRUCK
1253-1255

FRIAR WILLIAM OF RUBRUCK

Rubruck was born in 1215 and died in 1270. He went to the East as an envoy of Louis IX (St. Louis) of France, who learning that Sartach, son of Batu the commander of Tartar troops in Russia, had become a Christian, desired to open communications with him.

The vast conquests of Chinghis Khan were at this time still intact, though they were not under a single ruler. When Rubruck set out on his journey in 1253 Mangu Khan, a grandson of Chinghis and elder brother of Kublai Khan, was the Great Khan and ruler on the Mongolian steppes. Rubruck reached the courts of Sartach and Batu and after some delay was ordered to visit the Great Khan at his court, near Caracarum. This involved a journey of five thousand miles.

The narrative of this journey is certainly one of the most interesting and intimate travel records in existence. It is full of colour and life and gives a splendid first-hand picture of the Tartars. Historically it is as important a record as Marco Polo's.

After many amazing experiences Rubruck at length returned to Christian soil in 1255. He had hoped to meet King Louis in Palestine, but the King had already made his pilgrimage and had returned to France. He therefore went to Acre and in the monastery of his Order wrote the report of his journey. This he sent to the King.

Roger Bacon met Rubruck several years later and spoke to him about his adventures and discoveries. He also examined Rubruck's travel record and made detailed notes which we find embodied in the famous *Opus Majus*. Little is known about the man personally excepting that he was honest, pious, stout-hearted, a keen observer, and like Friar Carpini, he, too, was a very heavy man. He has left us a record and narrative of a journey that has few superiors in the whole Library of Travel.

THE JOURNAL OF
FRIAR WILLIAM OF RUBRUCK

*A Frenchman of the Order of the Minor Friars, to the
East Parts of the World, in the Years 1253 to 1255*

Chapter 1

OF THE CITIES ❧ AND LANDS WE PASSED IN GOING TO THE LAND OF THE TARTARS

To his sovereign, the most Christian Louis, by God's grace the renowned king of France, Friar William of Rubruck, the meanest of the order of Minor Friars, wishes health and continual triumph in Christ.

It is written in the book of Ecclesiasticus concerning the wise man: "He shall travel into foreign countries, and good and evil shall he try in all things." This, my lord and king, have I achieved: however, I hope that I have done it as a wise man, and not as a fool. For many there be, who perform the same action which a wise man does, not wisely but more foolishly: of which number I fear myself to be one. Nevertheless, in whatever way, I have done it because you commanded me, when I departed from your Highness, to write all things unto you, which I should see among the Tartars. You wished also that I should not fear to write long letters: I

have done as your Majesty enjoined me, yet with fear and
reverence, because I want words and eloquence sufficient to
write to so great a majesty.

Be it known then to your sacred Majesty, that in the year
of our Lord 1253, about the nones of May [7th], we entered
into the sea of Pontus [Black Sea], which the Bulgarians
call the Great Sea. It contains in length 1008 miles, as I
learned of certain merchants, and is divided, as it were, into
two parts. About the middle thereof are two provinces,
one towards the north, and another towards the south. The
south province is called Synopolis, and it is the castle and
port of the Sultan of Turkey; but the north province is
called by the Latins, Gasaria [Crimea]: but by the Greeks,
who inhabit the shore thereof, it is called Cassaria, that is
to say Cæsarea. And there are certain headlands stretching
forth into the sea towards Synopolis. Also there are three
hundred miles of distance between Synopolis and Cassaria.
The distance from those points or places to Constantinople,
in length and breadth, is about seven hundred miles: and
seven hundred miles also from there to the east, namely
to the province of Georgia.

We arrived at the province of Gasaria, or Cassaria, which
province is triangular, having a city on the west part called
Kersona, wherein St. Clement suffered martyrdom. And
sailing before the said city, we saw an island on which a
church is said to be built by the hands of angels. About the
middle of the said province toward the south, upon a sharp
point, is a city called Soldaia [Sudak], directly over against
Synopolis. And there all the Turkish merchants who traffic in the north countries, in their journey outward, arrive,
and also they who return homeward from Russia, and the
northern regions, and wish to pass into Turkey. The merchants carry ermines and grey furs, with other rich and

costly skins. Others carry clothes made of cotton, and silk, and various kinds of spices. But upon the east part of the said province stands a city called Matrica, where the river Tanais [Don] discharges its streams into the sea of Pontus, through a mouth twelve miles in breadth. This river, before it enters into the sea of Pontus, forms a little sea, in breadth and length seven hundred miles, and it is in no part above six paces deep; therefore, great vessels cannot sail over it. But the merchants of Constantinople, arriving at the city of Matrica, send their barks as far as the river of Tanais to buy dried fish, sturgeon, barbel, and an infinite number of other fishes. The said province of Cassaria is encompassed by the sea on three sides: on the west, is Kersona, the city of St. Clement; on the south, the city of Soldaia where we arrived; on the east, Maricandis, and there also stands the city of Matrica upon the mouth of the river Tanais.

Beyond the mouth stands Zikia, which is not in subjection unto the Tartars: also the people called Suevs and Hibers towards the east, who likewise are not under the Tartars' rule. Moreover, towards the south, stands the city of Trebizond, which has its own governor, named Guido, who is of the lineage of the emperors of Constantinople, and is subject to the Tartars. Next is Synopolis, the city of the Sultan of Turkey, who likewise is in subjection unto them. All the land from the mouth of Tanais westward as far as the Danube is under their subjection. Even beyond the Danube, towards Constantinople, Wallachia, which is the land of Assani, and Lesser Bulgaria as far as Solonia, all pay tribute to them. And besides the tribute imposed, they have also of late years exacted of every household one axe, and all such iron as they found unwrought.

We arrived therefore at Soldaia the twelfth of the calends of June [May 21]. And merchants of Constantinople, who arrived there before us, reported that certain messengers were coming from the Holy Land, who were desirous to travel into Sartach. However, I myself had preached on Palm Sunday, within the Church of St. Sophia, that I was not your nor any other man's messenger, but that I was going among these unbelievers according to the rule of our order. After arriving, the merchants cautioned me to take diligent heed what I spoke: because they having reported me to be a messenger, if I should say the contrary, I would not be allowed to pass. Then I spoke in this manner to the governors of the city, or rather to their lieutenants, because the governors themselves had gone to pay tribute unto Batu, and had not as yet returned. We heard of our lord Sartach, I said, in the Holy Land, that he has become a Christian: and the Christians were exceeding glad thereof, and especially the most Christian King of France, who is there now on a pilgrimage, and is fighting against the Saracens to redeem the Holy Places out of their hands: therefore, I am determined to go unto Sartach, and to deliver to him the letters of my lord the king, wherein he admonishes him concerning the good and welfare of all Christendom. And they received us favourably, and gave us lodgings in the cathedral church. The bishop of this church had been to Sartach, and he told me many good things concerning him, which later I failed to discover for myself.

Then they gave us our choice, whether we would have carts and oxen, or pack-horses to transport our effects. The merchants of Constantinople advised me not to take carts of the citizens of Soldaia but to buy covered carts of mine own, such as the Russians carry their skins in, and to put into them all our effects, which I would not require daily: because, if I should use horses, I must at every stopping place take down my things and lift them up again on other horses' backs: and besides, that I should ride a more gentle pace by the oxen drawing the carts. By accepting their evil counsel, I was travelling to Sartach two months which I could have done in one had I gone by horse.

I brought with me from Constantinople, on advice of the merchants, pleasant fruits, muscadel wine, and delicate biscuit bread to present unto the governors of Soldaia, to the end I might obtain free passage: because they look favourably upon no man which comes with an empty hand. All of which things I bestowed in one of my carts, for they told me, if I could carry them as far as Sartach, that they would be most acceptable unto him. We took our journey, therefore, about the first of June, with four covered carts of our own, and with two other which we borrowed of them, wherein we carried our bedding to rest upon in the night, and they allowed us five horses to ride upon. There were just five persons in our company: namely, I myself and mine associate, Friar Bartholomew of Cremona, and Goset the bearer of these presents, the man of God Turgemannus, and Nicolas, my servant, whom I bought at Constantinople with some part of the alms bestowed upon me. Moreover, they allowed us two men, which drove our carts and looked after our oxen and horses.

There are high points of land on the shore from Kersona to the mouth of Tanais. Also there are forty castles between Kersona and Soldaia, every one of which has its own language: among them there were many Goths, whose language is Teutonic.

Beyond these mountains towards the north there is a most beautiful wood growing on a plain full of fountains and rivulets. And beyond the wood there is a mighty plain which stretches out for five days' journey to the very border of the province northward, and there is a narrow isthmus or neck land, having sea on the east and west sides, so that there is a ditch made from one sea to the other. In this plain before the Tartars came were the Comans, who compelled the mentioned cities and castles to pay tribute unto them. But when the Tartars came a great multitude of the Comans entered into this province, and all fled to the sea shore, being in such extreme famine, that they who were alive were obliged to eat up those who were dead; and a merchant who saw it with his own eyes reported to me that the living men devoured and tore with their teeth the raw flesh of the dead, as dogs would gnaw upon corpses.

Towards the border of the said province there are many great lakes; upon their banks are brine springs, the water of which as soon as it enters the lake becomes salt as hard as ice. And out of these salt pits Batu and Sartach have great revenues: for they come here from all Russia for salt; and for each cart-load they give two pieces of cotton amounting to the value of half an *yperpera*. There come also by sea many ships for salt, which pay tribute every one of them according to the quantity.

The third day after we departed out of Soldaia, we found the Tartars. When I found myself among them I thought I had arrived into a new century. Their life and manners I will describe to your Highness as well as I can.

Chapter 2
OF THE TARTARS AND OF THEIR HOUSES

THEY have in no place any settled city to live in, neither do they know where their next will be. They have divided all Scythia among themselves, which stretches from the river Danube to the rising of the sun. And every captain, according to the great or small number of his people, knows the bound of his pastures, and where he ought to feed his cattle, winter and summer, spring and autumn. In the winter they descend into warm regions southward. And in the summer they ascend to the cold regions northward. In winter when snow falls upon the ground, they feed their cattle upon pastures without water, because then they use snow instead of water.

Their houses in which they sleep, they base upon a round frame of wickers interlaced compactly: the roof consists of wickers, meeting above into one little roundell, out of which ascends a neck like a chimney, which they cover with white felt, and oftentimes they lay mortar or white earth upon the said felt, with the powder of bones, that it may shine white. And sometimes also they cover it with black felt. The felt on the collar they decorate with various beautiful pictures. Before the door they hang a felt curiously painted with vines, trees, birds, and beasts.

These houses they make so large that they are often thirty feet in breadth. Measuring once the breadth between the wheel-ruts of one of their carts, I found it to be twenty feet over: and when the house was upon the cart, it stretched over the wheels on each side five feet at least. I counted twenty-two oxen in one team, drawing a house upon a cart, eleven in one order according to the breadth of the cart, and eleven more before them: the axletree of the cart was of huge size, like the mast of a ship. And a fellow stood in the door of the house, upon the forestall of the cart, driving the oxen.

Moreover, they make certain square baskets of small slender wickers as big as great chests: and afterward, from one side to another, they frame a hollow lid or cover of like wickers, and make a door in the front. And then they cover this chest or little house with black felt rubbed over with tallow or sheep's milk to keep the rain from soaking through; this they decorate also with paintings or with feathers. In such chests they put their whole household stuff and treasure. Also the same chests they strongly bind upon other carts, which are drawn with camels, so that they may wade through rivers. Neither do they at any time take down the chests from their carts.

When they take down their dwelling houses, they turn the doors always to the south: and then they place the carts with chests, here and there, within half a stone's throw of the house: so that the house stands between two ranks of carts, as it were, between two walls. The matrons make for themselves most beautiful carts, which I am not able to describe unto your Majesty but by pictures only: for I would right willingly have painted all things for you, had my skill been in that direction. A single rich Moal [Mongol], or Tartar, has two hundred or one hundred such carts with chests. Chief Batu has sixteen wives, every one of which has one great house, besides other little houses, which they place behind the great one, being as it were chambers for their serving girls to dwell in. And to every one of the houses belong two hundred carts.

When they take their houses off the carts, the principal wife places her court on the west front, and so all the rest in their order: so that the last wife lives upon the east side: and one court is distant from another by about a stone's throw. The court of one rich Moal will appear like a great village, though very few men will be found. One woman will guide twenty or thirty carts at once, for their country is very flat, and they bind the carts with camels or oxen, one behind another. And there sits a wench in the foremost cart driving the oxen, and all the residue follow on a like pace. When they chance to come to a bad place, they let them loose, and guide them over one by one. They go at a slow pace, as fast as a lamb or an ox might walk.

Chapter 3
OF THEIR BEDS ❧ AND OF THEIR DRINKING POTS

HAVING taken down their houses from their carts, and turned the doors southward, they place the bed of the master of the house at the north side. The women's place is always on the east side, namely, on the left hand of the master of the house, sitting upon his bed with his face southwards; but the men's place is upon the west side, namely, at the right hand of their master. Men, when they enter the house, will not in any case hang their bows on the women's side.

Over the master's head is always an image, like a puppet, made of felt, which they call the master's brother: and another over the head of the good wife or mistress, which they call her brother, is fastened to the wall: and higher up between both of them, there is a little lean one, which is as it were the guardian of the whole house. The mistress of the house places aloft at her bed's feet, on the right hand, a goat-skin stuffed with wool or some other material, and near that a little image or puppet looking towards the maidens and women. Next to the door, also on the women's side, there is another image with a cow's udder, for the women that milk the cows. It is the duty of their women to milk cows. On the other side of the door, next to the men, there is another image with the udder of a mare, for the men milk the mares.

And when they come together to drink and make merry, they sprinkle part of their drink upon the image which is above the master's head: afterward upon other images in order: then a servant goes out of the house with a cup full of drink sprinkling it three times towards the south, and bowing his knee at every time: and this is done for the honour of the fire. Then he performs the same towards the east, for the honour of the air: and then to the west for the honour of the water: and lastly to the north in behalf of the dead.

When the master holds a cup in his hand to drink, before he drinks he pours part upon the ground. If he drinks sitting on horseback, he pours out part upon the neck or mane of his horse. After the servant has so discharged his cups to the four quarters of the world, he returns into the house: and two other servants stand ready with two cups, and two basins, to carry drink to their master and his wife, sitting together upon the couch. And if he has more wives than one, she with whom he slept the night before sits by his side the day following: and all his other wives must that day resort to her house to drink: and there the court is held for that day: the gifts also which are presented that day are laid up in the chests of that wife. A bench, bearing a vessel of milk or of other drink and drinking cups, stands at the door.

Chapter 4

OF THEIR DRINKS ◄ AND HOW THEY PROVOKE ONE ANOTHER TO DRINKING

In winter they make an excellent drink of rice, of millet, and of honey, being well and highly coloured like wine. Also they have wine brought to them from far countries. In summer they care not for any drink but *cosmos* [mare's milk]. And it stands always within the entrance of the door, and next to it stands a minstrel with his guitar. I saw there no lutes or violins such as we have, but many other musical instruments which are not used among us. And when the master of the house begins to drink, one of his servants cries out with a loud voice, "Ha!" and the minstrel plays upon his guitar. And when they make any great solemn feast, they all of them clap their hands and dance to the noise of music, the men before their master and the women before their mistress.

When the master has drunk, his servant cries out as before, and the minstrel stops his music. Then they drink all around, both men and women: and sometimes they carouse for the victory very filthily and drunkenly. Also when they desire to provoke any man, they pull him by the ears to the cup, and so lug and draw him, clapping their hands and dancing before him. Moreover when some of them will make great feasting and rejoicing, one of the company takes a full cup, and two others stand, one on his right hand and another on his left, and so they three come singing to the man who is to have the cup handed to him still singing and dancing before him: and when he stretche forth his hand to receive the cup, they leap suddenly back, returning again as they did before, and so having deluded him three or four times by drawing back the cup until he is merry, and has a good appetite, then they give him the cup, singing and dancing and stamping with their feet, until he has finished drinking.

Chapter 5
OF THEIR FOOD ✿ AND VICTUALS

CONCERNING their food and victuals, be it known that they do, without exception, eat all their dead animals. And amongst so many droves, it cannot be but some cattle must die. However, in summer, so long as their *cosmos* lasts, they care not for any other food. And if they chance to have an ox or a horse die, they dry the flesh thereof by cutting it into thin slices and hanging it up against the sun and the wind. It is presently dried without salt, and also without any evil smell. They make better sausages of their horses than of their hogs, which they eat fresh. The rest of the flesh they reserve until winter. They make of their ox-skins great bladders, or bags, which they dry wonderfully in smoke. Of the hinder part of their horse hides they make very fine sandals and shoes.

They give to fifty or a hundred men the flesh of one ram to eat, for they mince it in a bowl with salt and water, they have no other sauce, and then with the point of a knife, or a little fork which they make for this purpose, such as we use to take roasted pears or apples out of wine, they give to every one of the company a mouthful or two, according to the number of guests. The master of the house, first of all, takes what he pleases. Also, if he gives to any of the company a special part, the person receiving it must eat it alone, and must not give any part of it. Not being able to eat it all up he carries it with him, or delivers it to his boy, if he is present, to keep it for him. If not, he puts it into his *saptargat*, that is to say a square bag which they carry about with them for the saving of all such provisions, and in this bag they also store their bones, when they have not time to gnaw them thoroughly, that nothing of their food be lost.

Chapter 6

HOW THEY MAKE THEIR DRINK CALLED COSMOS

THEIR drink called *cosmos* is prepared in this manner. They fasten a long line to two posts standing firmly in the ground, and to the line they tie the young colts of the mares which they mean to milk. Then come the mothers who stand by their foals, and allow themselves to be milked. And if any of them be too unruly, then one takes her colt and puts it under her, letting it suck a while, and presently taking it away again, and the milker takes its place. After they have got together a good quantity of this milk, being as sweet as cow's milk, while it is fresh they pour it into a great bladder or bag, and they beat the said bag with a piece of wood made for the purpose, having a club at the lower end shaped like a man's head, and being hollow within: and as soon as they beat the bag it begins to boil like new wine, and to become sour and sharp to the taste, and they beat it in that manner until it turns to butter. Then they taste it, and when it is mildly pungent, they drink it. It bites a man's tongue like the wine of grape, when it is drunk. After a man has taken a draught thereof, it leaves behind it a taste like the taste of almond milk, and goes down very pleasantly, intoxicating weak brains: also it causes wine to be avoided in great measure.

Likewise *caracosmos*, that is to say, black cosmos, for great lords to drink. They make this in the following manner. First they beat the milk as long as the thickest part of it descends right down to the bottom like the lees of white wine, and that which is thin and pure remains above, being like whey or white must. The lees or dregs being very white, are given to slaves, and will cause them to sleep. That which is thin and clear their masters drink: and indeed it is agreeably sweet and wholesome liquor.

Chief Batu has thirty cottages, or granges, within a day's journey of his abiding place: every one of which serves him daily with *caracosmos* of a hundred mares' milk, and so all of them together with the milk of three thousand mares, besides white milk which other of his subjects bring.

For as the husbandmen of Syria bestow the third part of their fruits and carry it unto the courts of their lords, so do the Tartars their mares' milk every third day. Out of the cows' milk they first churn butter; boiling the butter until it is dry, they put it into rams' skins, which they reserve for the same purpose. Neither do they salt their butter: and yet by reason of the long boiling it spoils not: and they keep it in store for winter. The churnmilk which remains of the butter, they let alone till it becomes as sour as possibly it may be; then they boil it and in boiling, it is turned into curds, which curds they dry in the sun, making them as hard as the slag of iron. This kind of food also they store up in bags for winter. In the winter season when milk fails them, they put the curds, which they call *gryut*, into a bladder, and pouring hot water into it, they beat it vigorously till they have resolved it. It is thereby made exceedingly sour, and they drink this instead of milk. They are very scrupulous, and take diligent heed not to drink pure water by itself.

Chapter 7

OF THE BEASTS WHICH THEY EAT ❧ OF THEIR GARMENTS ❧ AND OF THEIR MANNER OF HUNTING

GREAT lords have villages in the south, from whence their tenants bring them millet and meal for the winter. The poor provide themselves with such necessaries, for the exchange of rams, and of other skins. The slaves fill their bellies with thick water, and with this are contented. They will neither eat mice with long tails, nor any kind of mice with short tails. They have also certain little beasts called by them *sogur* [marmots], which lie in a cave twenty or thirty of them together, all the whole winter sleeping there for the space of six months. These they take in great abundance. There is also a kind of conies having long tails like cats, and on the outside of their tails grow black and white hairs.

They have many other small beasts good to eat, which they know very well how to distinguish. I saw no deer there, and but a few hares, but a great number of gazelles. I saw wild asses in great abundance, which are like mules. Also I saw another kind of beast called *artak* [Ovis Poli], having in all resemblance the body of a ram, and crooked horns, which are of such bigness that I could scarce lift up a pair of them with one hand. Of these horns they make great drinking cups. They have falcons, gerfalcons, and other hawks in great plenty; all which they carry upon their right hand; and they always put about their falcons' necks a thong of leather, which hangs down to the middle of their breasts. When they cast them off the fist at their game, with their left hand they bow down the heads and breasts by this thong, lest they should be tossed up and down, and beaten with the wind, or lest they should soar too high. They get a great part of their food by hunting and hawking.

Concerning their garments and attire, you must know that out of Cathay and other regions of the east, out of Persia also and other countries of the south, there are brought to them stuffs of silk, cloth of gold, and cotton cloth, which they wear in summer. But out of Russia, Moxel, Great Bulgaria, and Pascatir, that is Great Hungary, and out of Kerkis, all which are northern regions and full of woods, and also out of many other countries of the north, which are subject unto them, the inhabitants bring them rich and costly skins of many kinds which I never saw in our parts, and which they wear in winter. And always in winter they make themselves two gowns, one with the fur inward and another with the fur outward, to defend them from wind and snow; these latter are usually made of wolves' skins, fox skins, or else of papions [badger, or variety of fox]. And when they sit within the house, they have a lighter one to wear. The poor make their upper gown of dogs' or of goats' skins.

When they go to hunt for wild beasts, there meets a great company together, and environing the place round about, where they are sure to find some game, by little and little they approach on all sides, till they have gotten the wild beasts into the midst, as it were, into a circle, and then they discharge their arrows at them. Also they make themselves breeches of skins. The rich Tartars sometimes wad their gowns with silk stuffing, which is exceeding soft, light and warm. The poor line their clothes with cotton cloth which is made of the finest wool they can pick, and of the coarser part of the wool they make felt to cover their houses and their chests, and use it for their bedding also. The same wool, being mixed with one-third part of horse hair, they use to make their ropes. They also make felt covers for their stools, and caps to protect their heads from the weather as well as saddle-cloths and rain cloaks; so they use a great quantity of wool. This much concerning the attire of the men.

Chapter 8

OF THE FASHION WHICH THE TARTARS USE IN CUTTING THEIR HAIR ❦ AND OF THE ATTIRE OF THEIR WOMEN

THE men shave a square plot upon the crowns of their heads, and from the two foremost corners they shave, as it were, two seams down to their temples. They shave also their temples and the back part of their head even to the nape of the neck. Likewise they shave the fore part of their scalp down to their foreheads, and upon their foreheads they leave a lock of hair reaching down to their eyebrows. Upon the two hindermost corners of their heads, they have two locks also, which they twine and braid into knots and so bind and knit them, one under each ear.

The women's garments differ not from the men's, saving that they are somewhat longer. But the day after one of their women is married, she shaves her scalp from the middle of her head down to her forehead, and wears a wide garment like the hood of a nun, but larger and longer in all parts than a nun's hood, open before and tied under the right side. For in this the Tartars differ from the Turks, because the Turks fasten their garments to their bodies on the left side, but the Tartars always on the right side.

They have also an ornament for their heads which they call *botta,* being made of the bark of a tree, or of some such other light material. It is so thick and round that it cannot be held but in both hands together, and it has a square sharp spire rising from the top more than a cubit high and fashioned like a column. This *botta* they cover all over with a piece of rich silk: it is hollow within, and upon the spire, or square top, they put a bunch of quills or of slender canes a cubit long and more. This tuft they beautify with peacocks' feathers, and round about its length with the feathers of a mallard's tail, and with precious stones.

Great ladies wear this kind of ornament upon their heads, binding it strongly with a certain hat, which has a hole in the crown fit for the spire to come through it. Under this ornament they gather up their hair in a knot, and they bind it strongly under their throats. When a great company of such gentlewomen riding together are beheld far off, they seem to be soldiers with helmets on their heads carrying their lances upright. All their women sit on horseback like

men, and they bind their hoods or gowns about their waists
with a blue silk scarf, and with another scarf they gird it
above their breasts. They also bind a piece of white silk like
a muffler or mask under their eyes, reaching down to the
breast. These gentlewomen are exceedingly fat, and the
smaller their noses, the fairer are they esteemed. They daub
over their faces with grease, and they never lie down in bed
when having their children.

Chapter 9

OF THE DUTIES OF THE TARTAR WOMEN ❧ AND OF THEIR LABOURS ❧ AND ALSO OF THEIR MARRIAGES

THE duties of women are: to drive carts, to lay their
houses upon the carts and to take them down again, to milk
cows, to make butter and *gryut*, to dress skins and to sew
them, which they usually do with thread made of tendons.
They divide the tendons into slender threads, and then
twine them into one long thread.

They make sandals and socks and other garments. However, they never wash any apparel, for they say that God
is thus angered, and that dreadful thunder will come if
washed garments be hanged out to dry. Yes, they beat such
as wash, and take their garments from them. They are ter-
ribly afraid of thunder, and when it thunders they put all
strangers out of their houses, and then wrap themselves in
black felt and lie hidden till the thunder is over.

They never wash their dishes or bowls, but when their
meat is cooked they wash the bowl with scalding hot broth
out of the pot, and then pour the broth into the pot again.
They also make felt and cover their houses with it.

The duties of the men are: to make bows and arrows, stir-
rups, bridles, and saddles; to build houses and carts; to keep

horses; to milk mares; to churn *cosmos*, and to make bags into which to put it; they keep camels also and lay burdens upon them. As for sheep and goats, both men and women tend and milk them.

With sheep's milk thickened and salted they dress and tan their hides. When they desire to wash their hands or their heads, they fill their mouths full of water and spout it into their hands a little at a time; and in this way they wet their hair and wash their heads.

As to their marriages, you must understand that no man can have a wife till he has bought her. Sometimes it happens their girls are very stale before they are married, for their parents keep them till they can sell them. They keep the first and second degrees of blood kin inviolable, as we do; but they have no regard of the degrees of affinity: for they will marry at one time, or by succession, two sisters. Their widows marry not at all, for this reason; because they believe that all who have served them in this life, shall do them service in the life to come. Therefore, they are persuaded that every widow after death shall return to her own husband. And hence comes an abominable and filthy custom among them, namely, that the son marries sometimes all his father's wives except his own mother. The court or house of the father or mother falls by inheritance always to the younger son. He is to provide for all his father's wives, because they are part of his inheritance as well as his father's possessions. And then if he will he uses them as his own wives; for he thinks it no injury if they return to his father after death. Therefore, when any man has bargained with another for a maid, the father of the said damosel makes him a feast; in the meanwhile she flies to some of her kinsfolk to hide herself. Then her father says to the bridegroom: "Lo, my daughter is yours, take her wheresoever

you can find her." He and his friends then seek her till
they find her, and having found her he must take her by
force and carry her off with a semblance of violence to his
own house.

Chapter 10

OF THEIR EXECUTION OF JUSTICE AND JUDGMENT ❦ AND OF
THEIR DEATHS AND BURIALS

CONCERNING their laws or their execution of justice, you
should know that when two men fight, no third man dare
intrude to part them. A father may not help his own son.
But he that has the worst of it may appeal to the court of
his lord. And if any one touches him after the appeal, he
is put to death. But he must appeal without any delay; and
he who has suffered the injury, leads the other as though he
were a captive. They punish no man with sentence of death,
unless he be taken in the act or confesses. But being accused
by the multitude, they put him into extreme torture to make
him confess. They punish murder with death, and carnal
copulation also with any other besides his own. By his own
I mean his wife or his maid-servant, for he may use his
slave as he pleases. Heinous theft or felony they punish also
with death. For a light theft, as for stealing a ram, the
person, if not apprehended in the act, is cruelly beaten. Also
false messengers, because they feign themselves to be messengers, and indeed are none at all, they punish with death.
Sacrilegious persons they use in like manner, because they
esteem such to be witches.

When any man dies, they lament and howl most piti-
fully for him; and the mourners are free from paying any
tribute for one whole year. Also whosoever is present at
the house where any adult lies dead, he must not enter into
the court of Mangu Khan for one whole year. If it were a

child deceased, he must not enter into the court till the next month. Near the grave of the deceased they always leave one tent. If any one of the nobles of the family of Chinghis, who was their first lord and father, dies, his grave is not known. And always about those places where they bury their nobles, there is a camp of men to watch the tombs. I could not learn if they hide treasures in the graves of their dead.

The Comans build a great tomb over their dead, and erect the image with his face towards the east, holding a drinking cup in his hand, at the height of his navel. Upon the monuments of rich men they erect pyramids, that is to say, little sharp houses or pinnacles; and in some places I saw mighty towers made of brick, in other places pyramids made of stones, even though there are no stones to be found thereabout. I saw one newly buried, in whose behalf they hung up sixteen horse hides, four facing each quarter of the world, between certain high posts; and they set beside his grave *cosmos* for him to drink, and flesh to eat: and yet they said that he was baptized. I beheld other kinds of tombs also towards the east, namely, large floors or pavements made of stone, some round and some square, and then four long stones pitched upright about the pavement towards the four corners of the world.

When any man is sick, he lies in his bed, and causes a sign to be set upon his house, to signify that there a sick person lies, so that no man may enter into the house; therefore, none at all visit any sick person, but his servant. Moreover, when any one is sick in their great courts, they appoint watchmen to stand round about the court, and they will not allow any person to pass within the bounds. For they fear lest evil spirits or winds should come with the persons that enter. They, however, call soothsayers and their priests.

Chapter 11

OF OUR FIRST ENTRANCE AMONG THE TARTARS ❦ AND OF THEIR INGRATITUDE

AND as we found ourselves among these barbarous people, I thought, as I said before, that I had entered into a new world. They came flocking about us on horseback, after they had made us wait a long time for them, sitting in the shadow under their black carts. The first question they asked was whether we had ever been with them before or not? Giving them answer that we had not, they began to beg most impudently for some of our provisions. We gave them some of our biscuit and wine, which we had brought with us from the town of Soldaia. Having drunk off one flagon of our wine they demanded another, saying that a man does not go into the house with one foot. However, we gave them no more, excusing ourselves on the ground that we had but a little.

Then they asked us whence we came, and whither we were bound? I answered them with the words above-mentioned: that we had heard concerning Chief Sartach that he had become a Christian, and that our determination was to travel to him, having your Majesty's letters to deliver. They were very inquisitive to know whether I came of mine own accord, or whether I had been sent? I answered that no man compelled me to come, neither had I come unless I myself had been willing; and therefore I had come according to mine own will, and to the will of my superior. I took diligent heed never to say that I was your Majesty's ambassador. Then they asked what I had in my carts; whether it were gold or silver, or rich garments to carry unto Sartach? I answered that Sartach should see what we had brought, and that they had no business to ask such questions, but should conduct me to their captain, and he, if he thought good, should cause me to be directed to Sartach; otherwise I would return.

Now, there was in the same province a relative of Batu called Scacatai, to whom my lord the Emperor of Constantinople had written letters of request to allow me to pass through his territory. With this answer of ours they were satisfied, giving us horses and oxen, and two men to conduct us. However, before they would allow us these necessaries for our journey, they made us wait a long while, begging our bread for their young brats, wondering at all things which they saw about our servants, as their knives, gloves, purses, and belts, desiring to have them. I excused myself on the ground that we had a long way to travel, and that we must not deprive ourselves of things necessary for so long a journey. Then they said that I was an impostor.

True it is that they took nothing by force from me; but they will beg that which they see very shamelessly. And if a man gives to them, it is but lost, for they are thankless wretches. They esteem themselves lords and think that nothing should be denied them by any man. If a man gives them nothing, and afterwards stands in need of their service, they will do nothing for him. They gave us of their cows' milk to drink after the butter was churned out of it; it was very sour, and they call it *apram*. And thus we departed from them. And it seemed to me that we had escaped out of the hands of devils. On the next day we came to their captain.

From the time when we departed from Soldaia till we arrived at the court of Sartach, which was the space of two months, we never lay in house or tent, but always under the starry canopy, and in the open air, or under our carts. We saw no village, nor any sign of building where a village had been, but the graves of the Comans in great abundance. The same evening our guide which had conducted us gave us some *cosmos*. After I had tasted it I sweated most extremely because of the novelty and strangeness, and because I never drank of it before. Nevertheless, I thought it was very savoury, as indeed it was.

Chapter 12

OF THE COURT OF SCACATAI ❧ AND HOW THE CHRISTIANS DRINK NO COSMOS

ON the next day we met with the carts of Scacatai laden with houses, and I thought that a mighty city came to meet me. I wondered also at the huge droves of oxen, and horses, and at the flocks of sheep. I could see but a few men that guided all these matters: therefore, I inquired how many men he had under him, and they told me that he had not above five hundred in all, the one-half of which number we had passed, as they lay in another direction. Then the servant which was our guide told me that I must present somewhat unto Scacatai; and so he made us stop, going himself ahead to give notice of our coming. By this time it was past three of the clock, and they unloaded their houses near a certain water; and there came unto us his interpreter, who being advised by us that we were never there before, demanded some of our provisions, and these we yielded upon his request. Also he required of us some garment for a reward, because he was to interpret our sayings to his master. We excused ourselves as well as we could. Then he asked us, what we would present to his lord? We took a flagon of wine, and filled a basket with biscuit, and a platter with apples and other fruits. But he was not contented, because we brought him no rich garment.

However, we entered so into his presence with fear and trembling. He sat upon his bed holding a guitar in his hand, and his wife sat by him; who, as I verily think, had cut and pared her nose between the eyes, that she might seem to be more flat and saddle-nosed; for she had left herself no nose at all in that place, having greased the very same place with a black ointment, and her eyebrows also; this sight seemed most ugly in our eyes. Then I rehearsed to him the same words which I had spoken in other places. For we had been cautioned to use the same speech in all places, and that amongst the Tartars we should never vary in our tale. Then I begged him to accept that small gift at our hands, excusing myself that I was a monk, and that it was against our profession to possess gold, or silver, or precious garments, and therefore that I had not any such thing to give him, but he should receive some part of our provisions instead of a blessing.

He caused our present to be received, and immediately distributed it among his men, who were met together for the purpose, to drink and make merry. I delivered also to him the letters from the Emperor of Constantinople. This was eight days after the feast of the Ascension. But the letters were written in Greek, and he had none about him that was skilful in the Greek tongue to translate them. He asked us also whether we would drink any *cosmos?* Those that are Christians among them, as the Russians, Grecians, and Alans, keep their own law very strictly, will in no case drink any *cosmos;* for they consider themselves no Christians after they have once drunk it, and their priests must bring them back into the church as if they had renounced the Christian faith. I answered him and said that we had as yet sufficient of our own to drink, and that when our drink failed us, then we would be constrained to drink such as should be given to us.

He inquired also what was contained in our letters, which your Majesty sent unto Sartach? I answered that they were sealed up, and that there was nothing contained in them, but good and friendly words. And he asked what words we would deliver to Sartach? I answered, the words of Christian faith. He asked again what these words were? For he was very desirous to hear them. Then I expounded unto him as well as I could, by mine interpreter who had no wit nor much fluency of speech, the Apostles' creed. After he had heard this, holding his peace, he shook his head. Then he assigned to us two men, who should watch over us, our horses, and our oxen. And he made us ride in his company, till the messenger whom he had sent to have the emperor's letters translated, had returned. And so we travelled in his company till the day after Pentecost.

Chapter 13
HOW THE ALANS CAME TO US ON PENTECOST OR WHITSUN EVE

ON Pentecost eve there came to us certain Alans, who are called Acias, being Christians after the manner of the Grecians, use Greek books and have Greek priests. However, they are not schismatics as the Grecians are, but without respect to persons, they honour all Christians. And they brought to us cooked meats, requesting us to eat of their food and to pray for one of their company who had died. Then I said, because it was the eve of so great and so solemn a feast day, that we would not eat any flesh at that time. And I explained to them the solemnity of the festival, at which they greatly rejoiced: for they were ignorant of all things regarding the Christian religion, except only the name of Christ.

They and many other Christians, both Russians and Hungarians, demanded of us, whether they might be saved, because they were required to drink *cosmos*, and to eat the dead carcases of such things as were slain by the Saracens and other infidels? Which even the Greek and Russian priests themselves consider as things strangled or offered unto idols; and because they were ignorant of the times of fasting, they could not have observed them.

Then I instructed them as well as I could and strengthened them in the faith. As for the flesh which they had brought we reserved it until the feast day. For there was nothing to be sold among the Tartars for gold and silver, but only for cloth and garments, of which kind of merchandise we had none at all. When our servants offered them coin called *yperpera*, they rubbed it with their fingers, and put it to their noses, to try to smell whether it were copper. Neither did they allow us any food but cows' milk only, which was very sour and filthy. The one thing most necessary was greatly wanting. The water was so foul and muddy by reason of their horses, that it was not fit to drink. And but for certain biscuits, which by the goodness of God still remained, we would undoubtedly have perished.

Chapter 14

OF A SARACEN WHO SAID THAT HE WOULD BE BAPTIZED ✿ AND OF CERTAIN MEN WHO SEEMED TO BE LEPERS

UPON the day of Pentecost there came to us a certain Saracen, to whom we expounded the Christian faith. He, hearing of God's benefits exhibited unto mankind by the incarnation of our Saviour Christ, and the resurrection of the dead, and the judgment to come, and that baptism was a washing away of sins, said that he desired to be baptized. But when we prepared ourselves for baptizing him, he suddenly mounted on horseback, saying that he would go home and consult with his wife what were best to be done. On the next day he told us that he could in no case receive baptism, because then he could drink no more *cosmos*. The Christians of that place affirm that no true Christians ought to drink this milk; and that without the said liquor he could not live in that desert. From this opinion I could not possibly turn him. So you see they are much estranged from the Christian faith by reason of that opinion, which has been implanted among them by the Russians, of whom there is a great multitude in that place.

The same day Scacatai, the captain, gave us a man to conduct us to Sartach, and two others to guide us to the next lodging, which was distant from that place five days' journey, as oxen travel. They gave us also a goat for victuals, and a great many bladders of cows' milk, and but a little *cosmos*, because it is so precious to them.

Taking our journey directly toward the north, I thought that we had passed through one of hell's gates. The servants who conducted us began to play the bold thieves with us, seeing us take so little care. At length, having lost much by their thievery, vexation taught us wisdom.

Then we came to the extremity of that province, which is fortified with a ditch from one sea to another; outside of it was the camp of these Mongols. As soon as we had entered, all the inhabitants there seemed to us to be infected with leprosy. Certain base fellows were placed there to receive tribute of all who took salt out of the salt pits. From that place they told us that we must travel fifteen days' journey, before we should find any other people. We drank *cosmos* with them, and gave to them a basket full of fruits and of biscuits. And they gave us eight oxen and one goat, to sustain us in so great a journey, and I know not how many bladders of milk. And so changing our oxen, we began our journey, which we finished in ten days, arriving at another camp. We found no water along the way, but only in certain holes made in the valleys, except two small streams.

From the time we departed out of the province of Gasaria, we travelled directly eastward, having a sea on the south side of us, and a waste desert on the north. This desert, in some places, is twenty days' journey in breadth, and there is neither tree, mountain, nor stone therein. But it makes most excellent pasture. Here the Comans, which were called Capthac, feed their cattle. The Teutons, however, call them Valans, and the province itself Valania. But Isidore [Isidorus of Seville] calls all that tract of land stretching from the river of Tanais to the lake of Mæotis, and as far as the Danube, the country of Alania. And the same land from the Danube to Tanais, which divides Asia from Europe, is the extent of two months' journey, even though a man should ride post as fast as the Tartars use to ride. It was all over inhabited by the Comans, called Capthac: even beyond Tanais as far as the river Volga. The space between the two rivers is a great and long journey to be travelled in ten days.

To the north of the same province lies Russia, which is full of wood in all places, and stretches from Poland and Hungary to the river Tanais. It has been ravaged all over by the Tartars, and is yet ravaged daily by them. They prefer the Saracens to the Russians, because they are Christians, and when they are able to give them no more gold or silver, they drive them and their children like flocks of sheep into the wilderness, there to herd their cattle.

Beyond Russia lies the country of Prussia, which the Teutonic knights of the order of St. Mary's hospital of Jerusalem have of late wholly conquered and subdued. And indeed they might easily win Russia, if they would put their hand to it. For if the Tartars should but once know that the great priest, that is to say, the Pope, did cause the sign of the cross to be displayed against them, they would all flee into their desert and solitary places.

Chapter 15

OF OUR AFFLICTIONS WHICH WE SUSTAINED ❦ AND OF THE COMANS' MANNER OF BURIAL

WE went on towards the east, seeing nothing but heaven and earth, and sometimes the sea on our right, the sea of Tanais, and the tombs of the Comans, visible two leagues off because of their custom of burying the whole family in one place. As long as we were travelling through the desert it went reasonably well with us. But I cannot sufficiently express in words the irksome and tedious troubles which I sustained when I came to any of their inhabited places. Our guide would have us go to every captain with a present, and our supplies could not extend so far. We were eight persons spending our wayfaring provisions each day, for the Tartars' servants would all of them eat of our supplies. We ourselves were five in number, and the servants our guides were three, two to drive our carts, and one to conduct us to Sartach.

The flesh which they gave us was not sufficient, neither could we find anything to be bought for our money. And as we sat under our carts in the cool shadow, by reason of the extreme heat which was there at that time, they did so shamelessly intrude into our company that they would even step on us to see the things we had. Having desire at any time to ease their stomachs, the filthy rascals had not the manners to withdraw themselves farther from us than a bean could be cast. Yes, like vile slovens they did their filthiness in our presence while they were talking with us, and many other things they committed which were most tedious and loathsome to us.

But above all things it grieved me to the very heart that when I would speak to them for their edification, my foolish interpreter would say: "You shall not make me become a preacher now: I tell you I cannot, nor I will not, repeat any such words." And true it was, for I discovered later, when I began to have a little smattering of the language, that when I spoke one thing he would say quite another, anything that came next to his witless tongue. Then seeing the danger I might incur in speaking through such an interpreter, I resolved to hold my tongue, and thus we travelled with great toil from lodging to lodging, till at length, a few days before the feast of St. Mary Magdalene, we arrived at the bank of the mighty river Tanais which divides Asia from Europe, much as the river Nile of Egypt divides Asia from Africa.

At the place where we arrived, Batu and Sartach did cause a certain cottage to be built upon the eastern bank of the river, for a company of Russians to dwell in, so that they might transport ambassadors and merchants in ferry boats over that part of the river. First they brought us over, and then our carts, putting one wheel into one boat and the other wheel into another boat, having bound both the boats together, and in this manner they rowed them over.

In this place our guide played the fool most extremely. For he, believing that the Russians dwelling in the cottage would provide us horses, sent home the beasts which we brought with us, that they might return to their own masters. And when we demanded some beasts of them, they answered that they had been exempted by Batu, and they were bound to do no other service but only to tend the ferry. Also that they received great tribute from merchants for this service.

We stayed, therefore, by the river's side for three days. The first day they gave us a great fresh fish, the second day they bestowed rye bread and a little flesh upon us, which the headman of the village had collected from every house for us, and the third day dried fishes, which they have there in great abundance. The river was as broad in that place as the Seine is at Paris. And before we came there we passed over many good waters full of fish, but the barbarous and rude Tartars do not know how to catch them; neither do they care for any fish, except it be so great that they may live upon it for a great while.

The river is the limit of the east part of Russia, and it rises out of the Mæotis, which fens stretch to the North Ocean. It runs southward for seven hundred miles before it falls into the sea called Pontus Euxinus [Black Sea]. And all the rivers we passed over ran with full stream into this sea. The same river has great woods growing upon the west side.

Beyond this place the Tartars ascend no farther unto the north; for at that season of the year, about the first of August, they begin to return back to the south. And therefore there is another cottage somewhat lower, where passengers are ferried over in wintertime.

In this place we were driven to great extremity because we could get neither horses nor oxen for our money. At length, after I had declared to them that my coming was for the common good of all Christians, they sent us oxen and men; but we ourselves had to travel on foot.

At this time they were reaping their rye. Wheat does not grow well in that soil. They have the seed of millet in great abundance. The Russian women dress their heads like our women. They embroider their safeguards or gowns on the outside, from their feet unto their knees, with coloured or grey stuff. The Russian men wear caps like the Dutchmen. Also they wear upon their heads certain sharp and high-crowned hats made of felt, much like a sugar loaf.

Then we travelled three days without finding any people. And when we and our oxen were exceeding weary and faint, not knowing how far off were any Tartars, suddenly there came two riderless horses running towards us, which we took with great joy, and our guide and interpreter mounted upon their backs, to see how far off any people were to be found. At length upon the fourth day of our journey, having found some inhabitants, we rejoiced like seafaring men who had escaped out of a dangerous tempest, and had reached port. Having taken fresh horses and oxen, we passed on from camp to camp, till at last, upon the second of the calends of August, we arrived at the camp of Sartach himself.

Chapter 16

OF THE DOMINION OF SARTACH ❦ AND OF HIS SUBJECTS

THE region lying beyond Tanais is a very good country, having stores of rivers and woods toward the north. There are mighty huge woods which two sorts of people inhabit. One of them is called Moxel [Finnish Mordwin people], being mere pagans and without law. They have neither towns nor cities, but only cottages in the woods. Their lord and a great part of themselves were killed in high Germany. At this they highly commended the brave courage of the

Germans, hoping to be delivered out of the bondage of the Tartars through them.

If any merchant comes to them, he must provide things necessary for him with whom he is first of all entertained, as long as he stays with them.   If any lie with another man's wife, her husband, unless he be an eye-witness thereof, regards it not; for they are not jealous.   They have abundance of hogs, and great stores of honey, wax, and many kinds of rich and costly skins, and plenty of falcons.   Next to them are other people called Merclas, which the Latins call Merdui, and they are Saracens.

Beyond them is the river of Volga, which is the mightiest river that I ever saw.   It flows from the north part of Bulgaria, and so trending southward, empties into a certain lake [Caspian] containing in circuit the space of four months' travel.   Of this I will speak later.   The two rivers, namely, Tanais and Volga, are only ten days' journey apart in the northern section, but southward they are greatly divided one from another.   For Tanais descends into the sea of Pontus: Volga empties into another sea or lake, made by the help of many other rivers which enter it and have their source in Persia.

We had to the south of us high mountains [Caucasus], upon the sides of which towards the desert do the people called Kerkis, and the Alans or Acis inhabit, who are as yet Christians and wage war against the Tartars.   Beyond them, next unto the sea or lake of Volga, there are certain Saracens called Lesgs, who are subjects of the Tartars.   Beyond these is Porta Ferrea, or the Iron Gate, which Alexander built to keep the barbarous nations out of Persia.   Of these I shall tell you later, for I travelled through them on my return. Between the two rivers, in the region through the which we passed did Comans of old time inhabit, before they were overrun by the Tartars.

Chapter 17

OF THE COURT OF SARTACH ❦ AND OF THE MAGNIFICENCE THEREOF

WE found Sartach lying within three days' journey of the river Volga, and his court seemed to us to be very great. He himself has six wives, and his eldest son also has three wives: every one of these women has a great house, and they have each one of them about two hundred carts. Our guide went to a certain Nestorian named Coiac, who is a man of great authority in Sartach's court. He made us to go very far to an officer named *Jamian.* For so they call him who has the duty of entertaining ambassadors. In the evening Coiac commanded us to come unto him. Then our guide began to inquire what we would present to him, and was greatly offended when he saw that we had nothing ready to bring him. We stood before him, and he sat majestically, having music and dancing in his presence. Then I spoke to him in the words before recited, telling him for what purpose I had come to his lord, and requesting favour at his hands to enable me to bring our letters to the notice of his lord. I excused myself also, that I was a monk, not having, nor receiving, nor using any gold or silver, or any other precious thing, save only our books and the vestments with which we served God. And this was the reason why I brought no present to him nor to his lord. For I who had abandoned my own goods, could not be a transporter of things for other men.

Then he answered very courteously, that being a monk and so doing. I did well; for so I should observe my vow;

neither did he require anything that we had, but rather was ready to bestow upon us such thing as we ourselves stood in need of. And he invited us to sit down, and to drink of his milk. Presently he requested us to say our prayers for him; and we did so.

He inquired also who was the greatest prince among the Franks? And I said the emperor, if he could enjoy his own dominions in peace. No, he answered, it is the King of France. For he had heard of your Highness through Lord Baldwin of Hainaut.

I found there also one of the Knights Templars, who had been in Cyprus, and had made report of all things which he saw there. Then we returned to our lodging.

On the next day we sent him a flagon of muscadel wine, which had lasted very well in so long a journey, and a box full of biscuits, and they were most acceptable to him. And he kept our servants with him for that evening. In the morning he commanded me to come to the court, and to bring the king's letters and my vestments and books with me, because he wanted to see them. Lading one cart with our books and vestments, and another with biscuit, wine and fruit, we did as he commanded. Then he ordered all our books and vestments to be laid before him. And there stood round about us many Tartars, Christians and Saracens on horseback, while we explained the books and vestments. At this he demanded whether I would bestow all those things upon his lord? His words made me tremble, and grieved me. However, hiding our grief as well as we could, we gave him this answer: "Sir, our humble request is, that our lord your master should accept our bread, wine, and fruits, not as a present, because it is too mean, but as a benediction, and in this way we would come with an empty hand before him. And he shall see the letters of my sovereign lord the king, and by them he shall understand the reason we have come to him, and then both ourselves and all that we have shall stand to his pleasure; for our vestments are holy, and it is unlawful for any but priests to touch them."

Then he commanded us to invest ourselves in the garments, that we might go before his lord; and we did so. I myself put on our most precious ornaments, took in mine arms a beautiful cushion, and the Bible which your Majesty gave me, and a most beautiful psalter, which the queen's grace bestowed upon me, in which there were goodly pictures. My associate took a missal and a cross; and the clerk, having put on his surplice, took a censer in his hand. And in this way we came into the presence of his lord; and they lifted up the felt hanging before his door, that he might behold us.

Then they caused the clerk and the interpreter three times to bow the knee, but of us they required no such submission. And they warned us to take heed that in going in, and in coming out, we touched not the threshold of the house, and requested us to sing a benediction for him.

Then we entered, singing *Salve Regina*. And within the entrance of the door stood a bench with *cosmos* and drinking cups. And all his wives were there assembled. Also the Moals, or rich Tartars, pressed in around us. Then Coiac carried to his lord the censer with incense, which he beheld very diligently, holding it in his hand. Afterward he carried the psalter to him, which he looked earnestly upon, as did his wife also that sat beside him. After that he carried the Bible; and Sartach asked if the Gospel were contained therein? Yes, said I, and all the Holy Scriptures besides. He took the cross also in his hand, and inquired concerning the image whether it were the image of Christ? I said it was. The Nestorians and the Armenians do never make the

figure of Christ upon their crosses. Either they seem not
to think well of his passion, or else they are ashamed of it.
Then he ordered them that stood about us to stand aside,
that he might more fully behold our ornaments. Afterward
I delivered to him your Majesty's letters, with translation
thereof into the Arabic and Syriac languages. I had them
translated at Acon into the character and dialect of both these
tongues. And there were certain Armenian priests which
had skill in the Turkish and Arabian languages. The knight
of the Order of the Temple had also knowledge in the
Syriac, Turkish, and Arabian tongues. Then we departed,
and put off our vestments, and there came to us certain
scribes with Coiac, and they translated our letters into Mongol. When Sartach heard our letters, he caused our bread,
wine, and fruits to be accepted. And he permitted us also
to carry our vestments and books to our own lodging. This
was done upon the feast of St. Peter [August 1].

Chapter 18

HOW WE WERE GIVEN IN CHARGE TO GO TO BATU ❧ THE FATHER OF SARTACH

THE next morning a certain priest came to us who was
brother to Coiac, requesting a little vase of holy oil, because
Sartach, he said, was desirous to see it; and so we gave it
him. In the evening Coiac sent for us, saying: "My lord
your king wrote good words to my lord and master Sartach.
But there are certain matters of difficulty in them, concerning which he dare not decide, without the advice and counsel
of his father. And therefore you must depart to his father,
leaving behind you in my custody the two carts, which you
brought here yesterday with vestments and books; because
my lord desires to examine them more carefully." I at once

suspecting what mischief might come by his greed, said to him: "Sir, we will not only leave those with you, but the two other carts also, which we have in our possession, will we commit to your custody." "You shall not," he said, "leave those behind you, but for the other two carts first named we will take care of them." I said that this could not conveniently be done; but that we must leave all with him.

Then he asked whether we meant to tarry in the land? I answered: "If you thoroughly understand the letters of my lord the king, you know that we are so determined." Then he replied, that we ought to be patient and humble, and with these words we departed from him that evening.

On the next day he sent a Nestorian priest for the carts, and we gave all the four carts to be delivered. Then came the brother of Coiac to meet us, and separated all the things which we had brought the day before to the court from the rest, namely, the books and vestments, and took them away with him. However, Coiac had commanded that we should carry those vestments with us which we wore in the presence of Sartach, that we might put them on before Batu, if need should require. But the priest took them from us by violence, saying: "You have brought them to Sartach, and would now carry them to Batu?" And when I gave him a reason he answered: "Be not too talkative, but go your way." Then I saw that there was no remedy but patience: for we could have no access unto Sartach himself, neither was there any other who would do us justice. I was afraid also of the interpreter, lest he had spoken other things than I said to him: for his desire was that we should have given away all that we had. There was yet one comfort remaining to me; for when I once discovered their intent, I took out from among our books the Bible, and the Sentences, and certain other books which I made special account of. However, I dared not take away the psalter of my sovereign lady the queen, because it was too well known by reason of the golden pictures that it contained. And so we returned with the two other carts to our lodging.

Then came he who was appointed to be our guide to the court of Batu, asking us to begin our journey at once. But I said that I would in no case have the carts to go with me. This he told to Coiac. Then Coiac commanded that we should leave them and our servant with him; and we did as he commanded. And so travelling directly eastward towards Batu, the third day we came to the Volga: when I saw the streams, I wondered from what regions of the north such huge and mighty waters should descend.

Before we departed from Sartach, Coiac, with many other scribes of the court, came to us and said: "Do not make report that our lord is a Christian, but a Moal." Because the name of a Christian seems to them to be the name of some nation. So great is their pride, that although they believe perhaps some things concerning Christ, yet will they not be called Christians, being desirous that their own name, that is to say Moal, should be above all other names. Neither will they be called by the name of Tartars. For the Tartars were another nation, as I was informed by them.

Chapter 19

HOW SARTACH ◈ AND MANGU KHAN ◈ AND KUYUK KHAN DO REVERENCE TO CHRISTIANS

AT the same time when the Franks took Antioch, a certain man named Con Khan had dominion over these northern regions. Con is a proper name: Khan is a name of authority or dignity, which means also a diviner or soothsayer. All diviners are called Khan amongst them. Whereupon their princes are called Khan, because the government of the people depends on divination. We do read also in the history of Antioch, that the Turks sent for aid against the Franks to the kingdom of Con Khan. For out of those parts the whole nation of the Turks first came. Con was of the nation of Kara-Cathay. Kara means black, and Cathay is the name of a country. This name was given the people of Cathay to distinguish them from those living eastward toward the ocean sea; concerning them we will speak later.

These Cathayans dwelt upon certain highlands over which I travelled. And in a certain plain country within those mountains, there lived a Nestorian shepherd, being a mighty governor over the people called Naimans, which were Christians, following the sect of Nestorius. After the death of Con Khan, the said Nestorian took possession of the kingdom, and they called him King John, reporting ten times more of him than was true. For this is the way of the Nestorians who come from those parts. They blaze abroad great rumours and reports upon just nothing. They said concerning Sartach that he had become a Christian, and the same also they reported concerning Mangu Khan and Kuyuk Khan: namely, because these Tartars pay more respect to Christians than they do to other people, and yet they themselves are no Christians. So likewise there went forth a great report concerning this King John. However, when I travelled along through his territories, there was no man, that knew anything of him, but only a few Nestorians.

In his pastures or territories lives Kuyuk Khan, at whose court Friar Andrew was. And I myself passed by it at my return.

This John had a brother, being a mighty man also, and a shepherd like himself, called Unc, and he inhabited beyond

the highlands of Cathay, being distant from his brother
John by the space of three weeks' journey. He was lord
over a certain village called Caracarum, having also
for his subjects people called Crit or Merkit, who were
Nestorian Christians. But their lord, abandoning the worship of Christ, followed after idols, retaining with him
priests of the idols, who all of them are worshippers of
devils and sorcerers.

Beyond his pastures, some ten or fifteen days' journey,
were the pastures of Moal, who were a poor and beggarly
nation, without governor and without law, except their
soothsayings and their sorcery, to which all apply their
minds. Near the Moal were other poor people called Tartars. Now, King John having died without male issue, his
brother Unc was greatly enriched, and caused himself to be
named Khan; and his droves and flocks ranged even to the
borders of Moal.

About the same time there was one Chinghis, a blacksmith among the people of Moal. This Chinghis stole as
many cattle from Unc Khan as he could possibly get, even
though the shepherds of Unc complained to their lord. Then
he got together an army, and marched up into the country
of Moal to seek for the said Chinghis. But Chinghis fled
among the Tartars, and hid himself amongst them. And
Unc having taken some spoils both from Moal and also from
the Tartars, returned home. Then Chinghis spoke to the
Tartars and to the people of Moal, saying: "Sirs, because we
are destitute of a governor and captain, you see how our
neighbours do oppress us." And the Tartars and Moals
appointed him to be their chieftain. Then having secretly
gathered together an army, he fell suddenly upon Unc and
overcame him, and Unc fled into Cathay. At the same time
the daughter of Unc was taken, and Chinghis married her

to one of his sons, by whom she conceived and brought forth the great Khan who now reigns, called Mangu Khan.

Then Chinghis sent the Tartars before him in all directions: and so was their name published and spread abroad; for in all places the people would cry out: "Lo, the Tartars come, the Tartars come!" However, through continual wars they are now almost all killed off and the Moals endeavour what they can to extinguish the name of the Tartars, that they may raise their own name instead. The country which they first inhabited, and where the court of Chinghis Khan still remains, is called Onankerule [Orchon River south of Lake Baikal]. But because Caracarum is the city from which they first spread, they esteem that as their royal and chief city, and there for the most part do they elect their great Khan.

Chapter 20

OF THE RUSSIANS ❧ HUNGARIANS ❧ AND ALANS ❧ AND OF THE CASPIAN SEA

Now, as for Sartach, whether he believes in Christ I know not. This I am sure of, that he will not be called a Christian. And it even seems to me that he scoffs at Christians. He is on the road of the Christians, as namely of the Russians, the Wallachians, the Bulgarians, the Soldaians, the Kirghiz, and the Alans; all of them must pass by him as they are going to the court of his father Batu to carry gifts. Therefore, he is most attentive to them. However, if the Saracens come, and bring greater gifts then they are dispatched sooner. He has about him certain Nestorian priests, who pray upon their beads and sing their devotions.

Also there is another under Batu, called Berta, who feeds his cattle toward the Iron Gate, where lies the passage of all those Saracens who come out of Persia and out of Turkey

to go unto Batu, and passing by they give presents to him.
He has become a Saracen, and will not permit swine's flesh
to be eaten in his dominions. At the time of our return
Batu commanded him to remove himself from that place,
and to inhabit the east side of Volga: for he was unwilling
that the Saracens' messengers should pass by the said
Berta, because he saw it was harmful.

During the four days we remained in the court of Sartach,
we had not any food at all allowed us, but once only a little
cosmos. And in our journey between him and his father
we travelled in great fear. Certain Russians, Hungarians,
and Alans being servants unto the Tartars, of whom they
have great multitudes among them, assemble twenty or
thirty in a company, and so secretly in the night take bows
and arrows with them, and whomever they find in the night
they put him to death. They hide themselves in the daytime. And having tired their horses, they go in the night
to a herd of other horses feeding in some pasture, and
change them for new, taking with them also one or two
extra horses, to eat them when they need. Our guide, therefore, was afraid lest we should meet with such companions.

On this journey we should have died of famine had we
not carried some of our biscuits with us. At length we came
to the mighty river Volga. It is four times greater than
the river of the Seine, and of a wonderful depth; and issuing from Great Bulgaria, it runs into a certain lake or sea,
which of late they call the Hircan Sea, according to the
name of a certain city in Persia which is located upon the
shore. Isidore called it the Caspian Sea. For it has the
Caspian mountains and the land of Persia on the south; and
the mountains of Mulidet, that is to say, of the people called
Assassins, towards the east, which mountains join the Caspian
mountains. On the north lies the desert which the Tartars

now inhabit. Here once dwelt certain people called Cangle. And on that side it receives the streams of Volga; which river rises in summer like the Nile in Egypt. Upon the west it has the mountains of the Alans, and Lesgs, and the Iron Gate, and the mountains of Georgia.

This sea therefore is compassed in on three sides with mountains, but on the north side by plain ground. Friar Andrew in his journey travelled round about two sides, the south and the east; and I myself about the other two, that is to say, the north side in going from Batu to Mangu Khan, and in returning likewise; and the west side in coming home from Batu into Syria. A man may travel round it in four months. And it is not true what Isidore reported, that this sea is a bay or gulf coming forth of the ocean; for it does in no part join with the ocean, but is surrounded on all sides by land.

Chapter 21

OF THE COURT OF BATU ❦ AND HOW WE WERE ENTERTAINED

ALL this country extending from the west shore of the sea, where Alexander's Iron Gate is located, and from the mountains of Alania, all along north to Mæotis, where the river of Tanais has its source, is called Albania. Of this country Isidore reports that there are dogs of such size, and so fierce, that they are able to seize bulls and to kill lions. The truth is, as I have heard told, that towards the North Ocean they make their dogs draw carts like oxen, so great is their size and strength.

Upon that part of Volga where we arrived, there is a new cottage built, where they have placed Tartars and Russians together, to ferry over and transport messengers going and coming to the court of Batu. Batu remains upon the farther side towards the east. From January until August both he and all other Tartars ascend by the banks of rivers towards cold and northerly regions, and in August they begin to return again. We passed down the stream, therefore, in a boat to his court.

From this place to the villages of Great Bulgaria to the north, it is five days' journey. I wonder what devil carried the religion of Mahomet thither. From the Iron Gate, which is upon the extreme borders of Persia, it is about thirty days' journey across the desert, and from there you ascend by the bank of Volga, into the country of Bulgaria. There is no city along this journey, but only certain cottages near the place where the Volga enters the sea. The Bulgarians are most wicked Saracens, more earnestly professing the damnable religion of Mahomet, than any other nation.

When I first beheld the court of Batu, I was astonished, for his houses, or tents, seemed like a mighty city, stretching out a great way in length, the people ranging up and down about it for the space of three or four leagues. And as among the people of Israel each man knew on which side of the tabernacle to pitch his tents; so every one here towards which side of the court he ought to place his house when he takes it off the cart. The court is called in their language *horda*, which signifies, the middle; because the governor or chieftain among them dwells always in the middle of his people; except only that towards the south no subject or person places himself, because in that direction the court gates are open. But to the right and left they extend as far as they will, according to the lay of the land, so long as they do not place their houses directly opposite the court.

At our arrival we were conducted to a Saracen, who gave us no food at all. The day following we were brought into the court. Batu had caused a great tent to be erected, because his house, or ordinary tent, could not contain so many men and women as were assembled. Our guide cautioned us not to speak, till Batu had given us order to do so, and that then we should speak briefly. Then he asked also whether your Majesty had sent ambassadors to the Tartars or not; I answered, that your Majesty had sent messengers to Kuyuk Khan; and that you would not have sent messengers to him, or letters to Sartach, had you not been persuaded that they had become Christians. Then he led us into the pavilion, and we were warned not to touch the cords of the tent, for they are held to represent the threshold of the house. There we stood in our robes and barefooted, and bareheaded, and we were a great and strange spectacle in their eyes. For, indeed, Friar John of Pian de Carpini had been there before my coming; and because he was the Pope's messenger, he changed his gown, fearing lest he should be slighted. Then we were brought into the very centre of the tent, and they did not require that we do any reverence by bending our knees, as they do of other messengers. We stood before him for the space that would take a man to say the psalm, *Miserere mei Deus,* and there was great silence kept of all men.

Batu himself sat upon a seat long and broad like a bed, gilt all over, with three stairs to ascend to it, and one of his ladies sat beside him. The men sat down, some on the right hand of the lady, and some on the left. Those places on the one side which the women did not fill, for there were only the wives of Batu, were taken by the men. Also, at the very entrance of the tent, stood a bench furnished with *cosmos,* and with stately great cups of silver, and gold, and they were richly set with precious stones. Batu beheld us earnestly, and we him; and he seemed to me to resemble in personage Monsieur John de Beaumont, whose soul now rests in peace. He had a fresh ruddy colour in his countenance. At length he commanded us to speak.

Then our guide asked that we should bow our knees and speak. I bowed one knee, as to a man, but he signalled that I should kneel upon both knees. I did so, not wishing to dispute over it. Again he commanded me to speak. Then thinking I was praying God, because I kneeled on both my knees, I began by saying: "Sir, we beseech the Lord, from whom all good thinges do proceed, and who hath given you these earthly benefits, that it would please him hereafter to make you partaker of his heavenly blessings: because the former without these are but vain and unprofitable." And I added further, "Be it known unto you of a certainty, that you shall not obtain the joys of heaven, unless you become a Christian: for God saith, Whosoever believeth and is baptized, shall be saved; but he that believeth not, shall be condemned." At this he smiled modestly; but the other Moals began to clap their hands, and to laugh at us. And my silly interpreter, of whom I should have received comfort in time of need, was himself abashed and stood dumbfounded. Then after silence was re-established, I said to him: "I came to your son, because we heard that he was a Christian; and I brought him letters on the behalf of my sovereign lord the King of France, and your son sent me here to you. The cause of my coming, therefore, is best known to you." Then he caused me to rise, and asked your Majesty's name, and my name, and the names of my associate and interpreter, and had them all put down in writing. He demanded also, because he had been informed that you departed from your own country with an army, against whom you waged war. I answered: "Against the Saracens, who had defiled the house of God at Jerusalem." He asked also whether your Highness had ever before that time sent any messengers to him, or not. "To you, sir," said I, "never."

Then he made us sit down, and gave us of his milk to drink, which they regard to be a great favour, especially when any man is admitted to drink *cosmos* with him in his own house. I sat looking down upon the ground and he commanded me to lift up my face, wishing to get a better view of us, or else because of superstition. They hold it a sign of ill-luck, or evil, when any man sits in their presence, holding down his head, as if he were sad; especially when he leans his cheek or chin on his hand.

Then we departed, and immediately after us came our guide, and conducting us unto our lodging, said to me: "The Lord King requests that you remain in this land, but Batu cannot grant this without the knowledge and consent of Mangu Khan. Wherefore you, and your interpreter must go to Mangu Khan. However, your associate and the other man shall return to the court of Sartach, waiting there for you, till you come back." Then the interpreter began to lament, deeming himself a dead man. My associate also protested, saying that they should sooner chop off his head, than take him out of my company. Moreover, I myself said, that without my associate I could not go; and that we stood in need of two servants at least, to attend upon us, because, if one should chance to fall sick, we could not be without another. Returning to the court, he told these things to Batu. And Batu commanded, saying: "Let the two priests and the interpreter go together, but let the clerk return to Sartach." And coming again to us, he told us. And when I desired to speak for the clerk to have him with us, he said: "No more words, for Batu has resolved; so it shall be, and I dare not go to the court any more." Goset the clerk had remaining of the alms money bestowed unto him, twenty-six *yperpera* [about 60 dollars], and no more: ten he kept for himself and for the lad, and sixteen he gave to the interpreter for us. Thus were we parted asunder with tears: he returning to the court of Sartach, and ourselves remaining here.

Chapter 22
OF OUR JOURNEY TOWARDS THE COURT OF MANGU KHAN

UPON the eve of the Assumption our clerk arrived at the court of Sartach. And on the next day the Nestorian priests were adorned with our vestments in the presence of Sartach. Then we ourselves were conducted to another host, who was appointed to provide us houseroom, food, and horses. But because we had nothing to bestow upon him, he did it all meanly. Then we rode forward with Batu, descending along by the bank of Volga, for a space of five weeks together: sometimes my associate was so hungry that he would tell me about it weeping, that it fared with him as though he will never eat any thing in all his life again.

There is a fair or market following the court of Batu at all times; but it was so far distant from us that we could not reach it. We were constrained to walk on foot for want of horses. At length certain Hungarians, who had once been clerks, found us, and one of them could sing many songs without book, and was looked upon by other Hungarians as a priest, and was sent to funerals of his deceased countrymen. There was another of them also well instructed in grammar; for he could understand the meaning of everything that we spoke, but could not answer. These Hungarians were a great comfort to us, bringing us *cosmos* to drink, and sometimes flesh to eat. When they requested to have some books of us, and I had not any to give them, for indeed we had none, but only a Bible, and a breviary, this grieved me. And I said unto them: "Bring me some ink and paper, and I will write for you as long as we shall remain here"; and they did so. I copied out for them the hours of the Blessed Virgin, and the office for the dead. Moreover, upon a certain day, a Coman accompanying us saluted us in Latin, saying: *"Saluite Domini."* Wondering at this, and saluting him in return, I demanded of him who had taught him that kind of salutation. He said that he was baptized in Hungary by our friars, and that from them he had learned it. He said, moreover, that Batu had asked many things of him concerning us, and that he told him the condition of our order.

Afterward I saw Batu riding in his company, and all his subjects that were householders or masters of families riding with him, and, in my estimation, there were not five hundred men in all.

At length there came a certain rich Moal to us, whose father was chief of a thousand, a great office among them, saying: "I am the man that must conduct you to Mangu Khan, and we have a journey of four months before us; and there is such extreme cold in those parts that stones and trees are split by the frost. Therefore, think it over whether you be able to endure it or not." I answered: "I hope by God's help that we shall be able to stand that which other men can endure." Then he said: "If you cannot endure it, I will forsake you by the way." And I answered him: "It would not be just for you to do so, for we do not go upon any business of our own, but because we are sent by your lord. Wherefore since we are committed to your charge, you ought in no way forsake us." Then he said: "All shall be well." Afterward he caused us to show him all our garments: and whatsoever he deemed to be useless for us, he asked us to leave it behind in the custody of our host.

Next day they brought to each of us a furred gown, made all of rams' skins, with the wool still upon them, and breeches of the same, and boots also of buskin according to their fashion, and shoes made of felt, and hoods also made of skins after their manner. The second day after the Elevation of the Holy Cross, we began our journey, having three guides to direct us. We rode continually eastward, till the feast of All Saints. All that region, and beyond it, was inhabited by the people of Cangle, who were by parentage descended from the Comans. Upon the north side of us, we had Great Bulgaria, and on the south, the Caspian Sea.

Chapter 23

OF THE RIVER OF URAL ❦ AND OF VARIOUS REGIONS OR NATIONS

HAVING travelled twelve days' journey from Volga, we found a mighty river called Jagac [Ural], which flows out of the north, from the land of Pascatir, falling into the Caspian Sea. The language of Pascatir and of the Hungarians is all one, and they are all of them shepherds, not having any cities. Their country borders upon Great Bulgaria, on the west frontier. From the northeast part of this country, there is no city at all. Great Bulgaria is the farthest country in this direction that has any city. Out of this region of Pascatir came the Huns of old time, who afterward were called Hungarians. Next to it is Great Bulgaria. Isidore reported that the people of this nation had swift horses with which they crossed the impregnable walls of Alexander, which, together with the rocks of Caucasus, served to restrain those barbarous and bloodthirsty people from invading the regions to the south. And that they had tribute paid to them from as far off as Egypt. Likewise they wasted all countries even as far as France. Therefore, they were more mighty than the Tartars. And to them the Blacians, the Bulgarians, and the Vandals joined themselves. For out of Bulgaria the greater, came the Bulgarians. Moreover, those who live beyond the Danube, near Constantinople, and not far from Pascatir, are called Ilac, which is Blac, for the Tartars cannot pronounce the better B; from them come those people who inhabit the land of Assani. They are both of them called Ilac in the language of the Russians, the Poles, and the Bohemians. The Sclavonians all speak one language with the Vandals, all of whom banded themselves with the Huns. But now for the most part they unite themselves to the Tartars; whom God hath sent from the remote parts of the earth, according to that which the Lord said: I will provoke them to envy, namely those who keep not the law, and are no people, and with a foolish nation will I anger them.

This prophecy is fulfilled to the letter upon all nations which observe not the law of God. All this which I have written concerning the land of Pascatir was told me by certain Friars Prædicants, who travelled there before ever the Tartars came abroad. But from that time they were subdued by their neighbours the Bulgarians, and became Saracens. Other matters concerning these people may be learnt from the chronicles. For it is manifest, that those provinces beyond Constantinople, which are now called Bulgaria, Wallachia, and Sclavonia, were of old time provinces belonging to the Greeks. Also Hungary was previously called Pannonia.

We were riding over the land of Cangle, from the feast of the Holy Cross until the feast of All Saints [September

15 to November 1], travelling almost every day, according to my estimation, as far as from Paris to Orleans, and sometimes farther, as we were provided with post horses. For some days we had change of horses twice or three times in a day.

Sometimes we travelled for two or three days without finding any people, and then we were required not to ride so fast. Of twenty or thirty horses we had always the worst, because we were strangers. For every one before us took their choice of the best horses. They provided me always with a strong horse, because I was very corpulent and heavy; but whether he ambled a gentle pace or not, I dared not inquire. Neither dared I complain, although he rode hard. Every man must be contented with his lot. Consequently, we were greatly troubled, for often our horses were tired before we could reach any people. And then we had to beat and whip our horses, and to lay our clothing upon pack horses; and sometimes two of us had to ride upon one horse.

Chapter 24

OF THE HUNGER AND THIRST ❦ AND OTHER MISERIES ❦ WHICH WE SUSTAINED ON OUR JOURNEY

Of hunger and thirst, cold and weariness, there was no end. . They gave us no food, but only in the evening. In the morning they used to give us a little drink, or some cooked millet. In the evening they bestowed flesh upon us, as a shoulder and breast of ram's mutton, and every man a measured quantity of broth to drink. When we had sufficient of the meat broth, we were marvellously well refreshed. And it seemed to me most pleasant, and a most nourishing drink.

Every Saturday I remained fasting until night, without

eating or drinking anything. And when night came I was obliged, to my great grief and sorrow, to eat flesh. Sometimes we had to eat flesh half cooked, or almost raw, and all for want of fuel. This happened when we were in the fields, or came to our journey's end after dark. We could not then conveniently gather together the dung of horses or oxen; for other fuel we found but seldom, except perhaps a few thorns in some places. Upon the banks of some rivers there are woods growing here and there, but they are very rare.

In the beginning our guide highly disdained us, and it seemed to him tedious to conduct such base fellows. Afterward, when he began to know us somewhat better, he directed us on our way by the courts of rich Moals, and we were asked to pray for them. Had I carried a good interpreter with me, I should have had opportunity to have done much good.

Chinghis Khan, who was the first great Khan, or Emperor, of the Tartars, had four sons, of whom there were many children, every one of whom does at this day enjoy great possessions; and they are daily multiplied and dispersed over that huge and waste desert, which is, in dimensions, like the ocean sea. Our guide directed us, as we were going on our journey, through many of their camps. And they marvelled greatly that we would accept neither gold, nor silver, nor precious and costly garments. They inquired also concerning the great Pope, whether he was of so great an age as they had heard. For there had gone a report among them, that he was five hundred years old. They inquired also of our countries, whether there were sheep, oxen, and horses there, and also regarding the ocean sea; they could not conceive of it, because it was without limits or bounds.

Upon the eve of All Saints, we forsook the way leading towards the east, because the people had now descended very much south, and we went on our journey by certain alps, or mountains, directly southward, for the space of eight days. In the desert I saw many asses, rather like our mules; these our guide and his companions chased very eagerly; however, they did but lose their labour, for the beasts were too swift for them. Upon the seventh day there appeared to the south of us huge high mountains, and we entered into a place which was well watered, and fresh as a garden, and here we found land tilled and manured.

On the eighth day after the feast of All Saints, we arrived at a certain town of the Saracens, named Kenchat, and the governor met our guide at the town's end with ale and cups. For it is their manner at all towns and villages, subject to them, to meet the messengers of Batu and Mangu Khan with meat and drink. At that time of the year, they already had ice on their roads. And before the feast of St. Michael [September 29] we had frost in the desert. I inquired the name of this province; but being now in a strange part, they could not tell me the name, but only the name of a very small city in the same province. And there descended a great river [Talas] down from the mountains, which watered the whole region, according as the inhabitants would give it passage, by making channels and sluices; neither did this river flow into any sea, but was absorbed into the earth; and it made many marshes. Also I saw many vines, and twice drank of the wine.

Chapter 25

HOW BURI WAS PUT TO DEATH ❧ AND CONCERNING THE HABITATION OF THE TEUTONS

THE next day, we came to another village near the mountains. I inquired what mountains they were, for I understood them to be the mountains of the Caucasus, which are stretched forth and continued on both parts to the sea, from the west unto the east; and on the west part they fall into the Caspian Sea, where the river Volga discharges its streams. I inquired also of the city of Talas, where there lived certain Teutons, servants of Buri, of whom Friar Andrew made mention. Concerning these men I also inquired very diligently in the courts of Sartach and Batu, but I could get no information of them except that their lord and master Buri was put to death upon the following occasion. This Buri was not placed in good and fertile pastures. And upon a certain day being drunk, he spoke in this way to his men: "Am not I of the stock and kindred of Chinghis Khan, as well as Batu?" For indeed he was brother or nephew to Batu. "Why then do I not go to the banks of the Volga, to feed my cattle there, as freely as Batu himself does?"

These speeches of his were reported to Batu. Whereupon Batu wrote to his servants to bring their lord bound before him. And they did so. Then Batu demanded of him whether he had spoken any such words. And he confessed that he had. But, because it is the Tartars' manner to pardon drunken men, he excused himself and said he was drunk at the time. "How dare you mention my name in your drunkenness?" said Batu. And with that he caused his head to be chopped off.

Concerning the Teutons, I could get no information till I had come to the court of Mangu Khan. And there I was informed that Mangu Khan had removed them out of the jurisdiction of Batu, for the space of a month's journey from Talas, eastward, to a certain village called Bolac: where they are set to dig gold, and to make armour. I passed very near their city in going, namely, within three days' journey of it, but I was ignorant that I did so: neither could I have turned out of my way, if I had known.

From the village I have mentioned we went directly eastward, by the mountains. And from that time we travelled among the people of Mangu Khan, who in all places sang and danced before our guide, because he was the messenger of Batu. For this courtesy they do afford each to other: the people of Mangu Khan receive the messengers of Batu in this same manner; and so likewise the people of Batu entertain the messengers of Mangu Khan. However, the subjects of Batu are stronger and show not so much courtesy to the subjects of Mangu Khan, as is shown to them.

A few days later we entered upon those alps where the Black Cathay people were wont to inhabit. And there we found a mighty river [Ili] in so much that we were obliged to cross it in a boat. Afterward we came to a certain valley, where I saw a castle destroyed, the walls of which were only of mud; and in that place the soil was tilled also. And there we found a certain village, named Equius, where there were Saracens, speaking the Persian language, though they dwelt a huge distance from Persia.

The day following, having passed over the hills, which descended from the great mountains southward, we entered into a most beautiful plain, having high mountains on our right hand, and on the left hand of us a certain sea or lake, which is fifteen days' journey in circuit. The plain is most commodiously watered with certain streams distilling from the mountains, all of which fall into the lake. In summertime we returned by the north shore of the same lake, and there were great mountains on that side also. Upon this plain there were a great many villages; but for the most part they were all ruined because of the fertile pastures that the Tartars might use for their cattle.

We found one great city there named Cailac, which contained a market, and great store of merchants frequenting it. In this city we remained fifteen days, waiting for a certain scribe, or secretary of Batu, who ought to have accompanied our guide to the court of Mangu.

All this country was once called Organum; and the people thereof had their proper language, and their peculiar kind of writing. But it was now inhabited of the people called Turcomans. The Nestorians likewise in those parts used the very same language and writing. Perhaps the Nestorians called them Organa, because they were wont to be most skilful in playing upon the organs, or guitars, so it was reported to me. Here first did I see worshippers of idols, of whom there are many sects in the east countries.

Chapter 26

HOW THE NESTORIANS ❧ SARACENS ❧ AND IDOLATERS ARE JOINED TOGETHER

THE first sort of these idolaters are called Jugures: their land bordered upon the land of Organum, within the mountains eastward; and in all their cities Nestorians and Saracens live together, and they are scattered also towards Persia. The citizens of the city of Cailac had three idol temples; and I entered into two of them, to behold their foolish superstitions.

In the first I found a man having a cross painted with ink upon his hand, and I supposed him to be a Christian; for he answered like a Christian to all questions which I asked of him. I asked him, why, therefore, he had not the cross with the image of Jesus Christ? And he answered: "We have no such custom." At this I concluded that they were Christians, but that for lack of instruction they omitted the above ceremony. I noticed behind a certain chest, which was to them an altar, where they set candles and oblations, an image having wings like the image of St. Michael; and other images also, holding their fingers as if they were blessing. That evening I could find out nothing more, for the Saracens shun these idolaters so much that they will not allow them to speak of their religion. And when I inquired of the Saracens concerning these ceremonies, they were offended.

On the following day, which was the first of the month and the Saracens' feast of Passover, I changed my host and took up my lodging near another idol temple. The citizens of this city of Cailac do courteously invite and lovingly entertain all messengers, every man according to his ability and station.

Entering into the temple, I found the priests of the idols there. Always at the first of the month they open their temples, and the priests put on their vestments and offer the oblation of bread and fruits. First I will describe to you those rites and ceremonies, which are held in all their temples; and then the superstitions of the Jugures, a sect distinguished from the rest. They all worship towards the north, clapping their hands together, prostrating themselves on their knees, and holding their foreheads in their hands. The Nestorians in these parts do not join their hands together in prayer, but hold their hands before their breasts.

Their temples are built east and west; and upon the north side is a chamber, in manner of a vestry. Sometimes, if it is a square temple, the vestry or choir place is built in the centre. Within this chamber they place a chest long and broad like a table, and behind this, facing south, stands their principal idol. The one I saw at Caracarum was as big as the image of St. Christopher. Also a certain Nestorian priest, who had been in Cathay, said that in that country there is an idol so huge that it may be seen two days' journey away. They place other idols round about the principal one, all of them finely gilt over with pure gold; and upon the chest, which is in manner of a table, they set candles and offerings. The doors of their temples always open towards the south, which is contrary to the customs of the Saracens. They have also great bells like we have. And that is the reason, I believe, why the Christians in the East will not use great bells. However, they are common among the Russians, and Grecians of Gasaria.

Chapter 27

OF THEIR TEMPLES AND IDOLS ❦ AND HOW THEY WORSHIP THEIR FALSE GODS

ALL their priests have their heads and beards shaved quite close and they are clad in orange coloured garments; and being once shaven, they lead a chaste life, in groups of a hundred or two hundred together in one cloister. On the days when they enter into their temples, they place two long benches inside. Upon these they sit facing the singing men in the choir. They have certain books in their hands, which sometimes they lay down upon the benches, and their heads are bare as long as they remain in the temple.

They read softly to themselves, hardly uttering any sound at all. Coming in amongst them, at the time of their devotions, and finding them all sitting mute, I attempted to get them to answer me, but could not by any means possible. They have with them also wherever they go, a certain string with a hundred or two hundred beads, much like our rosaries, which we carry about with us. And they always utter these words: *Ou mam Hactani* ("God thou knowest," as one of them expounded it unto me). And so they expect a reward at God's hands, as often as they pronounce these words in remembrance of God.

Round about their temple they always make a court, as though it were a churchyard, which they enclose with a good wall. And upon the south part of this they build the main gate, where they sit and talk. And upon the top of this gate they set up a long pole, raising it, if they can, above all the whole town. And by this pole all men may know, that there stands the temple of their idols. These rites and ceremonies are common to all idolaters in these parts.

I found certain priests sitting in the outer gate of this temple, and those which I saw seemed to me, because of their shaven beards, as if they had been Frenchmen. They wore certain paper ornaments upon their heads. The Jugure priests wear such attire wherever they go. They are always dressed in their orange coloured jackets, which are very straight and are laced or buttoned from the bosom down, after the French fashion. And they have a cloak upon their left shoulder which falls around the chest and back to the right side, like a deacon carrying the chasuble in time of Lent.

Their kind of writing is like the Tartars'. They begin to write at the top of their paper, drawing their lines right down; and so they read and multiply their lines from the left hand to the right. They do use certain papers and characters in their magical practices, and their temples are full of such short scrolls hung round. Also Mangu Khan has

sent letters to your Majesty written in the language of the
Moals, but in the script of the Jugures.

They burn their dead according to the ancient custom, and
lay up the ashes in the top of a pyramid. Now, after I had
sat a while by the priests, and entered into their temple and
seen many of their images both great and small, I demanded
of them what they believed concerning God: and they answered: "We believe that there is only one God." And I
demanded further: "Do you believe that he is a spirit or
some bodily substance?" They said: "We believe that he
is a spirit." Then said I: "Do you believe that God ever
took man's nature upon him?" They answered: "No."
And again I said: "Since you believe that he is a spirit, then
why do you make so many images to represent him? Since
also you believe not that he was made man: Why do you
make him more like the image of a man than of any other
creature?" Then they answered, saying: "We do not make
these images to represent God, but when any rich man
amongst us, or his son, or his wife, or any of his friends dies,
he has the image of the dead person made and placed here.
We, in remembrance of him, do reverence to it." Then I
replied: "You do these things only for the friendship and
flattery of men." "No," they said, "only for their memory."

Then they questioned me, as if in derision: "Where is
God?" To which I answered: "Where is your soul?"
They said, in our bodies. Then said I: "Is it not in every
part of your body, ruling and guiding the whole body, and
yet it is invisible? Even so God is everywhere and ruleth
all things, and yet is he invisible, being understanding and
wisdom itself." Then, just as I wanted to have some more
conversation with them, my interpreter became weary, and

was not able to express my words, so he made me keep silent.

The Moals of this sect believe that there is but one God; but they make images of felt, in remembrance of their dead, covering them with five most rich and costly garments, and putting them into one or two carts, which carts no man dare touch; and these are in the custody of their soothsayers, who are their priests, and of whom I shall tell you further on. These soothsayers, or diviners, always attend upon the court of Mangu and of other great personages. The poor have none, but only those of the family and kindred of Chinghis. And when they are to move or to take any journey, the said diviners go before them, as the cloudy pillar went before the children of Israel. They appoint ground where the tents must be pitched, and first of all they take down their own houses: and after them the whole court does the same. Also upon their festival days or calends they take their images and place them in a circle within the house. Then come the Moals and enter into the same house, bowing themselves before the said images and worship them. Moreover, it is not lawful for any stranger to enter into that house. Once I myself would have forced my way in, but was most rudely treated.

Chapter 28

OF VARIOUS NATIONS **❧** AND OF CERTAIN PEOPLE WHO EAT THEIR OWN PARENTS

THOSE Jugures, who live among the Christians and the Saracens, by their sundry disputations, as I suppose, have been brought to believe that there is but one only God. They dwell in certain cities, which afterward were brought in subjection to Chinghis Khan, who then gave his daughter in marriage to their king. Also the city of Caracarum itself is in a manner within their territory; and the whole country of the king, Prester John, and of his brother Unc, is near their dominions; though they inhabit certain pastures northward, while the Jugures live between the mountains towards the south.

So it happened that the Moals adopted their letters from them. And they are the best scribes and nearly all the Nestorians know their writing. Beyond them, between the mountains eastward, are the nation of Tangut, who are a most valiant people, and once took Chinghis in battle. But after peace was made he was set at liberty by them, and afterwards he subdued them.

These people of Tangut have oxen of great strength, with tails like horses, and with long shaggy hair upon their backs and bellies. They have legs shorter than other oxen have, but they are much stronger. These oxen draw the great houses of the Moals. Their horns are slender, long, straight, and so sharp that their owners must cut off the ends. The cows will not let themselves be milked unless they whistle or sing to them. They have also the character of bulls, for if they see a man clothed in red, they run upon him immediately to kill him.

Beyond these are the people of Tibet, men which are in the habit of eating the carcases of their deceased parents; that for pity's sake they might make no other sepulchre for them, than their own bowels. However, of late they have left off this custom, as they became abominable and odious to all other nations on account of it. But they still to this day make fine cups of the skulls of their parents, so that when they drink out of them, they may, amidst all their jollities and delights, call their dead parents to remembrance. This was told me by one who saw it.

The said people of Tibet have a great deal of gold in their land. Whoever wants gold, digs till he has found some quantity, and then taking so much of it as will serve his turn, he lays up the residue within the earth; because, if he should put it into his chest or storehouse he thinks that God would withhold from him all other gold within the earth. I saw some of these people, but they were very deformed creatures.

In Tangut I saw lusty tall men, but brown and swart in colour. The Jugures are of a middle stature like our Frenchmen. Amongst the Jugures remains the original and root of the Turkish and Coman languages. After Tibet are the people of Langa and Solanga, whose envoys I saw in the Tartars' court. They had brought more than ten great carts with them, every one of which was drawn with six oxen. They are little brown men like Spaniards. Also they have jackets, resembling the upper vestment of a deacon, saving that the sleeves are somewhat straighter. And they have mitres upon their heads like bishops. But the fore part of their mitre is not as hollow within as the back part; neither is it sharp-pointed or cornered at the top, but it is square and is of a kind of buckram which is made rough and rugged with extreme heat, and is so polished that it glistens in the sun like glass, or a helmet well burnished. And at their temples they have long bands of the same stuff fastened to their mitres, which hover in the wind as if two long horns grew out of their heads. When the wind tosses them up and down too much, they tie them over the top of their mitre from one temple to another: and so they lie circlewise over their heads. Moreover, their principal messenger to the Tartars' court had with him a table of polished elephant's tooth, about a cubit in length and a hand in breadth. And whenever he spoke to the emperor himself, or to any other great personage, he always held this table, as if he had found there the things which he wanted to say. Neither did he cast his eyes to the right hand, or to the left, or look in the face of him with whom he talked. Likewise, when coming into the presence of the lord, and when leaving it, he looked nowhere but upon his table.

Beyond them, as I understand of a certainty, there are other people called Muc, having villages, but who take no cattle to themselves. There are many flocks and droves of cattle in their country, and no man appointed to herd them. When any one of them wants any beast, he climbs a hill, and there calls, and all the cattle which are within hearing come flocking about him, and allow themselves to be handled and taken, as if they were tame.

When any messenger or stranger comes into their country, they shut him up in a house, ministering there things necessary to him, until his business is dispatched. For if any stranger should travel through that country, the cattle would flee away at the very scent of him, and so would become wild.

Chapter 29

OF CATHAY OR CHINA ❦ THE DEATH OF KUYUK KHAN ❦ AND THE CONSPIRACY AGAINST MANGU KHAN HIS SUCCESSOR

BEYOND is the great Cathay, of which the inhabitants were anciently the Seres. Because from them come the good cloths of silk, or seric, so called from the name of the people. And the people have received their name from one of their cities. I have been informed that in this country there is a city with walls of silver and of gold. In this land there are many provinces of which several do not obey the Moals. Between them and the sea is India. These inhabitants of Cathay are small in build and speak through their noses.

Like all Orientals, they have small eyes. They are very skilled workers in all the crafts, and their doctors know well the virtues of herbs and understand diseases through the taking of the pulse; but they have no knowledge of urines; this, at least, is what I have observed. Many of them inhabit Caracarum and exercise the same profession as their fathers; it is necessary that all the sons continue the paternal profession. That is why the tax is the same for all because one pays each day to the Moal a thousand five hundred *iascot* or their value in *cosmos*, that is to say, fifteen thousand marks without counting the cloths of silk, the provisions and the services that they receive.

All these people are spread throughout the Caucasus or rather to the north of these mountains up to the Eastern Ocean, and they are to the south of Sithia, which the nomadic Moals inhabit. All are their tributaries. They are given over to idolatry and tell a great number of fables of their gods, of the genealogy of these gods and of certain deified men, as our own poets do.

Among them are found Nestorians and Saracens who are held as foreigners in Cathay. In fifteen cities of Cathay one sees Nestorians, and in one city called Segin [Hsi-an Fu] there is a bishop. The rest are pure idolaters. The priests of the idols of these people wear large yellow coloured hoods. If it is necessary to believe what I have heard, there are also hermits who live very austere lives in the woods. However, they say their prayers and have sacred books in Syrian that they do not understand. This results in their chanting as do the monks in our country who know nothing of grammar. They are above all usurers, drunkards and some live with the Tartars and have like them several wives. When they enter a church they wash the lower parts of their bodies like the Saracens; they eat meat on Friday and hold their banquets in the manner of the Saracens. The bishop rarely visits their country, perhaps only once in fifty years. At that time all the little male children are ordained priests, even those who are still in the cradle, which explains why almost all the men are priests. Then they marry, which is completely contrary to the teaching of the Fathers, and they are bigamists because after the death of their first wife they take a second. They are also all simoniacs, not administering any sacrament without pay. They are very attentive to their wives and children and consequently they are more occupied in gaining money than in propagating the faith. Those among them who bring up the children of noble Moals, while teaching them the gospel and faith, manage to alienate them from the practice of Christian virtues, through the bad example of their habits and above all through their cupidity because the life of the Moals themselves and of the Tuins, who are idolaters, is more pure than the life of these priests.

We left Cailac on the day of the feast of St. Andrew [November 30] and arrived three leagues distant at a village of Nestorians. We entered their church and sang joyfully with our clearest voice, *"Salve regina!"* because it was a long time since we had seen a church. Three days afterwards we were on the confines of this province and on the shore of this sea [the Ala Kul], which to us seemed as stormy as the ocean. And in the middle we saw a large island. My companion approached the shore and moistened a cloth in it to taste the water, which was salty but drinkable. Between the south and the east there is a valley surrounded by high mountains and another lake between them and a stream crosses this valley from one lake to another.

The wind blew almost continually in this valley and with so much force that travellers ran the risk of being blown into the lake. However, we crossed this gorge, making our direction toward the north through high mountains covered with snows like the rest of the country. On the day of St. Nicholas we began to make haste because we no longer found any inhabitants other than the *iams*, that is to say, men placed one day's journey apart to take care of ambassadors. In many places in the mountains the road is narrow and the grazing bad, so that between morn and night we covered the distance of two *iams*, in this way making two days' journey into one. We travelled more by night than by day. It was intensely cold there, so we turned our sheepskins with the wool outside.

The second Sunday in Advent [December 7] we came to a certain place where there were steep and jagged rocks, and our guide asked me to say a prayer which could chase away the demons because in this place the devils were known to carry away men without their knowing what was happening to them. Sometimes they took away a horse and abandoned the rider; sometimes they tore away his entrails, leaving his skeleton on the horse, and many other things of this nature happened there. Then we sang loudly *"Credo in unum Deum,"* and by the grace of God we passed through safe and sound. Then they asked me to write cards [charms] for them to carry on their heads, and I said to them: "I will teach you the word that you will carry in your heart and by which your body and soul would be saved through eternity." But my interpreter failed to repeat it. However, I wrote for them the "Credo" and the "Pater," saying: "Here are written what a man must believe of God and the prayer through which one asks God all that is necessary for man; believe then firmly all that is written here even without understanding it and ask of God that he do for you what is contained in the prayer written here, which he gave himself with his own mouth to his disciples, and I hope he will save you." I could not do more, for it was dangerous to speak of doctrines through the medium of an interpreter; it was even an impossibility because he did not know how.

We then entered into the plain where Kuyuk Khan held his court. It was once the country of the Naimans who were the true subjects of that Prester John, but I saw his court only upon my return. However, I will tell you what happened to his family, his son and his wives. When Kuyuk died [1248 A.D.], Batu wished that Mangu replace him as the Khan. But of how he died I would not be able to say anything definite. Friar Andrew says that he lost his life following the taking of a certain medicine which was administered to him by the order, one believes, of Batu. However, there is another story: Kuyuk Khan had invited Batu to come to render him homage and Batu set out in great state, but not without great fear, he and all his men. He sent on ahead his brother named Stican who when he had arrived in the presence of Kuyuk and had to present him the cup, a quarrel then arose between them and they killed each other. The widow of Stican kept us for two days so that we might give her benediction and ·pray for her.

So Kuyuk being dead, Mangu was elected by the will of Batu and he was already elected when Friar Andrew visited these countries. Kuyuk had a brother named Siremon who, on the advice of the widow of Kuyuk and his vassals, went with great pomp to Mangu as if to render him homage but in reality with the project of killing him and destroying all his court. And when he was not more than one or two days' march away from Mangu one of his chariots broke and had to remain on the road. While the driver was endeavouring to repair it one of the men of Mangu came by and aided him in his work. This man inquired so much regarding their journey that the driver revealed to him what Siremon proposed to do. Then Mangu's man, retiring with an air of indifference, took the best horse he could find among all the horses, and riding day and night, arrived at the court of Mangu and announced to him what he had just learned.

Then Mangu promptly called together all his men and arranged all those who were armed in three circles about his court, so that no one could enter. He sent the others against this Siremon, who did not suspect that his scheme was discovered. They seized him and led him to the court with all his men. Mangu charged him with the crime and he confessed at once. Then he was put to death and with him the eldest son of Kuyuk Khan, and with them three hundred of the chief men among the Tartars. Messengers were sent to find the women who were whipped with red-hot brands in order to obtain from them a confession. And after they confessed they were all killed. The youngest of the sons of Kuyuk, who could not have given advice or had knowledge of what was planned, had his life spared and was given the possession of the court of his father with all its belongings. We passed that way on our return and my guides, in going or coming, did not dare to go to that side because "the mistress of nations sat in sorrow, and there was no one to console her."

Chapter 30

OUR DEPARTURE ❦ AND OUR ARRIVAL AT THE COURT OF MANGU KHAN

WE took again the road of the mountains, going always toward the north. Finally on the day of the Blessed Stephen

[December 26] we entered into a plain, as vast as the ocean, in which we did not discover a single hillock, and the following day on the feast of St. John the Evangelist we arrived in the presence of the great Khan. When we were at a distance of five days from there, the *iam* with whom we were staying wished to conduct us by a roundabout way that would have delayed us for over fifteen days and the motive, if I understood it correctly, would make us pass through Onankerule, the real country where Chinghis Khan had his court. Others said that they wished to take a longer road so as to magnify the power of their lord. It is thus, indeed, that they usually act to people who come from countries not subject to them. And it was with the greatest difficulty that our guide was made to take the direct road. This hesitation made us lose a good part of a day, from dawn to the third hour.

In this journey the secretary we had awaited in Cailac said to me that, in the letters Batu was sending to Mangu Khan, there was a request asking for an army and to aid Sartach against the Saracens. I was astonished and troubled then because I was acquainted with the tenor of your letters and I knew in them mention was not made of this request, except that you advised him to be the friend of all Christians, to honour the Cross and be the enemy of all the enemies of the Cross. And yet because the interpreters were Armenians of Great Armenia, greatly hating the Saracens, I feared lest they should have translated something in a manner harmful to the Saracens. I prudently remained silent because I did not wish to contradict the words of Batu nor to involve myself without a good cause.

So we arrived in the court on the day that I just mentioned to you. A great house was assigned to our guide, but to us only a little shelter where we could hardly store our things. Our guide received many visits and there was brought him rice wine in long narrow-necked bottles. I could not in any manner distinguish this drink from the best wine of Auxerre, excepting only by the odour which was not that of wine. We were called and closely questioned as to the purpose of our trip. I answered: "We have heard that Sartach was Christian; we wished to come to him. We bring him letters addressed to him by the king of the French. Sartach sent us to his father. His father sent us here. He himself must have written the purpose of our mission."

They asked us if you wanted to make peace with them. I replied: "He sent letters to Sartach as to a Christian and if he had known that he was not a Christian he would never have sent him letters. As to making peace, I tell you he has never done you the least harm. If he had done something that would justify your declaring war on him or on his people, he would hasten, as an upright man, to make apology and ask you for peace. If you, on the contrary, wanted without any cause to make war on him or his people, I hope that God, who is just, would aid them." And they always very astonished repeated: "Why do you come if you do not come to make peace?" For they are so haughty they imagine that the whole world seeks them out to ask to live in peace with them. Still if it were allowed me, I would preach war against them throughout the world. But I did not want to tell them openly why I came among them, fearing to pronounce a single word contrary to what Batu had ordered me to say. So it seemed to me sufficient to say that the cause of my coming was the mission I had from Batu.

The following day we were conducted to the court, and I thought I could go barefooted as we do in our own countries; that is why I left my shoes behind. Those who come to the court get off their horses within an arrow's shot from the dwelling of the Khan, and there leave the horses with the grooms entrusted to their care. When we had alighted and our guide proceeded to the Khan's dwelling, we found there a Hungarian servant, who recognized us—that is, our Order. Those surrounding us gazed at us with amazement, especially because we were barefooted, and they asked us why we considered our feet of so little importance. The Hungarian explained to them the reason for it, telling them that it was a rule of our Order. Then came the first secretary, who was a Nestorian Christian, by whose advice everything is done at the court. He looked at us attentively, called over the Hungarian and asked him many questions. Then we were told to go back to our lodging.

Chapter 31

AN ARMENIAN MONK IN THE COURT OF MANGU KHAN

As I was going back, I noticed, before the east end of the court, at a distance of two cross-bow shots, a house with a little cross on it. I rejoiced at it, for I supposed there was some vestige of Christianity there. I entered with confidence and found an altar beautifully bedecked; I saw, on a cloth of gold, embroidered the images of the Saviour, of the Holy Virgin, of St. John the Baptist and two angels, the lines of the bodies and of the garments designed with pearls. There was also a great silver cross, of which the middle and corners were mounted with precious stones, and many other ornaments; an oil lamp with eight lights was burning before the altar; and there was seated there an Armenian monk, dark, thin, dressed in a tunic of very rough haircloth, reaching midway to his thighs, over it a black jacket lined with wool and under the haircloth an iron belt. As soon as we entered, and even before greeting the monk, we kneeled down and sang: "*Ave regina cœlorum*," and he arose and prayed with us. Then, having saluted him, we sat down beside him. He had a dish with some fire in it. We told him the reason of our coming, and he began encouraging us, telling us we ought to speak boldly, for we were the messengers of God, who is greater than all men.

Then he told us how he came to that country, only a month before we did; that he had been a hermit in the outskirts of Jerusalem, and that God had appeared before him three times, enjoining him to go and seek the leader of the Tartars. And as he delayed to obey, God threatened him the third time, and ordering him to kneel in reverence, said he would die if he did not obey. He determined at last to encourage Mangu Khan to become a Christian, assuring him that the whole world would then come under his rule and that the Franks and the great Pope would be loyal to him, and he advised me to speak in like manner. Then I answered: "Brother, I will willingly tell him to become a Christian; for I have come for that, and I will give this advice to the whole world. I will also make him see how much the Franks and the Pope will rejoice at it, and will promise him that they will look upon him as a brother and friend; but that they would become his slaves and would pay him tribute, that will I never promise, for then would I be speaking against my conscience." So the monk remained silent, and we went to our lodgings where we found it cold, and we had not eaten anything all day. We cooked a little meat and some millet with water, for our supper. Our guide and his companions had got drunk at the court and quite ignored us.

Chapter 32

WINTER IN CARACARUM

THERE were then at Mangu Khan's dwelling, the ambassadors of Vastacius, but we did not know it. At dawn, next day, some men of the court made us get up in haste. I went with them, barefooted, by a narrow path to the lodging of the ambassadors, and they asked them if they knew us. Then a Greek knight, recognizing the Order to which I belonged, and also my companion whom he remembered having seen at the court of Vastacius with Friar Thomas, our provincial, gave, with his companions, excellent testimony of us all. They asked us then, if you were at peace or at war with Vastacius. "Neither at peace nor at war," I answered; and they said: "How can that be?"—"Your country and ours," I answered, "are so remote from each other, that they have nothing to discuss together." Then the envoy of Vastacius said that it meant peace, and this made me cautious and I kept silent.

That morning my toes were so frozen that I could no more go without sandals. For the cold in these regions is very sharp, and when freezing begins, there is no interruption until the month of May, even till the middle of May. Every morning there was a frost that only the heat of the sun-rays melted. But in winter the frost was continuous on account of the wind. And if the wind blew there in winter as in our country, it would not be possible to live; for the atmosphere there is always calm till April, and then the wind rises. When we were there about Easter time a great number of animals died on account of the cold prevailing with the wind. There is little snow in winter, but towards Easter, that is, at the end of April, so much of it fell that all the streets of Caracarum were covered and it had to be

taken away in carts. They brought us, from the court, some
cloaks and some doublets of sheepskin and sandals, which
my companion and my dragoman took with much delight.
As for me, I did not think I needed them because the fur
coat I had from Batu sufficed me.

Chapter 33

OF THE AUDIENCE WITH MANGU KHAN ❦ WHAT MESSAGE WE DELIVERED TO HIM ❦ AND HOW HE REPLIED

In the octave of the Innocents [January 3, 1254], we
were conducted to the court, and Nestorian preachers, whom
I would not know whether they were Christians or no, approached and asked us in what direction we turn to pray.
I answered, "To the east." They asked us this because we
had our beards shaved, at the advice of our guide, so as to
appear before the Khan according to the custom of our
country. It was this that made them take us for Tuins, that
is, idolaters. They also made us explain certain passages
of the Bible. Then they asked us what ceremony we would
observe before the Khan—theirs or ours? I answered them,
"We are priests consecrated to the service of God. In our
country, our noblemen do not allow priests to kneel before
them, if it be not to honour God. We come from afar; so,
first, if it please you, we will sing praises to God who has
conducted us in safety from so far, then we will do all that
shall please your master, except that which would be contrary to the worship and glory of God."

They entered the house and repeated my words to the
Khan, who was pleased. Having stopped before the door
of which the curtain of felt was raised, and as it was the
Nativity, we began to sing.

A solis orbu cardine
Et usque terre limitem
Christum canamus principem
Natum Maria virgine

When we had sung the hymn, they felt our legs, our chests, our arms, to see if we had knives upon us. They also called our interpreter and forced him to remove his belt on which hung his knife, and leave it in the custody of the usher. Then we entered and we noticed, at the entrance, a bench with *cosmos*. There they made the interpreter stop. But us they made sit on a bench opposite some women. The house was all covered with a cloth of gold, and in a grate in the centre was burning a fire of briars and worm-wood roots, which grow in abundance in these regions, and of cattle dung.

The Khan was seated on a couch, dressed in a spotted and very glossy fur skin, like that of a seal. He is a man of medium height, aged forty-five years; at his side was his young wife, and a grown girl, very plain, called Cherina was seated with some other little children on a couch placed behind that of their parents. This house had belonged to a Christian lady, whom the Khan had loved very much and of whom he had this girl. Afterwards he married his young wife, but the young girl is the lady of all the court that had once been her mother's.

Then the Khan requested that we be asked what we wanted to drink, wine or rice wine, which is a kind of mead made with rice, or *caracosmos*, which is the pure milk of the mare, or *bal*, which is an extract of honey. They drink these four drinks in the winter. To the questions I an-swered: "My lord, we are not men who seek our pleasure in drink; whatever will please you, suits us." He then had poured for us the rice drink, limpid and sweet like white wine, of which I drank a few sips by mere politeness. But to our misfortune, the butler had given our interpreter so much to drink, that he became intoxicated.

Then the Khan had falcons and other birds brought, placed them on his hand and amused himself looking at them. At last, after a long interval, he bade us speak. Then we had to bend our knees. The Khan had his interpreter, a certain Nestorian of whom I would not know whether he was a Christian, and we had ours, such as he was, though drunk. Then I said: "First we render thanks to the glory of God, who let us come from a country so far away to see Mangu Khan to whom God has given such a great power on earth, and we pray Christ, by whose will we live and die, that he grant him a happy and long life." It is the wish of all, in this country, that one pray for their lives. Then I told him, "My lord, we have heard that Sartach was a Christian, and all the Christians rejoiced at hearing it, principally the king of the French. That is why we came to him, and our lord the king sent him letters by us in which were words of peace, and among other things the proof of the kind of men we are. He begs him, too, to let us remain in his country. For it is our duty to teach men to live according to God's law. But he, Sartach, sent us to his father Batu, and Batu has sent us here to you. You are the one to whom God has given great power in the world. We pray then your mightiness to grant us the permission to remain in your empire, so that we may accomplish our divine mission in your service and in the service of your wives and your children. We have neither gold nor silver nor precious stones to offer you, we have only ourselves and we offer ourselves to you to serve God and to pray him to give you his blessings. At least, let us remain here till the cold is over, for

my companion is so feeble that he would succumb of fatigue
if he continued travelling on horseback."

My travelling companion had told me of his infirmity
and begged me to get permission for him to stay, for we
thought we would have to return to Batu, if we did not get
permission to stay. Then Mangu Khan replied: "Even as
the sun scatters its luminous rays everywhere, so does my
power and that of Batu's spread everywhere. Therefore,
we have no need, neither of your gold nor of your silver."
Until now I always understood my interpreter, but since his
state of drunkenness, I could no longer understand him. It
seemed to me that Mangu Khan himself was staggering a
bit. His reply, however, seemed to show that he was not
pleased that we went to visit Sartach before him. Seeing
that I lacked an interpreter, I remained silent and begged
him only not to be displeased if I talked to him of gold and
silver. I made him see that I did not mention these things
because he lacked or desired them, but because we wanted
to honour him temporally and spiritually.

Then he made us rise and sit down again, and a little
later, after saluting him, we left, and with us his secretaries
and his interpreter, who was bringing up one of his daughters. They asked us many questions, inquiring if there were
in France many sheep and cattle and horses, as if they
were about to invade us and take possession of all. And I
forced myself to conceal my indignation and my anger. I
answered: "There is much riches there, which you will see
if you ever go there."

Then they appointed some one to take care of us, and we
rejoined the monk. As we went out to reach our lodging,
the above-mentioned interpreter came to us and said:
"Mangu Khan has pity for you and allows you to stay here
two months. Then the cold will be over; he informs you

at the same time that at ten days' journey from here there is a goodly city called Caracarum. If you want to go there, he will have you provided with all that you will require; if, on the contrary, you want to stay here, you shall also have all you need. However, it will fatigue you to ride with the court."

I replied: "May the Lord keep Mangu Khan and grant him a long and happy life. We have met a monk here, whom we believe to be a holy man, come to this country by the will of God. So we would willingly remain with him, for we are monks like him and we will pray together for the life of the Khan." Then the interpreter left us without a word.

Chapter 34

THE RETURN OF OUR GUIDE ◀ AND THE WOMAN FROM LORRAINE

WE went to a large house that we found cold and without a supply of fuel. We were still without food and it was night. Then he to whom we had been entrusted, procured a fire and a little food for us. Our guide returned to Batu after asking of us a carpet that we had left by his order at the court of Batu. We gave it to him and he went away in peace, asking our hand and pardon for letting us suffer of hunger and of thirst during the voyage. We pardoned him, asking pardon, too, of him and of all his suite if we have shown them a bad example in anything.

A woman of Metz, in Lorraine, called Paquette, and who had been a prisoner in Hungary, found us out and prepared for us a feast of the best she could. She belonged to the court of that lady who was Christian and of whom I have already spoken; she told us of the unheard-of misery she had suffered before coming to the court. But she was fairly

well off, for she had a young Russian husband who made her
the mother of three little children, and he was a carpenter,
which is a good position among the Tartars.

Chapter 35

OF WILLIAM ❦ THE GOLDSMITH OF PARIS ❦ WHO IS EMPLOYED BY THE KHAN ❦ AND OF OTHER ENVOYS

AMONG other things, she told us that there was in Caracarum a goldsmith, named William, originally from Paris.
His family name was Buchier, the name of his father Lau-
rant Buchier. She believed too that he had a brother who
lived on the Grand Pont and who was called Roger Buchier.
She also said that this goldsmith had with him a young man
whom he treated as his own son and who was an excellent
interpreter. Mangu Khan had given this master artisan
three hundred *iascot*, that is, three thousand marks, and fifty
workmen to make a certain work of art; that is why she
feared he would not be able to spare his son.

At the court it had been said: "Those who come from
your country are good men, and Mangu Khan converses
willingly with them, but their interpreter is worth nothing."
Which explains why she was so concerned about us. So
I wrote to this goldsmith, telling him of our arrival and asking him to send his son to us if that were possible. He answered that he could not do so that month, but that his work
would be completed the following month and he would then
send him to me.

We stayed there with the other ambassadors. The ambassadors are not treated in the same manner at the court of
Batu as in the court of Mangu Khan. At the court of Batu
there is an *iam* on the west side who receives all those who
come from the West; it is likewise arranged for all other

parts of the world. But at the court of Mangu, all are assembled under the same *iam* and may mutually visit and talk to each other. At the court of Batu they do not know each other, and one does not know whether another is ambassador, for they do not know each others' lodgings and do not see each other at the court. And so when one is summoned, another perhaps is not. One goes to the court only when he is summoned there. We met also a Christian from Damascus, who said he came on behalf of the Sultan of Mont Real and of Crac, to pay tribute to the Tartars and ask for their friendship.

Chapter 36

OF THE CLERK THEODOLUS ❦ AND THE SPIES OF THE KHAN

THE year before my arrival in these parts, there was here a clerk from Acon, who called himself Raymond but whose real name was Theodolus. He travelled from Cyprus in company with Friar Andrew; he went with him as far as Persia and there got certain musical instruments from Ammoric and remained there after the departure of Friar Andrew. Friar Andrew once departed, he continued his journey with his instruments and reached the court of Mangu Khan, who asked him why he had come. Theodolus answered him that he had come with a holy bishop to whom God had sent letters written in heaven in letters of gold, and had ordained to give them to the lord of the Tartars who should be the man of all lands. He was also to persuade the populations to make peace with him.

Then Mangu Khan said: "If you bring me these letters that come from heaven and from your Lord, you are welcome." Theodolus replied that he had letters but that they were together with his other wares on a wild horse that had

got loose and escaped through the forest and over mountains so that everything was lost. And, in truth, accidents
of that kind happen frequently. It is, therefore, important
for a man always to hold his horse, when he has to descend
from it. Then Mangu asked him the name of this bishop;
he replied that he was called Oto. Then he said that he
was from Damascus and that master William was the clerk
of the lord legate. And the Khan asked him too in what
kingdom he dwelt; to which he replied that he was the subject of a certain kind of the Franks, called Moles. For
he had heard speak of what happened on the plains of Men-
sura [the battle of Mansurah in 1249] and he wanted to
make believe that he was one of your subjects. Then he
added that the Saracens intervened between the Franks and
the Khan and barred the passage for him; that if the road
were open, the Franks would send ambassadors to make an
alliance with him. So Mangu Khan asked him if he would
conduct ambassadors to that king and bishop. He answered,
yes, even to the Pope. Then Mangu Khan had brought a
very strong bow that two men could hardly bend and two
arrows with heads of silver, full of holes and which whis-
tled like flutes when they were darted. He told a Moal
whom he entrusted to accompany Theodolus: "You will
go to this king of the Franks, followed by this man, and
you will offer him these objects from me; and if he wants
to live in peace with us, we will conquer the land of the
Saracens as far as his country, and we will yield to him the
rest of the earth to the west. If not, you will bring back
the bow and the arrows, after telling him that with like bows
we can reach far and hit hard."

He then dismissed this Theodolus, and his interpreter
was the son of the master William. That young man heard
Mangu Khan say to this Moal: "You will go with this

man; observe the country well, the roads, the villages, the fortresses, the men and their arms." Then he reprimanded Theodolus, saying that he did wrong to take Tartar ambassadors, for they were ordered to spy. He answered that he would conduct them by sea so they would not know from where they came nor how to return.

Mangu also gave the Moal his tablet, that is, a plate of gold the breadth of a palm and a cubit's length on which are written his orders. He who carries it can command whatever he desires and his wish is at once granted.

In this manner Theodolus reached Vastacius, and was wishing to go as far as to the Pope and deceive him as he had deceived Mangu Khan. Vastacius asked him if he had letters for the Pope, since he was ambassador and entrusted to accompany the Tartar envoy. And as he was unable to show any letters, Vastacius had him seized, stripped of all he had and thrown into prison. As for the Moal, he was stricken with a malady and died there. Vastacius had the bull of gold returned to Mangu Khan himself by the attendants of the Moal, whom I met on the road at Erzerum, on the border of Turkey. I learned through them what had befallen this unhappy Theodolus. There are the like impostors the world over whom the Moals put to death whenever they can get them.

Chapter 37

THE MONK SERGIUS ❧ AND THE FEAST AT THE HOME OF THE KHAN

But the feast of the Epiphany [January 6] was drawing near, and the monk of Armenia, named Sergius, told me that he would baptize Mangu Khan on that day. And I begged him to do all he could to let me be present at the ceremony and bear witness of it. That he promised me.

The day of the ceremony the monk did not call me, but on the sixth hour I was invited to the court, and I saw the monk returning from the court with the priests and his cross, the priests carrying the censer and the book of the Gospels. For on that day Mangu Khan offered a feast and it was the custom that on such days, that his soothsayers call holy, and that some Nestorian priests call sacred, the Khan holds court. Then the Christian priests come first in grand magnificence and pray for him and bless his cup. After they leave, come the Saracen priests and do likewise. Then the priests of idols arrive and they do the same. The monk told me that the Khan believes only the Christians, but that he wants everybody to pray for him. The monk lied, for the Khan believes in no one, as you shall soon learn. Every one seeks the court as flies seek honey and they leave it satisfied, each imagining he has the prince's favours, and showering blessings on him.

So we were seated before his court at some distance, and they brought us meat to eat. We told them we would not eat there, and if they wanted to offer us food, we would accept it in our lodgings. Then they said to us: "Return to your lodgings then, for you have been called only to eat." So we went back with the monk, who blushed for the lie he told us. I did not want to say a word to him. However, the Nestorians persuaded me that the Khan was baptized. I answered them that I did not believe it and that I could not speak of it to others, for I saw nothing.

We reached our lodgings that were cold and empty. We were supplied with beds and coverings. They brought us also fuel for a fire and some meat of a lean sheep, and of it a very small quantity for the three of us for six days.

Every day they gave us a bowl of millet and a quart of millet mead, and a saucepan and a tripod to cook the meat. We boiled the millet in the bouillon of that meat. Such was our food, and it would have been enough, if we could have eaten it in peace. But there are so many poor there dying of hunger, they would rush in on us when they saw us preparing our meals. Then I had proof of what martyrdom it was to give in charity when in poverty.

Chapter 38

OF THE COURT OF MANGU KHAN ❧ AND THE RELIGIOUS CEREMONIES

As the cold began to be severe, Mangu Khan sent us three coats of monkey skins, the fur outside, and we received these gifts with gratitude. We were also asked if we had enough food, to which I replied that we require little food, but that we had no suitable house where we could pray for Mangu Khan. Our lodging, in fact, was so small that we could not stand up in it and read our books when there was a fire. This answer was repeated to the Khan and he sent word to the monk asking if he would receive us at his home, to which he replied that he would gladly receive us.

From then on we were provided with better lodgings and we stayed with the monk opposite the court where no one but we and the Tartar soothsayers lived; but they were nearer and opposite the court of the first wife of the Khan. We, on the contrary, were placed at the opposite extremity towards the east, in front of the court of his last wife. It was on the eve of the octave of the Epiphany [January 12]. The next day, that is, on the octave of the Epiphany, all the Nestorian priests assembled in their chapel before dawn, struck on the table, sang matins solemnly, donned their vestments and prepared the censer and incense. And as they were thus waiting in the church, the first wife, called Cotota Caten, entered the chapel with several ladies and her oldest son Baltu, followed by several of his brothers. They prostrated themselves, touching the ground with their foreheads, according to the custom of the Nestorians; they also touched with their right hand all the images, kissing their hand each time after touching an image, then extending their hand to all the bystanders. Such is the ceremony that the Nestorians observe when they enter the church.

Then the priests sang a long time, placing the incense in the queen's hand and she putting it on the fire, and they incensed her. Finally, at the wake of day, she took off her head-dress, called *botta*, and I saw that she was shaved; she bade us leave, and as I was leaving, I noticed that they brought her a silver vase. I do not know whether she was baptized or no, but I do know that the Nestorians do not celebrate mass under a tent, they need a substantial church. At Easter I saw them baptize and consecrate fonts in great solemnity, which they did not do at the time I speak of.

And as we returned to our house, Mangu Khan himself came and entered the church, or oratory, and they brought him a couch of gold on which he sat down with his wife, opposite the altar. Not knowing of the arrival of Mangu, we were summoned to the church, and those who stood at the door searched us, fearing that we had knives on us. But entering the oratory, I carried only the Bible and my breviary. I bent before the altar, then before the Khan, and in passing we kept between the monk and the altar. Then they made us sing and intone a psalm according to our rites. We sang this prose: "*Veni, Sancte Spiritus.*"

The Khan had our books brought to him, the Bible and the breviary, and he asked with much curiosity what meaning the images had. The Nestorians answered whatever they wanted to, for our interpreter did not come with us. When I was before him for the first time, I also had the Bible and he asked to see it and examined it a long while.

Then he left, but the queen remained and distributed presents to all the Christians there. To the monk she gave one *iascot* as well as to the archdeacon of the priests. Before us she had placed a *nasic*, which is a large drape, very long, and as broad as a bed-cover, also a *buccaran* [quilted material]. I did not think I had to accept them, and they gave them to the interpreter who kept one and carried the other (*nasic*) to Cyprus where he sold it for eighty Cyprian *bezants*, but it was spoiled during the voyage. Then they brought us mead to drink, made of rice and of red wine like the wine of La Rochelle, and *cosmos*. Then the queen, taking a full cup, knelt and asked for our blessing, and all the priests sang in a loud voice, while she emptied her cup. When she drank once more, we had to sing, for it was our turn. Every one was a little drunk; meat of a sheep was brought, which was quickly devoured; after that fish, that is, carp without salt, and without bread; I had to eat of these. So they passed the day until evening. And then the queen herself, tottering with drunkenness, mounted her chariot in the midst of the singing and the howling of the priests, and went her way.

The following Sunday, the day when the Evangel is read: "*Nuptie facte sunt in Chana*," the Khan's daughter, whose mother was a Christian, came and did likewise, but not with such solemnity, for she gave no presents, but only drink, to the priests, enough to make them drunk, and she offered them parched millet to eat.

Before the Sunday of Septuagesima, the Nestorians fast for three days; they call these days the fast of Jonah, preached by him to the Ninevites. The Armenians then fast for five days, and they call them the fast of St. Serkis who is their greatest saint; the Greeks claim he was a canon. The Nestorians commence their fast Tuesday and end it Thursday, so that on Friday they eat meat. I saw the chancellor then, who is the secretary of state, Bulgai by name, send to them on Friday some meat, and they blessed it with pompous ceremony, like the paschal lamb is blessed. But he did not eat of it, according to the counsel of master William of Paris who sees him a good deal. The monk himself enjoined Mangu to fast this week, which he did as I heard tell. That is why, on the eve of Septuagesima [February 8], when the Armenians celebrate Easter, we went in procession to the dwelling of Mangu, and the monk and we two, having been previously searched lest we have knives on us, were introduced to the presence of the Khan.

Chapter 39

THE DIVINATION OF BURNT BONES ❧ AND THE FOUR DWELLINGS THAT WE VISITED

As we entered, a person came out carrying some bones of the shoulder blades of a sheep, all burnt, and I was very curious to know what he wanted to do with them. Having asked later what that signified, I learnt that they undertake nothing of importance without first consulting these bones; no one is allowed to enter the Khan's dwelling if he has not consulted these bones first. It is a form of divination; when the Khan wishes to undertake something, he has brought to him three of these bones, and holding them between his hands, he thinks about what he wants to do; will he do it or will he not? Then he gives these bones to one of his men to burn them. For that, there are near his home two little houses in which these bones are burnt and where the greatest care is taken of them. Once charred black, they are brought to the Khan who examines them very attentively to see if the heat of the fire has left them intact throughout their entire length. If so, he deems that he can carry out his intentions. If, on the contrary, he notices the least crevice there, or that any fragment is detached, he does nothing.

When we found ourselves in the presence of the Khan, warned in advance not to touch the threshold, the Nestorian priests brought over to him the incense, and he put a portion of it in the censer, and they incensed him. Then they sang, blessing his drink; the monk did the same after them, and we followed. And as he saw that we held Bibles before us, he had them brought to him and looked them over very carefully. After he had drunk and the high priest had taken his cup, he gave it to the other priests. Then we went out; my companion stayed a little behind. However, when we were outside, my companion, while following us, turned towards the Khan to bow to him and hit, by accident, the threshold of the house; and as we were hastening to reach the home of Baltu, his son, those who were charged to guard the threshold seized my companion and prevented him from following us; they called some one to take him to the house of Bulgai, who is the first secretary of the court and who condemns the guilty to death. Well, I did not know this. However, looking back and not seeing my companion coming, I thought they had detained him to give him some lighter garments, for he was weak and so laden with furs that he could hardly walk. They then called our interpreter and made him sit by him.

We went to the home of the oldest son of the Khan, who already had two wives and who is lodged on the right of his father's court; as soon as he saw us coming, he got up from the couch on which he was sitting, prostrated himself to the ground, striking the ground with his forehead and worshipping the cross. Getting up, he had it placed with the greatest veneration in an elevated place, on a new cloth, very near him. His master is a certain Nestorian priest, called David, a veritable drunkard who gives him lessons. Then he made us sit down and gave the priests to drink. He drank after them, receiving their blessings.

We then went to the court of the second wife of the Khan. Her name is Cota and she is an idol worshipper. We found her ill and lying in her bed. The monk then made her get up, and bade her to worship the cross on bended knees while striking the ground with her forehead; he was standing with the cross on the west of the house, and she on the east. That done, they changed places, and the monk went with the cross to the east and she to the west; and he commanded, with the same boldness, this woman, so feeble that she could scarcely stand on her feet, to prostrate herself again three times to worship the cross of the east, according to Christian fashion, which she did. He told her also to make the sign of the cross on her forehead and chest. Then she lay down again in her bed, and we prayed for her and we went our way towards the third dwelling, where the Christian lady used to live. After her death, she was succeeded by a young girl who, with the daughter of her master, received us gladly, and every one in the house worshipped the cross devoutly and they placed it on a cloth of silk in an elevated place. Then they brought some meat, that is, the meat of a sheep; it was placed before the mistress, and then distributed among the priests. We, the monk and I, neither ate nor drank. We had then to go to the apartment of that damsel Cherina, which was behind the great house and had been her mother's. At the sight of the cross she threw herself on the ground and worshipped it very devoutly, for she had been well enlightened in her religion, and put it in an elevated place on a cloth of silk, and all the cloths on which the cross was placed belonged to the monk.

This cross had been brought over by a certain Armenian who came with the monk, as he said, from Jerusalem; it was of silver and weighed four marks and had four precious stones in the angles and one in the center. The image of the Saviour was not on it, for the Armenians and the Nestorians are ashamed to see Christ attached to the cross. The monk presented it to Mangu, who asked him what he desired. He answered that he was the son of an Armenian priest, whose church the Saracens had destroyed and begged him to help restore it. Mangu then asked him at what price he could rebuild it, and he answered for two hundred *iascot*, that is, two thousand marks. And the Khan ordered that letters be given him to the one who receives the taxes in Persia and Great Armenia, so that he should pay him this sum of money. The monk carried the cross with him everywhere and the priests. seeing how it profited, began to be jealous of him.

So we were at the house of this damsel, and she made the priests drink a good deal. From there we went to the fourth dwelling, which was the last in importance, for the lord seldom visited this lady, and her dwelling was falling into decay, and she herself was not pleasing. But after Easter, the Khan made her a new dwelling and new carts. She, like the second wife, knew very little of Christianity; she was an idol worshipper and consulted the soothsayers. Still, at our entrance, she worshipped the cross as the monk and the priests had taught her. There the priests again drank and then we returned to our oratory, which was not far away, accompanied by priests who sang or rather howled, being in a state of drunkenness, which is in these parts a thing not reprehensible, neither in man nor in woman.

Then my companion was brought in, and the monk re- proached him severely for having touched the threshold. The next day Bulgai arrived, the great judge, and he made close inquiries whether any one had warned us not to touch the threshold and I answered: "My Lord, we had no inter- preter with us; how could we understand?" So he par- doned him, but never again was he allowed to enter a house of the Khan.

Chapter 40

A VISIT TO THE SICK PRINCESS ❦ AND HOW THE MONK CURED HER

THE lady Cota, who was ill since the Sunday of Sexage- sima, became even more sick; she was about to die, and the sorcerers and the idolaters could do nothing for her. So Mangu sent to the monk, asking him if he could do some- thing for her, and the monk replied rashly enough that he would deliver his head to the Khan, if he did not cure her. After that reply, the monk called us, telling us of the affair with tears and imploring us to pray with him the whole night long, which we did. He had a certain root, called rhubarb; he made it into powder and put it in water with a little cross adorned with the image of the Saviour. He claimed to know by it whether the sick person would recover or die. If he was to escape death, it would stick to his breast as if glued; if, on the contrary, he was to succumb, it would not stick. As for me, I was convinced that this rhubarb was something holy that he had brought from the holy land of Jerusalem. And he gave that water to all sick persons to drink, and it naturally happened that their intestines were strangely tormented by a draught so bitter. This movement of the body was considered like a miracle.

While he was preparing this remedy, I told him to make it with the holy water of the Roman Church, for it had a great virtue in chasing demons, and that we had understood that the princess was possessed of a demon. At his request we made holy water for him, and the monk mixed it with the rhubarb and put the cross in it to soak all night. I told him also that if he was a priest, the sacerdotal order would give him power to expel devils. He answered me that he had never received the Order, that he was even illiterate, being a cloth-weaver by profession; this I later learned in his own country, which we passed through in returning.

The next morning, then, we went to the sick princess, the monk and I and two Nestorian priests. She was in a little apartment behind her principal abode. At our entrance, she raised herself from her couch, worshipped the cross, had it placed near her on a cloth of gold, drank the holy water mixed with rhubarb, and washed her chest with it; the monk requested me to read the Gospel over her. I read the Passion of the Lord according to St. John. At last she was glad, for she was feeling better, and she had brought four *iascot* of silver, which she first placed at the foot of the cross; she then gave one to the monk and presented me with another which I did not accept. So the monk extended his hand and took it. Then she gave one to each of the priests, thus distributing the value of forty marks. Then she caused to be brought some wine, gave it to the priests to drink, and I had to drink three times from her hand in honour of the Trinity. She also wanted to teach me her language and laughed at me because I was silent, not having an interpreter with me.

The next day we went back to the house of the princess,

and Mangu Khan, having learned that we were there, called us before him. He had heard that the lady was better. We found him with several attendants, drinking what looked like liquid mud, that is, a pasty dish for comforting the head, and before him were the burnt bones of a sheep's shoulder-blade; he took the cross in his hand. But I did not see whether he kissed it or worshipped it; he looked at it, asking I know not what.

Then the monk asked him for permission to carry the cross at the end of a lance, for I had said something of that to the monk, and Mangu replied: "Carry it as you judge best." Then we saluted him and we went to the home of the princess, and we found her well and of good cheer, and she drank again of the holy water, and we read the Passion over her. These miserable priests had never taught her anything of the faith, neither talked about baptizing. I sat, silent, not able to say anything, and she again taught me some of her language.

The priests did not condemn her for having recourse to sorcery, for I saw at her home four swords half drawn from the scabbard, one at the head of her bed, the other at the foot, and two others at each side of the door. I also saw there a chalice of silver, like our chalices, which had perhaps been taken from some church in Hungary. It was full of cinders and suspended on the wall, and on the cinders was a black stone and the priests had never told her that it was evil. On the contrary, they themselves do as much and teach it by their example.

For three days we visited the princess, and she was completely restored to health. Then the monk made a banner covered with a cross and asked for a long reed like a lance, and we carried the cross at the end of that rod. I honoured that monk as a bishop, because he knew the language of the

country. However, he did many things that displeased me.
He had a pliable seat made for himself like the bishops
ordinarily have, and gloves, and a hat with peacock feathers and a little cross of gold on it. He had rough nails and
covered them with unguents. He was presumptuous in
speech. The Nestorians also recited verses of the psalm book
over two joined twigs which two men held between their
hands. The monk was present at all that, and there were
many other ridiculous things about him that displeased me.
Nevertheless, we did not abandon him on account of the
veneration we had for the cross. We carried it on high
everywhere we went, throughout the whole camp, singing:
"*Vexilla regis prodeunt,*" at which the Saracens were stupe-
fied.

Chapter 41

OF THE JOURNEY TO CARACARUM ❦ OF PEOPLE WHO GLIDE OVER ICE ❦ AND OTHER NATIONS

SINCE the day we arrived at the court of Mangu Khan,
this prince went but twice to the south and then he began
going back towards the north, that is, towards Caracarum.
During the journey, I noticed only one thing which, at
Constantinople, Baldwin of Hainaut, who had been there,
told me; that is, one mounts all the time while marching
and one never descends. In fact, all the rivers flow from
east to west, either in a straight direction or otherwise, that
is, reaching the north or south. I asked the priests of Cathay,
and they told me that from the place where I met Mangu
Khan to Cathay was a distance of twenty days' journey.
While to Onankerule, the true country of the Moals, where
is the court of Chinghis Khan, was a ten days' journey in a
straight direction eastward, and in these countries of the east
there was not one city. One meets there, however, people

called Su-Moal, that is, "Moals of the waters" for *su* in Tartar language means "Water." They live by fishing and hunting, not having any oxen or sheep.

Likewise towards the north, there is no city, but a pastoral people called Kirghiz. There are also there Oengai who attach to their feet polished bones and glide like that over ice or frozen snow, with such rapidity that they catch birds and beasts. There are still other miserable people towards the north spreading as far as the cold permits them and reach the west in the land of Pascatir, or Great Hungary, of which I have already spoken. The limit of this corner of the north is unknown because of the extreme cold, for there are mountains of snow there that never melts.

I asked about the existence of the monsters or of these monstrous men, of which Isidore and Solinus speak. They tell me that never the like was seen, and I was greatly astonished at it. All these nations, though poor, must serve the Moals in one way or another; it is an order of Chinghis that no one is exempt from work, except when old age forbids it.

Chapter 42

OF THE DEFORMED CREATURES ❦ AND OF CATHAY

ONE day a priest of Cathay came and sat by me, and he was clothed in a red cloth of a most beautiful colour, and I asked him from where such a colour is got. He told me that in the east of Cathay there are very high rocks where live certain creatures who have the form of a human being, except they cannot bend knees. Also, they move about, I do not know just how, but by jumping. They are not more than a cubit tall and their body is all covered with hair. These beings live in inaccessible caverns. The hunters bring them mead to get them drunk; they make holes in the rocks

in the form of vases and pour the mead in them. Cathay
has no wine but they are beginning to plant vines there and
they make a drink of rice.

So these hunters hide themselves and the jumping creatures come out of their caves, taste this mead, and cry: *"Chin,
chin."* It is because of this cry that they got their name,
for they are called "Chinchin." Then they assemble in
crowds, gorging this drink, and, becoming drunk, they fall
asleep on these rocks. Then the hunters approach and bind
the hands and feet of these sleepers. After that they open
a vein in their necks, draw three or four drops of blood, and
then send them back free. This blood, according to the
story of the priest of Cathay, is excellent for colouring purple
or scarlet. They told me also, which I do not believe, however, that beyond Cathay there is a province where no man
grows old, no matter what his age.

Cathay touches the ocean, and master William of Paris
told me that he saw there emissaries of certain people called
Caule [Korea] and Mance; they live on islands surrounded
by a sea covered with ice in the winter, so that the Tartars
can invade them. They also offered the Tartars, to be allowed to live in peace, thirty times two thousand *tumen* of
iascot annually.

Chapter 43

THE PAPER MONEY USED IN CATHAY ❧ AND HOW THEY WRITE

THE ordinary money of Cathay is a paper made of cotton
the length and breadth of a palm, stamped with lines similar
to those of the seal of Mangu Khan. The Cathayans write
with a brush like painters use, and a single figure comprises
several letters, signifies a word. The Tibet people write as
we do, from left to right, and have characters quite similar
to ours. The people of Tangut write from right to left

as the Arabs, and multiply the lines going upwards. The Jugures, as I have said before, write up and down. The ordinary money of the Ruthenians consists of different little skins, green and grey.

When we came to live at the home of the monk, he kindly advised us to abstain from eating meat, but he added that our domestic could eat it with his servants, and that he would provide us with flour, oil and butter. We complied with his wishes, though my companion suffered greatly on account of his weakness. Our food thus consisted of millet and butter, a dough cooked in water or sour milk, and unleavened bread baked on a fire of cattle or horse dung.

Chapter 44

OF THE LENTEN SERVICES ❧ AND THE COMPLAINT OF THE GATE-KEEPER

THEN came Quinquagesima [February 23], which is the first day of Lent in all the East, and Cotota, the greatest of the ladies, fasted with her women all that week. She came every day to our oratory and distributed food for the priests and other Christians, who gathered there in crowds during that first week to be present at the services. She gave me, as well as my companion, a tunic and breeches of grey samite, lined with woolen stuffing, because my companion often complained of the weight of his skins. I accepted them out of compassion for him, excusing myself for not wearing such clothes, and gave them to my interpreter.

The gate-keepers of the court, seeing that every day such a crowd filled the church, which was in the boundary of the domain of the court, sent one of their number to the monk with the order to tell him that they did not want so many people to congregate there, just beyond the limits of the court. The monk answered him harshly, he wanted to know if they gave this as the order of Mangu, and threatened to bring complaint against them to Mangu. But they forestalled him and accused him to Mangu, saying he talked too much and assembled too many people around him.

We were then called to the court on the Sunday Quandragesima, and the monk was shamefully searched to see that he carried no knife, and they compelled him to take off his shoes. We were brought before the Khan; and he held in his hand a charred sheep's shoulder-blade and was looking at it closely, as if he read something there. Then he reprimanded the monk and asked him why he talked so much to the men, instead of praying to God as he ought to. I was standing behind, my head uncovered. The Khan further said to him: "Why do you not uncover your head, when you are before me, as this Frank does?" And he made him approach. The monk, confused, took off his hat, contrary to the custom of the Greeks and the Armenians; and when the Khan lectured him right harshly we went out. Then the monk asked me to carry the cross to the oratory, for he did not want to entrust it to himself on account of his confusion.

Some time later he became reconciled with the Khan, promising him to go and find the Pope and to make his power recognized by all the nations of the West. After leaving Mangu and returning to the oratory, he questioned me about the Pope. He asked me if I thought he would receive him if he presented himself to him in behalf of Mangu, and to furnish him with horses as far as St. James of Compostella [Spain]. He asked me further, concerning you, if I believed that you would send your son to Mangu. I warned him then to be careful about making false promises to Mangu, for the last lie would be worse than the first, and that God had no need of our lies.

Chapter 45

OF THE THEOLOGICAL DISCUSSION ❧ AND THE PROVISIONS FROM THE KHAN

AT this time a difficulty arose between the monk and a certain priest, called Jonas, a well-educated man, whose father had been archdeacon, and whom the other priests looked upon as their teacher. The monk said that man had been created before paradise, and that it was so written in the Gospel. I was then called to decide the question. I, not knowing about what they differed, said that paradise had been created on the third day, with the trees of the earth, and that man was created on the sixth day. So the monk said: "Has not the devil brought, on the first day, earth from the four parts of the world, and did he not of this mud, form the human body, in which God had breathed the soul?" Hearing this Manichean heresy, and publicly upheld with so much impudence, I upbraided him sharply and told him to put his finger on his mouth, since he did not know the Holy Scriptures, and to thus avoid repeating his error. But he scoffed at me because I did not know the language. So I left and returned to my lodgings.

Then the priests and he went in procession to the court, without inviting me, because the monk, since the reprimand, did not speak with me and did not want to take me along as was his habit. When they came in the presence of Mangu, the Khan, not seeing me among them, asked them where I was and why I was not with them. The priests were afraid and excused themselves. When they returned they told me the words of Mangu and complained of the monk.

After that the monk became reconciled with me and I with him, and I asked him to aid me to understand the language of the country, promising to aid him in the study of the Holy Scriptures; for the brother who is aided by a brother is like a strong city.

The first week of the fast having passed, the princess no longer visited our oratory and ceased to favour us with the food and mead as she had done. The monk did not allow that any of it be brought to us, saying it was prepared with the fat of mutton. Too, he did not give us any oil, or rarely gave it to us. So we had nothing to eat but some bread baked on ashes and dough cooked in water to make soup, and even the water was of snow, or melted ice, which is very bad. My companion suffered from it. I told of our necessity to David himself, the master of the Khan's eldest son, and he told the Khan, who immediately ordered that we be given wine, flour, and oil.

The Nestorians and the Armenians never ate fish during Lent. So they gave us a leather bottle of wine. The monk said that he ate only on Sunday. The princess sent us cooked dough with sour wine for supper. But the monk had near him, under the altar, a basket of almonds, grapes, dried prunes and many other fruits, which he ate every day when he was alone. We ate but once a day and in great misery; for when they learned that Mangu Khan had given us wine, they rushed upon us impudently and like dogs, these Nestorian priests who every day became drunk at court, and these Moals and these attendants of the monk. The monk himself, when any one visited him and he wanted to give him to drink, sent to us for wine. That is why that wine was to us more an affliction than a consolation, for we could not refuse it to him without offending him. If we gave him

of it, we were short, and when it was done, we dare not ask
for more at the court.

Chapter 46

OF THE PALACE OF MANGU KHAN AT CARACARUM

TOWARDS the middle of Lent the son of master William,
the goldsmith, brought a beautiful silver cross, made after
the French style, with a Christ of silver over it. Seeing it,
the monks and priests stole it, and the young man was to
have presented it on the part of his master to Bulgai himself, the first secretary of the court. I was greatly scan-
dalized when I learned this news. The young man also
told Mangu Khan that the task that he had ordered him to
do was finished. I will give you a description of it.

Mangu has a large palace at Caracarum, under the walls
of the city, enclosed within a high wall as our monks' pri-
ories are enclosed. There is a palace there where he gives
a great feast twice a year, at Easter when he passes through,
and in summer when he leaves. This last feast is the
greater, for then come to his court all the nobles who are
more than a two months' journey away from it; and the
lord distributes garments and gifts and displays his glory
and all his magnificence. There are also many houses there,
long as barns, in which are enclosed his provisions and his
treasures. At the entrance of this great palace—for it would
not seem fit to bring there goat-skin bottles of milk or other
drinks—master William of Paris placed a great silver tree,
at the foot of which are four silver lions having a spout and
all pouring forth mare's white milk. Four spouts are introduced in the tree at its top, and from there they pour
out their milk from the mouths of gilded serpents whose
tails twine around the trunk of the tree. From one of these

channels flows the wine, from another *caracosmos*, or purified mare's milk, from the third *bal*, or honey-drink, and
from the fourth rice mead; and each liquor is received at
the foot of the tree in a special vase.   On top the artist had
placed an angel with a trumpet and underneath the tree he
had made a vault in which a man can hide.   There is a pipe
extending upwards through the middle of the tree to the
angel.   At first he made bellows, but they did not produce
enough wind.   Outside the palace is a cavern where the
drinks are kept and where there are servants ready to pour,
at the first sound of the angel's trumpet.   And the branches
of the tree are of silver and the leaves and fruits also.
When the head cup-bearer wants a drink, he calls to the
angel to sound the trumpet.   Then the man hidden in the
vault blows in the pipe that reaches the angel; the angel
places the trumpet to his mouth and the trumpet blows very
loudly at a distance.   At this resounding voice the servants
who are in the cavern, each pours his liquor into the spout
assigned, and the spouts pour it into the vases standing at
the foot of the tree, and then the cup-bearers draw of that
liquor and carry it to the men and women of the palace.

The palace is like a church having a nave in the centre
and two side aisles separated from the nave by two rows of
pillars.   There are three doors on the south side, and in
front of the middle door, inside, is this tree.   The Khan
has his seat to the north, on a platform, so that he can be
seen by all, and it is reached by two rows of steps leading
up to it; by one his food is brought to him, the other is used
for descending.   The space between the tree and these stairs
is empty, for there stands the servant assigned to give the
Khan the foods he wishes to eat, and the ambassadors who
bring him gifts; and he is seated on high like a god.   To
his right, that is, to the west, are the men, to his left, the

women; for the palace extends lengthwise from north to south. On the right, near the pillars, are raised benches in the form of an amphitheatre where the sons and the brothers of the Khan sit, and to the left his wives and daughters. Only one woman is seated at his side, but on a seat less elevated than his own.

When the lord had heard that master William had completed his work, he ordered him to put it in place and fix it there well. Towards Passion Sunday, the artist left with his little tents, leaving the big ones behind him. The monk and we accompanied him and he gave us a goat-skin bottle of wine. He crossed mountains where the wind was high and the cold intense, and where snow fell in abundance. He also sent to ask us, in the middle of the night, to pray God to temper the cold wind, for all the animals of the land were in danger, especially those about to bring forth young. So the monk sent him incense, telling him that he himself should sprinkle it on coals and offer it to God. I do not know whether he did either of these things, but the storm that had lasted for two days subsided at the approach of the third day.

Chapter 47

OF CARACARUM ❤ AND HOW WE MARCHED WITH THE CROSS ON HIGH

ON Palm Sunday we were at Caracarum. At the first rise of the morning's sun we blessed some boughs upon which buds were not yet visible, and towards the ninth hour we reached the city, the cross on high and banner unfurled, and passed the Saracens' quarters and their public places, to the church. The Nestorians came in procession to meet us. Once in the church, we found them ready to celebrate mass; and this finished, they all communicated and asked me if I wanted to communicate with them. I answered them that I had already drunk and that the sacrament could only be received at fasting.

The mass said, evening approached, and master William took us with him to his home for supper, in great joy. His wife was the daughter of one Larraine, and born in Hungary, she spoke French and Coman well. We met there another European, named Basil, the son of an Englishman and born in Hungary, and who spoke the same languages. The supper passed in real joy, and afterwards the Tartars conducted us to lodgings that they had prepared for us, not far from the church and oratory of the monk.

The next day the Khan entered his palace, and the monk, the priests and I followed him. They did not allow my companion to accompany us, because he had once trod on the threshold. As for me, I hesitated a long while; should I or should I not go? If I withdrew from the other Christians, I feared it would cause a scandal; moreover, the Khan wanted me. Fearing, on the other hand, to interfere with the good I wished to obtain, I at last decided to appear at the court, even though I saw it devoted to sorcery and idolatry. I did nothing but pray in a loud voice for the church and for the Khan himself, so that God might lead them in the way of eternal salvation.

So we entered the court, which is quite well arranged and in the summer is watered by canals. We then went into the palace full of men and women, and we stood before the Khan, having behind us the silver tree which occupied, together with the vases, the largest part of the palace. The priests brought two little loaves of blessed bread and fruit in a basin and presented it to him, after blessing it. The butler took it to the Khan who was seated on a highly elevated platform. Mangu at once ate one of these breads and had the other given to his son and to a younger brother, who was brought up by a Nestorian priest and knew something of the Scriptures. Also he asked to see my Bible.

After the priests, the monk said his prayer, and I after him. Then Mangu promised us to come the next day to the church, which is quite large and beautiful, being entirely covered with silken cloths embroidered in gold. But the next day he continued on his way, making excuses to the priests that he dared not come to the church because he learned that the dead were brought there. But we remained at the court of Caracarum with the monk and the other priests to celebrate Easter there.

Chapter 48

EASTER AT CARACARUM ❧ AND HOW WE BAPTIZED OVER SIXTY PERSONS

THEN Holy Thursday was approaching and Easter, too. I did not have my priestly garments, and I was observing the manner of consecration of the Nestorians, and I was very anxious. Will I receive the sacrament from them? Or will I myself consecrate in their vestments, with their chalice and on their altar? Or will I wholly abstain from the sacrament? There were a swarm of Christians there, Hungarians, Alans, Ruthenians, Georgians, Armenians, all of whom had been deprived of the sacrament since their captivity, for the Nestorians would not admit them in their church, unless they were baptized by them. However, these priests raised no objections to us in this regard. On the contrary, they recognized that the Roman Church was the head of all churches, and that they themselves would have to receive their patriarch from the Pope if the roads were open. And they liberally offered us their sacrament

and placed me at the head of the choir so that I could see
the way they baptized on the eve of Easter.

They claimed they had some ointment with which Mary
Magdalene had anointed the feet of the Saviour and they
pour oil into this, equal to the amount taken out, and dip
their bread in it. Also, all those of the East put into their
bread either fat, or butter, or tallow of a sheep's tail, or oil,
instead of yeast. They also say that they have flour of which
was made the bread consecrated by our Lord, and that they
put in as much as they take out of it. They have a room
beside the choir of the church and an oven where they bake
the bread that they must consecrate with great reverence.
Thus with this oil they make a bread the size of a hand; this
they divide into twelve parts in memory of the twelve
Apostles. They then subdivide these parts into as many
pieces as there are people; the priest places the body of Jesus
Christ into the hand of each, and every one receives it with
profound reverence and lifts his hand to the top of his head.

Then I heard their confession, as well as I could through
an interpreter, and I explained to them the Ten Commandments of God, and the seven principal sins and all that is
necessary to be penitent and absolved. They justified their
sin of theft, saying that they could not live without stealing,
for their lords deprived them of food and clothes. So, in
consideration of privations so unjust, I told them that they
could share of their masters' belongings all that they found
necessary, and I was ready to uphold this theory before
Mangu Khan himself. There were also soldiers who de-
fended their going to war on the grounds that otherwise
they would be put to death. These I strongly forbade to
march against the Christians or to do them the least harm,
and told them rather to suffer death, for they would then be
martyrs. I added, that if any one intended to complain

before Mangu Khan of my doctrine, I was quite ready to preach it before him; for the Nestorians of the court were present at my teachings, and I suspected they might repeat them.

Then master William had an iron made for us to form wafers with, and had made some vestments for himself, for he had a little learning, and performed the functions of a clerk of the church. He also had made, in French style, an image of the Holy Virgin, and on the panels of the partition he sculptured with talent the figures of the Gospel. To him is credited a silver box to enclose the body of Christ and relics in the little cavities made inside. Finally, he constructed an oratory on a chariot, beautifully painted, on which were represented the scenes of the Holy Story. So I accepted these ornaments and blessed them and we made, in our way, very beautiful wafers, and the Nestorians let me use their baptistery where there was an altar. Their patriarch sent them a skin from Bagdad, quadrangular like a portable altar, anointed with cream, which they used in place of a consecrated stone. So I celebrated mass, on Holy Thursday [April 9], with their silver chalice and their paten, both of which were large vases; likewise on the day of Easter. And we gave communion to the people, with the blessing of God, I hope. More than sixty persons were baptized, on the eve of Easter, in very good order, and the joy among the Christians was very great.

Chapter . 49

OF THE ILLNESS OF MASTER WILLIAM AND THE NESTORIAN PRIEST

THEN it happened that master William fell gravely ill. And when he was convalescing, the monk visited him and gave him to drink tea of rhubarb, which nearly killed him. When I in my turn visited him, I found him so weakened that I asked him what he had drunk or eaten. He told me what potion the monk had administered to him, and that he had drunk two full bowls of it, thinking it was holy water. Meeting the monk, I said to him: "Conduct yourself as an apostle doing miracles by the virtue of prayer and the Holy Spirit, or else be a physician that observes the rules of the art of curing. You give to drink a large dose of medicine to men who are too sick to drink it, as if it were something holy; you would be much rebuked for it, if that were known to the public." So he began to have fear and to mistrust me.

At this time, the priest who passed for the archdeacon of the Nestorians, also fell ill, and his friends sent for a Saracen soothsayer who said to them: "A lean man, who does not eat or drink or sleep in a bed, is angry with him. If he could obtain his blessing, he would get well." They understood that he meant the monk, and toward midnight, the wife, the sister, and the son of the priest went to the monk and begged him that he give his blessing to the sick man. They invoked us even, to ask the monk. And when we begged him, he said: "Do not trouble about him, for he and three others like him had formed the project to go to the court and induce Mangu Khan to chase you and me out of the country."

Now a controversy arose among them because Mangu and his wives had sent, on the eve of Easter, four *iascot* and some cloths of silk to be distributed among the monk and the priests, and one of the four pieces of money was counterfeit, being of copper. Also, it seemed to the priests that the monk had had too large a share; it was also possible that something they had said was reported to the monk.

At daybreak I went to the priest who was suffering from

acute pains in his side and was spitting blood; from which I concluded that it was an abscess. So I advised him to recognize the Pope as the father of all Christians, which he at once did, promising that if God returns him his health, he will go and kiss the feet of the supreme Pontiff, and act so that the Holy Father would send his blessings to Mangu Khan. I advised him also to give back all that did not belong to him. He told me he had nothing belonging to others. I spoke to him again of the sacrament of the extreme unction. He replied: "It is not our custom, and our priests do not know how to do it; I beg you to do whatever you judge right." I told him also of the confessions which they do not have. He whispered something to one of his companions. Then he felt better and he asked me to go and get the monk. I did so.

At first the monk did not want to come; however, when he learned that the man was feeling better, he came with his cross, and I carried the box of master William where was the body of Jesus Christ that I had reserved from the day of Easter at my compatriot's request. Then the monk began kicking the sick man, and the other kissed his feet with great humility. I said to him: "It is the custom in the Roman Church that the sick receive the body of Christ, as a viatic and a protection against the snares of the enemy. Here is the body of Christ that I have conserved since Easter day. You must confess and desire it." Then he said in a very strong faith: "I demand it with all my heart." When I exposed the consecrated wafer, he said with great fervor: "I believe that this is my Creator and my Saviour who gave me life and will give it to me again after death on the day of the general resurrection." And so he received from my hands the body of Jesus Christ that I had made according to the fashion of the Roman Church.

The monk remained with him and administered to him, in my absence, I do not know what potion. The following day the patient began to suffer again all the pains of death. So I took the oil that the Nestorians held as holy, and I anointed him with it according to the rites of the church, thus complying with the prayer for the dying. I did not have our oil with me, because the priests of Sartach had retained everything. And as we were commending his soul to God and as I wanted to be present at his death, the monk sent word that I leave, for if I stayed, I could not again be in the presence of Mangu Khan during all that year. The friends I questioned on this point said it was true and advised me to leave, so as not to be deprived of pursuing the good I was doing.

The sick man died, and the monk said to me: "Be not troubled; I have killed him with my prayers. He was the only scholar, and was hostile to us. The others know nothing. Henceforth, all of them and Mangu Khan himself will be at our feet." Then he told me what the priest had said about asking the Khan to send us away, but I did not believe it. I inquired among the priests, friends of the dead man, to learn if it was true. They told me that it was so, but they did not know if he had been asked or not.

I learned afterwards that the monk had the soothsayer and his wife come to his chapel, made them sift some dust and draw prophecies from it. He also had with him a Ruthenian deacon who helped him in this. Learning all this, I was horrified at his folly and said to him: "Brother, a man filled with the Holy Ghost, who teaches all things, should not consult soothsayers, and not be inspired with what they say; all this is forbidden and those who give themselves to such practices are excommunicated." He assured me he did nothing of all that. And I could not leave him, for I was lodged at his house by the order of Mangu Khan and I could not go elsewhere without his special orders.

Chapter 50

OF THE BROTHERS OF MANGU KHAN ❧ AND THEIR ARMIES

As to the city of Caracarum, you must know that but for the exception of the palace of the Khan himself, it is not as important as the village of Saint-Denis, and the monastery of Saint-Denis is worth twice as much as the palace. There are two quarters in it, one of the Saracens where the markets are and where the merchants leave their wares on account of the court which is at a short distance of it, also on account of the many ambassadors. The other quarter is that of the Cathayans all of whom are artisans.

Besides this palace there are great palaces which are inhabited by the secretaries of the court. There are twelve temples dedicated to the idols of the different nations, two mosques where they observe the laws of Mahomet, and one church of Christians at the far end of the city. The city is surrounded by a mud wall which has four doors. On the eastern side is sold millet, and on the others, grain, which, however, is very rare; on the west, they sell sheep and goats; on the south, oxen and carts, and on the north side, horses.

Following the court, we arrived here on the Sunday before Ascension. The next day we were called by Bulgai, first secretary of state and a great judge, as well as the monk and his whole family and all the ambassadors and the strangers who frequented the monk. We were separately brought into the presence of Bulgai, first the monk, then we; and they asked us where we came from, and why, and what we wanted. And they proceeded to question us minutely, because it was reported to Mangu Khan that forty Assassins had arrived under various disguises to kill. About this time, the lady of whom I have previously spoken, fell ill again and sent for the monk. But he would not go to her, answering: "She has already called idolaters, let them cure her if they can. I shall not go there again."

On the eve of the Ascension [May 20] we went through all the houses of the Khan, and I noticed that whenever he was about to drink, they sprinkled *cosmos* on his felt idols, which made me say to the monk: "What is there that is common between Christ and Belial? What connection is there between the Cross and these idols?"

Furthermore, Mangu Khan had eight brothers, three full brothers, and five half-brothers. He sent one of his full brothers to the country of the Assassins, whom they call Mulidet, with the order to kill them. Another went towards Persia; he has already entered, it is believed, Turkey, and will send from there an army against Bagdad and Vastacius. One of the other brothers [Kublai] he sent to Cathay, to subdue those who did not yet recognize his supremacy. He kept near him his youngest full brother, called Arabuccha, who governs the court of their mother, a Christian, in whose service is master William. One of his half-brothers captured this prisoner in Hungary, in a city called Belgrade, where there was a Norman bishop from Belleville near Rouen and a nephew of this bishop whom I had seen at Caracarum. He gave master William to the mother of Mangu, for she very much wanted to have him. After her death, the goldsmith passed into the service of Arabuccha with all those who belonged to her court. Mangu Khan knew him through Arabuccha and, having ordered the work of which I have already spoken, gave him one hundred *iascot*, that is, a thousand marks.

On the eve of the Ascension, Mangu Khan wanted to visit his mother at the court, for he was not far from her. The monk said he wished to accompany him and give his blessing to his mother's soul. That pleased the Khan. During the evening of the Ascension, the condition of the princess became worse and the chief of the soothsayers sent orders to the monk not to beat his board. The next day those of the court of the Khan left, but the court of the princess continued. When we arrived at the spot where the court was to stop, an order was given to the monk to move farther away from the court than usual. This he did. Then Arabuccha approached his brother, the Khan. The monk and we, seeing that he would pass at a little distance from us, came forward toward him with the cross. And he recognized us, because he had once visited our oratory, extended his hand and give us his blessing like a bishop. Then the monk mounted his horse and followed him, carrying some fruit with him. But Arabuccha stopped before the court and waited for his brother to return from the chase. The monk descended there also and presented him some fruit which he accepted. Two great men of the Khan's court, two Saracens, were seated near him. But Arabuccha, knowing the differences that separated the Christians from the Saracens, asked the monk if he knew the two Saracens. The monk replied: "I know them, for they are dogs. Why are they near you?" And these replied: "Why do you abuse us, since we do not talk to you?" And the monk insisted: "It is true," he said to them; "I repeat that you and your Mahomet are abominable dogs." So they started blaspheming against Christ, and Arabuccha stopped them, saying: "Do not talk like that, for we know that Messiah is God." Just then so great a wind arose over the whole country, as though demons were chasing it; shortly after, the news was spread that the princess Cota had died.

The following day Arabuccha returned to the court by another road; for it is a superstition among the Tartars never to return by the same road by which they come. For the same reason, nobody dares pass, either on foot or on horseback, the place where the court has stopped, as long as there remains after its departure, a trace of the fire that was built there. The same day, several Saracens joined the monk on the road, provoking and disputing with him. As he could not defend himself by reasoning, and as they were jeering at him, he wanted to hit them with the whip he held in his hand, and he carried on so much that his words were reported to the court. Also we were ordered to stop elsewhere with the other ambassadors than in front of the court, as we were in the habit of doing.

Then, too, I was always hoping for the arrival of the king of Armenia.[1] Also near Eastertime came a person from Bolat, where are the Germans whom I almost resolved to go and see. Some one had told me that a German priest was to arrive at the court. Because of that, I never dared ask Mangu whether I was to remain or go. In reality, he had given us permission to remain in his land only two months, but four months had already passed, and the fifth was nearing its end. For it was the end of May, and we had been there during January, February, March, April and May.

Not hearing anything said about the king or this priest, and fearing that we would be obliged to return in the winter, whose severity we had already felt, we asked Mangu Khan what he intended doing with us, for we would have willingly

---

[1] The King of Little Armenia, Heythum I, left his capital Sis in Cilicia for the court of Mangu Khan in 1254

remained with him, if he wished it; but if we had to go, it would be better to leave in the summer. He at once sent word that I remain, for he wished to speak with me the next day. I answered instantly that if he desired to speak to me he would have to send for the son of master William, as my interpreter was incompetent. The one who was addressing me was a Saracen, and once ambassador to Vastacius. Bribed with his presents, he advised him to send ambassadors to Mangu Khan. During these conferences, time would pass, for Vastacius believed that the Tartars would soon invade his countries. He then sent ambassadors, and after learning from them what sort of people the Tartars were, he scorned them and refused to make peace with them, and they did not invade his lands. Nor could they, for he dared defend himself against them; for they never conquer a country, but by ruse, and when they make peace with any one, it is only to destroy them.

This Saracen began making inquiries about the Pope and the king of France and which route to take to go to them. And the monk cautioned me secretly not to answer him, for he wanted to procure means to send them ambassadors. I, therefore, kept silent, not wishing to answer him. And he addressed me, in I do not know what injurious words, for which they wanted to indict him, or kill him, or whip him till he bled, but I would not let them.

Chapter 51

HOW THE KHAN ORDERED THE DIFFERENT PRIESTS TO DEFEND THEIR OWN RELIGIONS ❦ AND OUR LAST AUDIENCE WITH MANGU KHAN

THE next day, the Sunday before Pentecost, I was conducted to the court. The secretaries of the state, of whom one was a Moal, served the drinks to the Khan, and the others, Saracens, asked me why I had come to their country. So I repeated what I had said already, how I came to Sartach and from Sartach to Batu, and how Batu had sent me here. I said to them: "I have nothing to say on the part of any man, for it ought to be known what Batu has written; I have only to preach the words of God, if they wish to hear them."

At these words, they asked me what were the words of God I wished to pronounce, for they thought I was going to foretell some good news, like so many of the others do. I answered them: "If you accept as divine the words I preach, give me an interpreter." They answered: "We have sent for one; speak by this one as best you can; we will understand you." And they pressed me to speak. So I said: "Of him to whom much has been given, much will be required. Likewise, he who has received much, must give much love."

After these divine words, I said to Mangu Khan, that God has given him a great power, and that the riches he has gotten were not from the idols of Tuins but from Almighty God who made the heavens and earth, in whose hand are all the kingdoms, and who removes the power of one nation to another because of the sins of man. So, if he loves God, all will be assured him; if not, he must know that he will have to account for his last farthing.

Then said one of the Saracens: "Is there a man who loves not God?" I answered: "It is God who knows: he who loveth me, obeyeth my commandments; and he who loveth me not, keepeth not my commandments. Thus he who does not observe the commandments of God, loves not God." At this the Saracen said: "Have you been to heaven that you know the commandments of God?" "No," said I, "but he has sent them from heaven to the holy men, and himself descended from heaven to teach all men, and it is in the Bible and we see it, by the works of men, when they observe them or no." But he replied: "Do you mean to say that Mangu Khan does not follow God's precepts?" And I answered, "The interpreter will come, you said; and if Mangu Khan authorizes me, I will tell which are the commandments of God, and he shall judge himself if he obeys them or not." They left me and reported to the Khan that I had said he was an idolater, or Tuin, and that he did not observe the commandments of God.

The following day the Khan sent his secretaries to me, and they said: "Our lord sent us to you to let you know that you here are Christians, Saracens, and Tuins. Each of you says that his law is the best and that his Scriptures, that is, his books, are the truest. That is why he wishes that you all assemble in the same place, and that each write down his laws, so that the truth may be known." So I said: "Blessed be God who has inspired the Khan with such a thought. But our Scriptures teach that the servant of God must not dispute, only be kind to all. I am thus ready to explain, without hatred, the faith and hope of the Christians to whoever wishes to question me."

They wrote down my response and took it to the Khan. The Nestorians were also ordered to write down all they wished to say, and the same was told to the Saracens and the Tuins. The next day, the secretaries again came to me, saying: "Mangu Khan wishes to know why you travel through these parts." I answered them, "He should know by the letters of Batu." So they said, "The letters of Batu are lost, and the Khan has forgotten what Batu has written, and he wishes to know through you." More assured, I said, "The duty that my religion imposes upon me is to preach the Gospel to all men. Also, when I had learned

of the famous Moal race, I desired to come here, and, ani-
mated with this desire, I learned that Sartach was a Christian. So I wended my way towards him. And the king of
the French, my lord, sent him letters which contained kind
words, and among other things he said who we were and
requested him to allow us to remain among the Moals. He
then sent us to Batu and Batu sent us to Mangu Khan; that
is why we have begged him and still beg him to let us remain here."

The secretaries wrote all that down and brought it to
him the next day. He again sent word to me: "The Khan
well knows that you have no message for him, and that you
come to pray for him, like the other righteous priests; but he
wishes to know if any ambassadors have come to us from
your country, or if any of ours have gone to your parts."
So I told them all that I knew of David and of the Friar
Andrew, and they put it in writing and brought it to him.

Then once more he sent me word, saying: "The Khan,
our lord, says you have stayed here a long time; he wishes
that you return to your country and asks if you would take
his ambassadors with you." I replied: "I would not dare
take his ambassadors out of their country, because there are
countries at war between us, and seas and mountains; and I
am only a poor monk; that is why I would not venture to
take them under my leadership." And they, writing it all
down, returned to him.

The eve of Pentecost arrived. The Nestorians wrote the
chronicle since the creation of the world to the Passion of
Christ, they said a few things about the Ascension and the
resurrection of the dead and of the last judgment. There
was much to reprove there, and I pointed it out to them. We
wrote the symbol of the mass: "I believe in one God." Then
I asked them how they wished to proceed. They answered

that they first wished to discuss with the Saracens. I made them see that it was not well, for the Saracens agreed with us that there is but one God: "You will thus from them have aid against the Tuins." They agreed with me. Then I asked them if they knew how idolatry came into the world. They did not know. I explained it to them and they said: "Tell them that and speak in our place, for it is difficult to talk through an interpreter." I answered: "Look how you will act regarding them. I will uphold the cause of the Tuins; and you will defend that of the Christians. Let us suppose that I am of that sect who claims there is no God; prove that God exists." For there is a sect who believe that all soul, all virtue there is in no matter what thing, is the God of that thing, and that there is no other God. And the Nestorians could not prove anything, only repeat what is written in the Bible. I said to them: "They do not believe in the Bible; you allege one thing and they another." Then I advised them to let me discuss with them, for if I were vanquished, they would still find a way to talk.

Therefore on the eve of Pentecost, we assembled in our oratory and Mangu Khan sent three secretaries as arbitrators—one a Christian, another a Saracen, and the third a Tuin; and these proclaimed: "This is the order of Mangu and no one dare say that the commandment of God differs from it. He orders that no one use disagreeable or injurious terms toward his adversary, nor cause a wrangle that may disturb the conference, under penalty of death." So all kept their silence. And there were a great number of people there, for each side had called the most learned of his race, and many others were present.

The Christians placed me in the centre and told the Tuins to discuss with me. But they who were there in crowds began to murmur against Mangu Khan, for never before had a Khan tried to get hold of their secret. They then placed me opposite some one who came from Cathay and had an interpreter. Mine was the son of master William; he said to me: "My friend, if you think you are not enough versed, get some one more learned than yourself." I was silent. Then the Tuin asked me about what I wished to discuss first, the origin of the world or the destiny of the soul after death. I answered him: "That should not be the beginning of our conference. All things pass from God, and he is the principal source of all things; we must begin to speak of God, of whom you have not the same idea as we, and Mangu wants to know the best opinion." The arbitrators judged that this was right.

He wished to begin with these questions for they had studied them better; for they are all of the heresy of Manicheans, and believe that one-half of things is evil, the other half good, and that there are at least two principles, and they all believe that the soul passes from one body into another. Also the most learned priest among the Nestorians asked me if the souls of animals can take refuge somewhere, without being held in slavery after death.

To confirm this error, so master William told me, there had been brought a child from Cathay who, from their judgment, was not more than three years old. He was, however, capable of all reasoning and it was said that he had been incarnated three times, and that he knew how to read and write. So I said to this Tuin: "We believe firmly and with all our heart, and we confirm with our mouth that there is a God and one God only, and of a perfect unity. What do you believe in?" And he answered: "Only fools say there is but one God, but the wise uphold that there are several. Are there not, in our country, several great lords, and a greater one here, who is Mangu Khan? Even so there are different Gods, for they are different in each country." I answered: "Your example is a poor one; there cannot be similarity between men and God; for in that case a powerful man in his country would be called God."

And, as I was about to destroy his comparison, he prevented me and asked: "What is then your God, that you say is the only one?" I answered: "Our God is all powerful, and there is no other than he, and he needs the help of no one; but we all need his protection. It is not so with man. No one can do all by himself; that is why it is necessary that there be several leaders on earth, for one alone can not govern by himself. Our God also knows everything, and needs no advice. Also, all science comes from him. He is infinitely good, and has no want of our goods. Too, we live and we move and we are in him. Such is our God. and he must not be thought of otherwise."

"No," said he, "he is not like that. It is true that there is a supreme God in heaven whose filiation we still do not know; but under him there are ten other Gods, and under us an inferior God. They are innumerable in the countries of the world." As he was going to weave more fables around it, I asked him if he believed that the supreme God was all powerful, and I questioned him about some other God.

Evading my question, he in turn asked me: "If your God is what you say, why did he create half the things evil?"—"It is not true," I said to him; "the one who created evil is not God. And all that is, is good." The Tuins were astonished at this reply, and they wrote it down as false or impossible.

I was then asked: "From where does evil come?"— "You put your question wrong," I replied. "You should first ask what is evil, before searching whence it comes. But let us go back to the first question: Do you believe that an all-powerful God exists? And I will answer you then all that you will ask me." He sat for a long time refusing to reply, so that the secretaries present had to order him, in the name of the Khan, to answer. At last he said that there did not exist a God all-powerful. Then all the Saracens laughed out loud.

Silence restored, I said: "Then none of your Gods can ever save you, for it can happen that he have no power. Besides, no one can serve two masters; how, then, can you serve so many Gods in heaven and on earth?" Those present told him to reply, but he did not. And as I wanted to develop before the entire assembly the reasons for the unity and the trinity of the divine essence, the Nestorians of the country said to me that it sufficed, and that they wanted to talk themselves. I then yielded, and as they were preparing to discuss with the Saracens, the others replied: "We agree that yours is the true law and that all that is in the Gospel is true; so on no account do we wish to argue with you." And they confessed that in all their prayers they asked God to accord them grace to die as the Christians die.

There was an old priest there, of the sect Jugures, who say there is one God yet who make idols. They talked a long time with him, telling him all that came to pass till the coming of the Antichrist into the world, and also proved the Trinity by analogy to him and the Saracens. Every one listened without raising the least objection. Yet no one said: "I believe; I want to become a Christian." Then the Nestorians and the Saracens sang together in a loud voice; the Tuins said not a word and afterwards everybody drank deeply.

On Pentecost day [May 31], Mangu Khan called me

and the Tuin with whom I had discussed; and before entering, my interpreter, the son of master William, told me that
we must return to our country and that I must make no
objection, for it was a thing decided. When I came before
the Khan, I had to bend the knees, and the Tuin and his
interpreter also. Then he said to me: "Tell me the truth;
did you say the other day, when I sent my secretaries to
you, that I was a Tuin?" I answered: "My lord, I did
not say it, and I will repeat my words if that will please
you." So I repeated what I said and he replied: "I well
believed you did not utter these words, for you could not
have thus spoken; it is your interpreter who misunderstood."
And he held out toward me the stick on which he was lean-
ing, and said. "Have no fear." And I, smiling, said in a
low tone: "If I had fear, I would not be here." And he
asked the interpreter what I had said, and he repeated it
to him.

Then he professed his faith to me. "We Moals," said he,
"we believe there is but one God, by whom we live and by
whom we die, and we have for him an upright heart." Then
I said to him: "May God grant you grace, for without
it you can do nothing." And he asked what I had said, the
interpreter repeated to him, and the prince added: "Even as
God has given several fingers to the hand, so has he given
man several ways. God has made us know the Holy Scriptures, and your Christians do not observe them. You do
not see in them that one should blame another, do you?"—
"No, my lord," I said, "but I told you from the start that
I did not want to have any differences with any one."—"I
do not speak," said he, "for you. Likewise, you do not find
there that a man should avoid justice for money."—"No,
my lord," I replied. "And surely, I did not come to these
parts to obtain money; on the contrary, I have refused that

which they wanted to offer me." And there was a secretary there who attested that I had refused an *iascot* and some silken cloths.

"I do not speak of that," he said. "God has given you a Testament and you do not follow it; to us, he has given soothsayers, and we do what they tell us and we live peacefully." He drank, it seems to me, at least four times before finishing his dialogue.

While I was waiting for him to confess still another phase of his faith, he began to talk of my return, saying: "You have been here a long while; I wish that you leave. You have said that you do not want to take my ambassadors with you; will you forward my letters or deliver my words?" And from then on, I no longer had the occasion or the time to explain to him the Catholic faith. For no one can speak before him longer than he wishes him to, at least if he is not an ambassador; but an ambassador can say all he wants, and they always ask him if he has anything more to say. As for me, I was not allowed to talk further, but had to listen to him and answer his questions.

So I replied that he should make me understand his words, and have them written down. I willingly undertook to convey them as best I could. He then asked me if I wanted gold or silver or fine clothes. I said: "We accept no such things; however, we have nothing with which to pay our expenses of the voyage, and without your aid, we cannot leave your country." Then he said to me: "I will see that you have all that is necessary. Do you wish for more?" I replied: "That suffices me."

Then he asked me: "How far do you wish to be conducted?" I replied: "To the kingdom of Armenia your power extends; if I could be conducted as far as there, it would suffice me." And he said: "I will have you con-

ducted as far as that place; after that, take care of yourself."
He added: "I have two eyes in my head, and though there
are two of them, they see one way; for where one eye looks,
the other turns to. You have come on the part of Batu
and you must return towards him."

When he had finished, I asked for permission to speak.
"Speak," he said. And I began: "My lord, we are not
men of war. We want that the authority of the world
belong to him who can govern it with most justice, according
to the will of God. Our work is to instruct men to live by
the will of God. For this reason have we come to your
country, and we would have remained gladly had you wished
it. But if it is your wish that we leave, so it will be. I will
go back, and I will take your letters as best I can and as you
wish. But I would like to ask your Majesty if, when I will
have taken your letters, you will allow me to come back here,
principally because you have, at Bolat, poor subjects who
speak our language and who have no priest to instruct them
and their children in their religion. I would gladly live in
their midst."

He answered me: "If your masters send you back towards
me, you will be welcome." So I said: "My lord, I do not
know my masters' intentions; but I have received from them
the permission to go wherever I wish, there where it is
necessary to preach the words of God, and I think it is necessary in your regions; that is why, whether the king sends
back ambassadors or no, if you allow it, I will return."

Then he remained silent for a long while as though
absorbed in his thoughts, and the interpreter told me to say
no more. But I, anxious, was awaiting a reply. At last he
said to me: "You have far to go, strengthen yourself with
food, so you may arrive in your country in good health."
And he had drink given me. Then he left and I did not

see him again. Had I the power to perform miracles like Moses, he would perhaps have humbled himself.

Chapter 52

OF THE SOOTHSAYERS ❧ THEIR CUSTOMS ❧ AND HOW THEY EVOKE THE DEVIL

THEIR soothsayers, as he himself said, were their priests, and all they command to be done, is executed immediately. I will tell you what their office is as best I can, after what master William and others told me. They are numerous and they have a superior, who is like a pontiff, and who has his dwelling opposite the principal dwelling of Mangu Khan, a stone's throw from it. Under his keeping are, as I have said, the chariots in which their idols are carried. The others are behind the court, in the places assigned them. These soothsayers are consulted by people from different parts of the world. For some among them are versed in astronomy, particularly the chief, and he predicts the eclipses of the sun and of the moon, and when that has to happen, the whole population provides itself with food, so that they need not leave their houses. And when the eclipse is taking place, they ring the bells and sound the trumpets, hurling loud cries; and there is much ado. The eclipse past, they give themselves to unbounded joy and excessive drinking and eating. They predict the lucky and unlucky days for all circumstances of life.

Also, war is never declared nor battles waged without their advice, and the Tartars would long since have returned to Hungary, had their soothsayers allowed them. These arrange to pass over fire all that is sent to the court, and for this they get a large part of it. They also purify with fire all furniture left by the dead. When any one dies, they take away all that has belonged to him, and no one in the court is allowed to touch the least object that is not purified. This is what I saw at the court of the princess who breathed her last while we were there, and that explains the double reason why they made Friar Andrew and his companions pass the fire; first, because they carried presents; secondly, because these gifts had belonged to Kuyuk Khan who had died quite recently. They did not act so with me, for I had nothing. If an animal or anything falls to the ground during purification by fire, it becomes the property of the soothsayer.

These lastly mentioned also are in the habit of assembling and of consecrating, on the ninth day of the month of May, all the white mares of the herd. The Christian priests then have to be present at this ceremony with their censers. They sprinkle on the ground *cosmos* newly made and it is a great feast they hold on that day, for they eat and drink of the new *cosmos* for the first time; as is practised in some of our countries during the vintage on the day of St. Bartholomew or of Holy Syxtus, and when the fruits are gathered, the day of St. James and St. Christopher. The soothsayers are also called in at the birth of a child, to foretell his fate, and when some one falls ill, to judge if the malady is natural or the result of witchcraft.

The wife from Metz, of whom I have spoken, told me something extraordinary regarding this. Once, a present of very valuable furs was given to the court of her mistress, a Christian, as I have already told you. The soothsayers had it passed over the fire, and retained more of it than was their due. A woman under whose care was the treasure of this lady, accused them of it before her, and the latter reprimanded them. Then it happened that this lady fell ill and suffered sudden pains over all parts of her body.

The soothsayers were called in, and keeping themselves at a distance from her, they ordered one of the young girls to place her hand on the painful spot, and to take off whatever she found. So the young girl arose, did what she was told and found under her hand a piece of felt or something like it. They told her to put it on the ground, and instantly that thing began to crawl like a living animal. They put it in water and it became like a leech, and the soothsayers said: "Madam, some sorcery has been cast on you and has hurt you." And they accused her, who had accused them of stealing the furs. Led outside the camp, she was beaten with a rod for seven days and she was made to suffer other tortures to make her confess. And during these tortures the lady died, and her servant, learning of the misfortune, said: "I know that my mistress is dead, kill me so that I may accompany her, for I have never done her any harm." And since she avowed nothing, Mangu ordered that she be let live, and then the soothsayers accused the nurse of that Christian lady's daughter, whose husband was one of the most honourable men among the Nestorian priests. She was led to the places of torture with one of her women, to make her confess. The servant testified that she had been sent by her mistress to consult a horse. That woman confessed that she had done that to be liked by her master and receive some favour for it, but that she did nothing that could have harmed him. They asked her if her husband knew about it. She made excuses for him saying that he had burned the characters and the letters that she herself had made. Then the nurse was put to death, and Mangu sent her husband, who was a priest, to his bishop in Cathay, to try him for it, though he was not found guilty.

About this time, it happened that the first wife of Mangu Khan gave birth to a son, and the soothsayers were called to predict the destiny of the child; all prophesied a happy future, saying that he would live long and would be a great prince. A few days later, the child died. So the mother, furious, called the soothsayers to her and said to them: "You said that my son would live and he is dead." They answered her: "Madam, we see the sorceress, the nurse of Cherina, who was put to death the other day. It is she who has killed your son, and we have seen her carry him off."

The dead woman was survived, in the camp, by a son and a daughter, already grown up, and the lady had them brought and put to death, the young boy by a man, the young girl by a woman, to avenge herself of the death of her own son, who the soothsayers said had been killed by their mother. A short time later the Khan had a dream; he dreamt of these children, and asked what had been done with them. His servants, fearing to tell him, and he, more and more aroused by curiosity, insisted on knowing where they were, for during the night they appeared before him in a dream. So they told him, and he forthwith sent for his wife and asked her why she had condemned a woman to death without his knowledge. He had her shut in a prison for seven days and forbade that she be given the least nourishment. He had the Tartar beheaded, the one who had killed the young boy, and had his head hung on the neck of the woman who had killed the young girl; then he had her beaten with hot fire-brands in the middle of the camp, and finally he ordered that she be put to death. He would also have put his wife to death if he did not have children by her; but he left her court and did not return there for a month.

The soothsayers disturbed the atmosphere by their incantations, and when the cold was very intense they naturally could do nothing; so they accused certain people in the camp of having caused this cold temperature and these were executed without delay.

A short time after my departure from here, one of the concubines of the Khan was ill and suffered greatly. The soothsayers pronounced some mysterious words over a slave of German origin, and she went to sleep for three days. When she awoke, they asked her what she had seen. She had seen a number of persons; they thought that all these would soon die, and because she had not seen among them their mistress, they concluded that she would not die of that sickness. I saw that young girl. She still felt great fatigue in her head from this long sleep.

Some of these soothsayers evoke demons. They assemble, at night, in their house those who wish to have answers from the devil; they put cooked meat in the centre of the dwelling, and the *cham* who invokes begins by saying mysterious words, and, holding a drum in his hand, he strikes it hard on the ground. Then he passes into a fury and they bind him. Then the devil appears in the midst of the darkness; the *cham* gives him this meat to eat and commands his answers.

Once, as was told me by master William, a Hungarian hid in the house of the soothsayers, and the devil, who was on the roof, complained that he could not enter for there was a Christian there. At this noise he fled, for they began to look for him. They had done that and many other things, too long to relate.

Chapter 53

OF THE FESTIVAL AT CARACARUM ❧ AND THE DIFFERENT AMBASSADORS

FROM the day of Pentecost, they began preparing the letters addressed to you. During this time, master William returned to Caracarum and organized a great festival in the octave of Pentecost [June 25], and wanted that all the ambassadors be present the last day. He sent for us also, but I had gone to the church to baptize three children of a poor German whom we had met in that city.

At this feast, master William was the chief cup-bearer, for he had made the tree from which flowed the drinks, and poor and rich sang and danced and clapped hands before the Khan. Then the Khan spoke to them. "I have separated," he said, "my brothers from me, have sent them in the midst of dangers in foreign lands. We will see now what you will do, when I shall want to charge you with the missions of my work, towards the strengthening of our power."

During the four days of the feast, he changed his garments every day, and all the raiment from shoes to turbans, was of the same colour. At this time I saw an ambassador of the Calif of Bagdad, who used to be brought to court in a litter between two mules, and I was told that he had made a peace with the Tartars, and was to give them ten thousand horses for their army. Others said to the contrary, that Mangu would not make a peace unless they destroyed their fortresses, and that the ambassador answered him: "When you have pulled off all the hoofs from your horses' feet, we will demolish all our fortresses."

I have also seen ambassadors of a Sultan of India, who had brought along eight leopards and ten greyhounds. They had trained the dogs to sit on the horses' backs as leopards do. When I inquired about this country of India, they pointed to the west. These ambassadors went back with me for about three weeks, always toward the west.

I also saw there ambassadors of the Sultan of Turkey; they brought with them precious gifts and told us, I heard this with mine own ears, that their lord lacked neither gold

nor silver, but men; from which I concluded they asked
help in case of war.

Chapter 54

OF THE LETTERS OF MANGU KHAN TO ST. LOUIS

THE day of St. John, the Khan held a great feast and I
counted a hundred and five carts loaded with mare's milk
and ninety horses; the same on the day of Apostles Peter and
Paul. Finally, the letters destined to you being finished,
they called me and interpreted them to me. Here is the
tone of it, such as I could understand it by the translation
of the interpreter:

"The eternal commandment of God is this: in heaven
there is but one eternal God; on earth, there is no other
master than Chinghis Khan, the Son of God Demugin, or
Chinghis the sound of Iron." (They call Chinghis, the
sound of iron, for he was once a blacksmith; and when full
of pride, they call him "son of God.") "This is the message
sent you. Wherever there are Moals, Naimans, Merkits
or Mustelmen, wherever ears can hear, or a horse can travel,
there you will hear and understand it. My orders will be
heard and understood and believed and those who do will
not want war to be waged against us, and those who heed
and make war against us shall see though they have eyes
and see not, and when they shall want to hold anything,
they shall be without hands; such is the order of God eternal.
By the eternal virtue of God, through the great world of the
Moals, the order of Mangu Khan is sent to the lord of the
French, King Louis, and to all the other lords, and to the
priests and to the great realm of the French, to understand
our words. And the order of the eternal God has become
the order of Chinghis Khan, and since Chinghis Khan or

others after him, this order has not reached you. A certain David came to you as pretended ambassador, but he lied, and you sent back with him ambassadors to Kuyuk Khan. Then Kuyuk Khan died and your ambassadors reached this court. Camus, his wife, sent you *nasic* stuff and letters. I will not say how this woman, viler than a dog, knew things about war and peace, and how to manage a great country and do good."—Mangu himself told me with his own lips that Camus was the worst of sorceresses and that by her witchcraft, she had her entire family destroyed.—"The two monks who came from you to Sartach, Sartach sent to Batu and Batu sent to us, for Mangu Khan is the greatest lord in the world of the Moals. And now to the end, that your people, your priests and your monks all live in peace and rejoice in their welfare and that the commandment of God is obeyed among you, we wanted to send you, with your priests, Moal ambassadors, but they answered us, that between us and you there are countries at war and many wicked men, and that the roads are bad. He, therefore, feared that they would not be able to take our ambassadors in safety as far as your country; but he proposed to bring them our letters containing our orders and offered to transmit them to King Louis himself. That is why we have not sent our ambassadors with them. We, therefore, are sending you the written order of the eternal God, by your above-named priests, the order of the eternal God that we are making you understand. And when you shall have received and believed it, if you want to obey us, you will send us your ambassadors, and you will thus let us know if you wish to be at peace or at war with us. When, by the power of the eternal God, from the rising of the sun to the west, the whole world shall be united in joy and in peace, thus shall it be known what we are to be. If you have heard and understood the order of the eternal God, and if you resist it, saying: 'Our land is far away, our mountains are high and many, our sea is big,' and, in this, believe that you may declare war against us, the eternal God knows that we know what we can do. He makes easy that which is difficult, and brings closer together that which is separated by distance."

In these letters, we were first given the title of "your ambassadors." So I said to them: "Do not call us ambassadors, for I have said that we are not ambassadors of King Louis."

Then the men of the Khan delivered our message. They returned and announced that he had done so as a compliment and that he now ordered them to write what I shall tell them. I requested them, then, to leave out the word ambassador and to call us simply monks and priests. During this parley, my companion heard that we had to return by way of the desert to reach the dwelling of Batu and that we would have a Moal guide, and he went, unknown to me, to Bulgai, secretary of state, and made him understand by signs that he would die if he took that road.

When the day of his departure arrived, that is, a fortnight after the feast of St. John [June 24], we were called to the court and the secretaries said to my companion: "Mangu wishes that your friar pass by the way of Batu, and you, you say that you are ill, which is evident. Mangu says if you wish to depart with your companion, do so, but at your risk and peril; for you may stop at the home of some *iam* who may not supply you with needs and you will be a burden to your companion. But if you wish, remain here, the Khan himself will provide you with all you will need, till the arrival of ambassadors, with whom you will be able to go back more slowly and by roads on which are cities." The friar replied: "May God grant the Khan a happy life!

I will remain." But I said to him: "Brother, realize what you are doing. I will not leave you."—"You," he said, "are not leaving me; it is I who leave you, for, if I go with you, I see danger for my body and soul for I can no longer bear such hardships."

They made us take three gowns or tunics, and they said to us: "You will not accept either gold or silver, and you have stayed here a long time to pray for the Khan. He begs you to accept at least a simple garment for each of you, so that you do not leave with your hands empty." We had to accept these objects out of respect for him, for they consider unfavourably those who refuse gifts from them. They made us ask for what we wanted, and we repeated the same thing, to make known that the Christians have disdain for these idolaters who seek nothing but presents. And they replied that we were foolish, for if the Khan wanted to give them his entire court, they would gladly take it and do wisely. So we accepted the gowns and they asked us to make a prayer for the Khan; which we did and, with his permission, left for Caracarum.

It happened, one day, when we were far away from the court with the monk and other ambassadors, that the monk beat repeatedly a board and with such violence that Mangu Khan heard the noise and inquired what it signified. They told him; he wanted to know why the monk was so far from the court. They answered: "Because it is difficult to send him each day horses and cattle to the court." They added that it would be better if this religious person were at Caracarum, near the church to pray there. So the Khan sent word to him to say that if he wished to stay at Caracarum near the church, he would lack nothing. But the monk replied: "I came here from the Holy Land by God's order, and I left a city where there are a thousand churches better

than the one in Caracarum.   If he desires that I stay here
and pray for him, as God commands, I will remain; if not,
I will return towards the country from which I came."
Then, that same evening, they sent him some cattle and
harnessed them to carts, and in the morning he was conducted back to the place he used to occupy before the court.

A little before our departure, arrived a Nestorian monk
who was considered a wise man.   Bulgai, the secretary of
state, had him established before the court, and the Khan
sent his children to him, so that he bless them.

Chapter 55

OF THE RETURN JOURNEY ◄ AND THE MEETING WITH SARTACH

THEN we arrived in Caracarum, and when we were in
the house of master William, my guide came and brought
me ten *iascot*.   He put five in the hand of master William
and told him to spend it in the name of the Khan for the
friar's needs; the other five he gave to the man of God, my
interpreter, ordering him to spend it on the voyage for my
needs.   Master William had told them to do it, without our
knowledge.   I, at once, had one of these *iascot* sold and
distributed the change among the poor who were there and
who all had their eyes fixed upon us.   We spent another of
the *iascot* buying what we were in need of, clothing or other
things.   With the third, the man of God bought various
things which were useful to him.   The rest of the *iascot* we
spent en route, for from the time we entered Persia we did
not receive anything that we needed, neither among the
Tartars, but we rarely found something to buy.

Master William, once your subject, sends you a girdle
ornamented with a precious stone, such as they wear here
against lightning and thunder.   He greets you enthusiasti-

cally, and prays for you always. For him, I cannot enough thank God and you. We have baptized there in all six persons; and we separated with tears in our eyes, my companion remaining with master William, I leaving alone with my interpreter, my guide, and a servant who had orders to get for us a sheep in four days. We came to Batu in two months and ten days.

During that time, we did not see a city or a sign of any dwelling, save some tombs all over and a village where we could find no bread to eat. In the space of two months and ten days, we did not rest except one single day, when we could not get any horses. We came back for the most part by the countries we had already crossed, and some others. We went in winter and came back in summer by mountainous and far countries of the north. But during fifteen long days we had to follow the windings of a river [Ulungur], in the middle of mountains where there was no grass to be seen, except on the banks of the river. Sometimes we ran great dangers, not seeing a living soul, lacking food and having tired horses.

After having ridden for twenty days, I received news of the King of Armenia. At the end of August, he went to Sartach, who was on the way to Mangu Khan with his herds and flocks, his wives and children. As to his great dwellings, they remained behind between the Volga and the Tanais.

I greeted Sartach, saying that I would have gladly stayed in his country, but that Mangu Khan wishes me to go back and take his letters. He replied that one should execute the bidding of Mangu Khan. I inquired of Coiac about my servants. He told me that they were at the court of Batu and well taken care of. I then asked for our sacred ornaments and our books and he said: "You did not bring them to Sartach?" I replied: "I brought them to Sartach but I did not give them to him, as you know." And I repeated what I said to him when he requested me to give them to Sartach himself. He answered me: "You speak the truth, and no one can resist the truth. I myself have left all your belongings in my father's home at Sarai, a new city that Batu had built on the Volga. But our priests are here with some of your vestments." I replied: "If you like any of the vestments, keep them, but just return my books. It is necessary that I have letters from you to your father so that he will give me back what belongs to me."

When we were about to go, he said to me: "The court of ladies is following us closely; stay there and I will send answer by this man." I was afraid he was deceiving me; however, I could not wrangle with him. In the evening, that man came to me, the one he showed me, bringing me two tunics which I thought was a piece of silk, uncut, and he said: "Here are two tunics; Sartach sends you one, and the other, if you consider it correct, give to the king on his part." I replied: "I do not wear such garments; I will give both tunics to the king as homage from your lord." "No," he said, "do with them what seems good to you." Now, it pleases me to send you the two tunics and I am sending them by the bearer of gifts. He also gave me some letters for his father Coiac, to return to me all that is mine, for he wanted nothing belonging to me.

Chapter 56

OF THE RETURN VISIT TO BATU ❧ AND THE JOY OF FINDING OUR PEOPLE

I ARRIVED at the court of Batu the same day that I had left the year before, that is, the second after the Elevation of the Holy Cross [September 16], and with joy I again saw my people well, though they had suffered privations without number, as I learned from Goset. Had it not been for the King of Armenia who comforted them and recommended them to Sartach, they would have been lost; moreover they thought I no longer existed. Already the Tartars were asking them if they knew how to guard cattle and milk mares, for, had I not come back, they would have made slaves of them.

After that, I was called before Batu and had interpreted for me the letters sent you by Mangu Khan. For Mangu had written him that he could add, change or strike out anything he wanted. Then he said to me: "Take these letters and make them understood." He also asked me which road I wanted to take, by sea or land. I replied that the sea was already closed, on account of the winter, that I would have to go by land. Also, I thought you were still in Syria and I started towards Persia. But had I known that you had already left for France, I would have gone through Hungary and arrived sooner in France, taking roads less difficult than through Syria.

We travelled thus a whole month with Batu before getting a guide. Finally, they procured us a Jugure who, thinking I would not give him anything, though I told him I wanted to go straight to Armenia, had letters given him which enjoined that he take me to the Sultan of Turkey hoping thus to receive from him a recompense and earn more passing through that country.

Chapter 57
OF SARAI AND SUMMERKEUR ❧ AND THE RETURN OF THE BOOKS

FIFTEEN days before All Saints' day [October 16], I started for Sarai, going directly south by descending the

Volga, which is divided in three branches; each is twice as large as the Nile at Damietta. Further on, the river forms four branches of minor size, so that we crossed in boats seven places. On the middle branch is the open city called Summerkeur, which is without walls, but is surrounded by water when the river overflows. The Tartars surrounded it for eight years before they were able to take possession of it. It was inhabited by Alans and Saracens. We found there a German and his wife, a good man, at whose home lived Goset; for Sartach had sent him there to rid his court of him. Toward Christmas, Batu and Sartach were in these parts; one on one side of the river, the other on the other side. It is crossed only when it is covered with ice. There are quantities of grass there, and the Tartars hide in the reeds till the ice thaws.

After receiving the letters of Sartach, Coiac's father returned my vestments to me, excepting three albs, an amice embroidered in silk, a stole, a girdle, an altar-cloth embroidered in gold and a surplice. He also gave me back my silver vases, excepting a censer, and the vase that contained the holy oil, for these objects had been taken by the priests who were with Sartach. Finally, he gave me my books, excepting the psalter of my lady which he kept with my permission. I could not refuse it to him for he said Sartach had liked it very much. He asked me, in case I return to these countries, to bring with me a man who knows how to make parchment; for he was having constructed, by Sartach's orders, on the west side of the river, a big church and a new manor, and he said that he wanted to make books for Sartach's use. Yet I know that Sartach does not interest himself in these things.

Sarai and the palace of Batu are situated on the east side of the river and the valley through which the waters of the different branches flow is more than seven leagues wide, and there is there an abundance of fish. A Bible in verse, a book in Arabic, worth thirty *bezants*, and several other objects, all were lost for me.

Chapter 58

THE COUNTRY OF THE ALANS

THUS taking leave of him on the feast of All Saints [November 1], and going towards the south all the time, we reached on the day of St. Martin [December 15], the mountains of the Alans. For fifteen days, between the encampment of Batu and Sarai, we met no one save one of Batu's sons who preceded him with hawks in charge of numerous hawkers, and we saw but one poor little village. In that space of time, since the day of All Saints, when we did not meet a living soul, we were in great danger one day and one night and until the next morning at the third hour, for we were without water.

The Alans in these mountains are not yet conquered by the Tartars, so that two out of every six men of Sartach must hold them to keep these mountaineers from taking their cattle in the plain which is between the Alans and the Gate of Iron. This is a two days' march. There the plain of Arcacc begins.

Between the sea and these mountains are Saracens, called Lesgs, who are mountaineers, independent of the Tartars; so that they who are at the foot of the mountains of the Alans had to give me twenty men to take us to the Gate of Iron. I was glad of it, but I hoped to see them armed; for, though I much desired to, I had never seen their arms.

Chapter 59

THE GATE OF IRON BUILT BY ALEXANDER

WHEN we came to the most dangerous passage, only two of the twenty men had coats of mail. Having asked them from where they got them, they told me that they took them from the Alans who are good modellers of these objects and excellent at forging them. I concluded from this that they have no other arms except arrows and bows and mail. I saw some of them covered with metal and their helmets were of iron of Persia, and I also saw two who came before Mangu dressed in tunics of very hard leather, very uncomfortable and badly fitted.

Before arriving at the Iron Gate, we saw a château of the Alans which belongs to Mangu Khan, for he conquered all that country. We found there first some vineyards and drank wine. The next day we entered the Iron Gate which Alexander the Great had constructed. It is a city whose eastern extremity is on the seashore. Between the sea and the mountains is a little plain from where the city stretches to the top of the mountain which reaches to the west. So it is absolutely necessary to cross the city by passing through an iron gate which is in the centre, for on one side are inaccessible mountains, on the other side, the sea. Hence the name "Gate of Iron" given that city, which is more than a mile long, and on the top of the mountain is a fortress; its width, however, is but a stone's throw. Thick walls without moats surround it, and its towers are built of enormous, polished stones; but the Tartars have destroyed the summits of the towers and the parapets of the walls, cutting down the towers to the walls' height. All around the city, the country once looked like a paradise.

Two days later we saw another city, called Samaron,

where there were many Jews, and passing through it, we noticed its walls which descend from the mountain to the sea. We left the road which runs through; we wended our way to the east toward the sea and we ascended the mountains toward the south.

The next day we crossed a valley where there were the remains of walls from one mountain to another, and not a road was there leading to the top. These were ancient ramparts put up at the time of Alexander to stop the wild populations, that is, the herdsmen of the desert, preventing them from entering the cities and cultivated lands. There are other shut-in places where Jews live; but I cannot tell you for certain, though there are many Jews in all the cities of Persia.

The following day we came to a big city called Samag [Shamake], and then, the next day, a vast plain called Moan, through which the Cur flows. This river gave its name to the Curges [Kirghiz], whom we call Georgians. It flows through the middle of the Tiflis, the capital of the Georgians, descending directly from the west to the east towards the Caspian Sea, and has excellent salmon. We found some more Tartars in the plain through which flows the Araxes, descending directly from Great Armenia between the south and west, from where it got the name Ararat country, which is Armenia itself. That is why it reads in the book of Kings that the sons of Sennacherib, after killing their father, fled from the country of the Armenians; in Isaiah, it is said that they escaped to the country of Ararat.

To the west of that magnificent plain is Curgia [Georgia] where once lived the Crosminians. At the foot of these mountains is a large city called Ganges, the ancient capital of the Crosminians; it kept the Georgians from descending into the plain.

We next arrived at a bridge of boats, held by iron chains stretched across the river into which flows the Tur, or the Cur, and the Araxes. But the Araxes loses its name here.

Chapter 60

OF THE BATTLE THAT TOOK PLACE BETWEEN THE TARTARS AND THE SULTAN OF TURKEY ◄ AND OF DIFFERENT COUNTRIES ◄ OF THE GENOESE MERCHANT ◄ AND THE ARRIVAL HOME

WE continued going up along the Araxes, of which the poet said: . . . *the Araxes disdains bridges,* and we left Persia on our left towards the south, the Caspian Mountains and Great Georgia on our right, and went toward Africa between the south and the west. We crossed the camp of Baachu, chief of the army there on the Araxes, which conquered the Georgians, the Turks and the Persians.

There is at Tauris, in Persia, another chief who is charged with the collecting of tributes, and whose name is Argun. Mangu Khan has called them both back to give up their places to his brother who came to that country. This country that I described to you is not really Persia; it is generally called Hircania. I went to meet Baachu in his home and he gave us wine to drink. He himself drank *cosmos* which I would have preferred myself had he offered it to me. Yet the wine was good, though new, but the *cosmos* would have been better for a man thirsty and famished.

So we ascended along the Araxes from the feast of St. Clement [November 23] to the second Sunday of Quadragesima [February 15] before reaching the source of the river. Beyond the mountain where it rises is a goodly city called Erzerum which belongs to the Sultan of Turkey and near which starts the Euphrates, towards the north, at the foot of the mountains of Georgia. I would have gone to see it, but there was so much snow that no one could cross the beaten path. On the other side of the mountains of the Caucasus, toward the south, is the source of the Tigris.

When we left Baachu, my guide went to Tauris to speak with Argun and took my interpreter with him. But Baachu had me conducted to a city called Naxua, which was once the capital of a large kingdom, a very large and very beautiful city. The Tartars completely ruined it. There used to be eight hundred churches of Armenians in it; the Saracens destroyed them and left only two very small ones. In one of them, I celebrated, as best I could, Christmas, with our clerk. The next day the priest who served this church, died, and a bishop came, with twelve monks of the mountains, to bury him; for all the Armenian bishops are monks, and the Greeks, too, for the most part. This bishop told me that nearby was a church in which St. Bartholomew was martyred, as well as the blessed Judas Thaddeus; but it could not be visited on account of the snow.

He told me also that they have two prophets; the first is Methodius, martyr, who was of their race and who predicted all that happened to the Ysmaelites, which prophecy was fulfilled in the race of the Saracens. The other prophet is called Acatron, who on his death-bed prophesied that the race of the Archers would come from the north and subdue all the countries of the Orient, but that God would spare the kingdom of the Orient to deliver unto them the kingdom of the West.—Our brothers, the Franks, like good Catholics, will not put any faith in these prophecies.—They [the Archers] would conquer the countries from north to south, would come as far as Constantinople and occupy its port; one of them, who will be called a sage, will enter the city, and, seeing the churches and the ceremony of the Franks, will be baptized and will show the Franks how to destroy the Tartars and kill their king! At this miracle, the Franks will be at the centre of the world, that is, Jerusalem, will fall upon the Tartars who will be on their frontiers, and with our nation's help, that is, the Armenians, will pursue them, so that the king of the Franks will hoist his flag on the walls of Tauris in Persia, and thus convert to the Christian faith all the Orientals and all the infidel nations, and there will be in the world a peace so great that the living will say to the dead: "Woe unto you, unfortunate ones, for you have not lived to see these times."

I had already read this prophecy at Constantinople, brought there by Armenians in that city, but did not give it any attention. But when the bishop talked to me of it, I recalled it and thought about it more. In all Armenia this prophecy is believed like the Gospel. The bishop added: "As the souls in limbo await the coming of Christ for deliverance, so do we await your arrival to be delivered from this bondage of which we are so weary for so long."

Near this city of Naxua are mountains in which is said to be Noah's ark; there are two of them, one more elevated than the other; the Araxes flows at its feet, and there is there a city called Cemanum. The name, which signifies "eight," was given it because it was built on the highest mountain by the eight persons who came out of the ark. Many of the travellers have tried to climb this mountain, but without success. This bishop also told me that a monk once had so great a desire to make that ascent that an angel brought him some wood of the ark, telling him no longer to torment himself. This wood is kept in the church of the convent, they told me.

This mountain is not as high as it seems. An old man explained to me the reason why no one can climb it. The name of the mountain is Massis, and in their language is of the feminine gender. "On the Massis," said he, "no one can climb, for it is the mother of the world."

In that same city of Naxua, I met Friar Bernard of Catalogna, of the Order of Friar Preachers; he had lived in Georgia with a prior of the Holy Sepulchre, who is there owner of a large domain. He had learned a little Tartar and was going with a friar of Hungary to Tauris to find Argun and ask his permission to be near Sartach. When they came to this city they could not obtain an audience and the Hungarian friar returned by way of Tiflis with a servant. As for Friar Bernard, he stayed at Tauris with a German lay-brother whose language he did not understand.

We left Naxua on the octave of the Epiphany [January 13], for we had to linger a long time on account of the snows. Four days later we reached the country of Sahensa, a Curgian prince very powerful at one time, but now tributary to the Tartars who destroyed all his fortresses. His father, Zacharius, had got this country from the Armenians by snatching it from the yoke of the Saracens. There are very beautiful habitations there of true Christians who have churches like in France. Every Armenian has, in the most conspicuous spot in his home, a hand of wood holding a cross before which burns a lamp, and what we do with holy water to chase away evil spirits, they do with incense. For every evening the Armenians burn incense and carry it to the corners of the house to preserve it from all sorts of enemies.

I dined with Sahensa, and he showed me great friendship, he, his wife and his son Zacharius, a handsome and excellent young man, who requested me to recommend him to you, in case you may wish to take him into your service. For this young man suffers so under the domination of the Tartars that, though he has an abundance of all things, he would prefer to wander to strange lands rather than bend under their bondage. Besides, the Armenians said they were the sons of the Roman Church, and if the Pope would send them some help, they would subject all the neighbouring nations to the Church.

Fifteen days after we left the city of this Sahensa, we came to the country of the Sultan of Turkey, and the first fortress we saw was Marsengen [Medshingert]. All its inhabitants are Christians; Armenians, Curges and Greeks, but they are all under the submission of the Saracens. There the governor, or castellan, told me that he had received orders to refuse provisions to the Franks and to the ambassadors of the King of Armenia and of Vastacius; so that from this castle to Cyprus, where I arrived eight days before the feast of St. John, we had to buy our food. My guide procured some horses; he received money to secure provisions, and he put it nicely into his pocket. When he came to a camp and saw a flock, he would carry off a sheep by force and would give it to his friends to eat, and he would wonder why I would not eat the products of his theft.

On the day of the Purification, I found myself in a city called Aini, in the dominion of Sahensa, whose position is strongly fortified. There are in it a thousand churches of Armenians and two synagogues of Saracens. The Tartars have a bailiff there. Five friar preachers came to meet me there, four of whom were of the province of France and the fifth joined them in Syria. They had with them only an infirm servant who knew Turkish and a little French. They were bearers of letters from the Pope for Sartach, for Mangu Khan and for Buri, letters like those you gave me and in which he asked them for permission for his monks to stop in their lands and to preach there the message of God.

When I related to them all that I had seen and how I had been sent back, they started toward Tiflis, where they have some of their friars, to consult them as to what they had to do. I told them that with these letters they could go where they wished, but that they would need much patience; I suggested to them to convince themselves as to the aim of their voyage, for if they had no other mission than that of preaching, the Tartars would show them little consideration, especially if they had no interpreter. What happened to these religious men, I do not know.

The second Sunday after Quadragesima we reached the head of the Araxes, and having passed the top of the mountain, we came to the Euphrates, which we descended westward as far as a fort called Camath. There the Euphrates turns southward toward Halapia. We crossed the river going toward the west by high mountains thickly covered with snow. There was that year an earthquake so terrible that alone in the city of Arsengen, ten thousand people of gentility perished, besides the poor whose names were not known. Riding about on horseback, for three days, we saw how the earth cracked in this terrible commotion and how pieces of earth were detached from mountains and heaped in the valleys, to such an extent that had the trembling been a little stronger, the words of Isaiah would have been fulfilled to the letter: "The entire valley shall be filled and all the mountains and hills made low."

We passed by the valley in which the Sultan of Turkey was defeated by the Tartars. To tell you how it happened would take too long. But a friend of my guide who was then in the Tartar army said that the latter had only ten thousand men in all, and a Curgian, prisoner of the Sultan, said that he had two hundred thousand men, all horsemen. The plain where the battle took place, rather the defeat, was transformed into a lake during the earthquake, and I said in my own heart that the whole plain opened up to receive the blood of the Saracens.

At Sebaste of Lesser Armenia, we arrived in the Greater Week. We visited the sepulchre of the forty martyrs. Here is also a church of St. Blaise, but I could not go there, for it is high up on a fortress. On the octave of Easter [April 4] we went to Cæsarea of Cappadocia where there is a church of St. Basil the Great.

Fifteen days later we came to Yconium; we travelled by short distances and we rested in many places, for we could not always get horses. My guide thus acted in a calculating manner, by arranging to get paid every three days in each city we stopped. I was very much grieved at it, but dared not complain for he could have sold me and my companions, or killed us, and there would have been no one to stop him.

I found, in Yconium, several Franks, a Genoese merchant from Acon, named Nicholas from Santo-Siro and one of his companions from Venice, called Benefatius de Molendino, who had got hold of all the alum in Turkey, so that the Sultan could sell none but to these two, and they made the price of it so high that what was worth but fifteen *bezants* sold for fifty.

My guide presented me to the Sultan and the Sultan told me that he would willingly have me conducted as far as the seas of Armenia or Cilicia. Then, the Genoese merchant, of whom I have spoken, knowing that the Saracens took little care of me and that I was very tired of my guide, who each day wearied me with his claims for presents, had me taken to Curta, port of the king of Armenia. I arrived on the eve of the Ascension [May 5] and remained there until the next day of Pentecost. I then learned that ambassadors had been sent by the king to his father.

I had my baggage taken to Acon, by sea, and I immediately went to the king's father to find out if he had any news from his son. I found him at Assis with all his children but one called Barunusin, who was having a fortress constructed. He had received ambassadors from his son saying he was coming back and that Mangu Khan had singularly reduced the tribute he owed him, and had granted him the privilege of not sending any ambassadors to him. On account of this, the old nobleman, with all his children and all his people, held a great feast. As for me, he had me accompanied to the sea, and to the port called Anax; from there I went to Cyprus and found my minister, or provincial, at Nicosia, and he took me to Antioch the same day. I found this city in a deplorable condition. We remained there for the feast of the Apostles Peter and Paul. From there we went to Tripoli where a chapter of our Order was held, on the day of the Assumption of the Holy Virgin.

The provincial decided that I choose the convent of Acon, not allowing me to go and meet you and ordering me to write you what I desired, by the bearer of these presents. Not daring to go against his wishes, I am doing what I can and have written you. I beg grace from your kindness, for what I may have said unseemly or too much or not enough, being little learned and not accustomed to writing such long stories. May the peace of God, which surpasseth all understanding, keep your heart and mind. I would gladly see you and some special friends that I have in your kingdom.

Therefore, if your Majesty does not find it inconvenient, I would dare to beg you to write to my provincial to let me come to you, but that I may return without delay to the Holy Land.

Of Turkey, you must know that not a tenth part of the inhabitants are Saracens; nearly all are Armenians and

Greeks. The country is governed by children. The Sultan, who was defeated by the Tartars, has a legitimate wife who is an Iberian and by whom he had a child, a weakling, who will be sultan after him. He had another by a Greek concubine, whom he gave to a powerful admiral; he had a third by a Turkish woman with whom Turks and Turkomans became affiliated to conspire against the lives of the children of Christians.

They had resolved further, as I was informed, to destroy, after victory, all the churches and to kill all those who would not become Saracens; but the son was defeated and many of his were killed.

He united his army a second time; then he was captured and thrown into prison. Pacaster, the son of the Greek woman, arranged with his half-brother that he let him hold the sceptre of the Sultan, for the other who was in the land of the Tartars was of delicate health. But all his relatives on his mother's side, Iberians or Georgians, were indignant at this conduct. Therefore, to-day a child reigns in Turkey, with few soldiers, little money, and many enemies. The son of Vastacius is feeble and at war with the son of Assan, who is also a child and under the domination of the Tartars; and if the army of the Church were to enter the Holy Land, it would then be very easy to conquer all the country and to pass through them.

The king of Hungary has no more than thirty thousand soldiers. From Cologne to Constantinople is not more than a forty days' march in a chariot. From Constantinople there are not as many days' travel to the country of the king of Armenia. Long ago brave men crossed these countries [Peter the Hermit in 1096] and won victories there, even though they had valiant warriors to combat, whom God has since removed from the earth.

It is not necessary to risk the dangers of the sea, nor to be at the mercy of the seamen; the money necessary to arm a fleet would suffice for the expenses of the voyage by land. I will tell you confidentially that if your peasants—I do not speak of kings or of knights—wanted to travel like kings of the Tartars and content themselves with the food of these potentates, they would become the leaders of the world.

It seems useless to me that another religious man like myself be sent or friar preachers go to the land of the Tartars; but if the Pope, who is at the head of all Christians, wished to send a bishop in fit manner, and answered all the letters that the Khan had three times addressed to the Franks— the first to Pope Innocent IV, of happy memory, and the second to you; the third time through the intermediary of David who deceived you, and finally by me—he would be able to tell the Khan all he wished to and execute all that is contained in his letters.

The Khan listens willingly to all an ambassador says and always asks if there is anything he wishes to add; but it is important that he have a good interpreter, even several, and money to spend for travelling, etc.

THE JOURNAL OF
FRIAR ODORIC
1318–1330

FRIAR ODORIC

Odoric is said to have been born in 1286 and at a very early age took the vows of the Franciscans and joined their convent in Udine. He soon became eminent for his ascetic sanctity. He lived on bread and water, went barefoot and alternately wore the haircloth and a shirt of iron mail. Miracles are ascribed to him long before he began his wanderings.

In about the year 1318 Odoric was sent to the East as part of an extended missionary movement. He reached western India in about 1321, and went from there to China, where he remained for three years.

During the course of his travels he saw the shrine of St. Thomas near Madras, he sailed in a junk to Sumatra, he visited Java, the coast of Borneo, he travelled overland in China and visited Fu-chow, Hang-chow and by way of the Great Canal reached Peking. He returned overland across Asia, through Tibet, Persia and the land of the famous Assassins. An Irishman named Friar James was his companion for a good part of these extensive travels. He died, the object of popular devotion, in the convent of Udine in January, 1331. Soon after his death his fame as saint and traveller spread far and wide.

He was the first traveller after Marco Polo to describe these far sections of the world. And more than this, he described many things which Marco Polo omits: such as the comorant fishing, the long finger nails of the natives and the binding of women's feet. Sir John Mandeville (if such a person there ever was) took the substance of his fraudulent travels directly from these travel records of Friar Odoric.

THE JOURNAL OF FRIAR ODORIC

Chapter 1

HERE BEGINS THE JOURNAL OF FRIAR ODORIC ❦ OF THE ORDER OF THE MINORITES ❦ CONCERNING STRANGE THINGS WHICH HE SAW AMONG THE TARTARS OF THE EAST

ALTHOUGH MANY STORIES and sundry things are reported by various authors concerning the customs and conditions of this world; yet I, Friar Odoric of Friuli, being desirous to travel unto the foreign and remote countries of the unbelievers, also saw and heard great and miraculous things, which I am able truly to account.

First of all, therefore, sailing from Pera by Constantinople, I arrived at Trebizond. This place is commodiously situated, being an haven for the Persians and Medes, and other countries beyond the sea. In this land I beheld with great delight a very strange spectacle, namely, a certain man leading about with him more than four thousand partridges. The man himself walked along the ground, and the partridges flew in the air. These he led to a certain castle called Zauena, being three days' journey distant from Trebizond. The partridges were so tame, that when the man desired to lie down and rest they would all come flocking about him like chickens. And so he led them to Trebizond, and to the palace of the emperor, who took as many of them as he pleased, and the rest the man carried to the place from whence he came.

In this city lies the body of Athanasius [who died in 373 A.D.], upon the gate of the city. And then I passed on further into Great Armenia, to a certain city called Erzerum, which had been very rich in old time, but now the Tartars have almost laid it waste. In this city there was abundance of bread and flesh, and of all other victuals except wine and fruits. This city also is very cold, and is reported to be higher than any other city in the world. It has most wholesome and sweet waters about it; for the veins of the waters seem to spring and flow from the mighty river of Euphrates, which is but a day's journey from the city. Also, the said city stands directly midway to Tauris.

I passed on to a certain mountain called Sobissacalo. In this country there is the very same mountain whereupon the Ark of Noah rested. This I would willingly have ascended, if my company would have waited for me. However, the people of this country report that no man could ever ascend the mountain, because they say it pleases not the Most High.

From this country I travelled on further, to Tauris that great and royal city, which was in old time called Susis. This city is, for traffic of merchandise, said to be the chief city of the world. There is no kind of provision, nor anything else belonging to merchandise, which is not to be had there in great abundance. This city stands very well situated, for to it all the nations of the whole world may resort for traffic. Concerning this city, the Christians in those parts are of opinion that the Persian emperor receives more tribute out of it than the king of France out of all his dominions. Near to the city there is a salt-hill yielding salt to the city; and of that salt each man may take what pleases him, not paying aught to any man therefor. In this city live many Christians of all nations, over whom the Saracens bear rule in all things.

Then I travelled on further unto a city called Soldaia, wherein the Persian emperor dwells in the summer season. But in winter he moves to another city which stands on the sea [Caspian] and is called Baku. This city is very great and is a cool place, having good and wholesome waters, to which also many kinds of merchandise are brought for sale.

Moreover, I travelled with a certain company of caravans toward Upper India, and after many days' journey, I came to the city of the three Wise Men [the three Magi] called Cassan, which is a noble and renowned city, saving that the Tartars have destroyed a great part of it. It abounds with bread, wine, and many other commodities. From this city to Jerusalem, where the three Wise Men were miraculously led, it is fifty days' journey. There are many wonders in this city also, which, for brevity's sake, I omit.

From here I departed to a certain city called Geste [Yezd], from which the Sea of Sand is one day distant. It is a most wonderful and dangerous thing.

In this city there is abundance of all kinds of victuals, and especially of figs, raisins, and grapes, more, I suppose, than in any part of the whole world. This is one of the three principal cities in all the Persian Empire. Of this city the Saracens report that no Christian can by any means live there more than a year.

Then passing many days' journey on forward, I came to a certain city called Comerum, which was a huge and mighty city in old time, containing well-nigh fifty miles of walls, and in times past did great damage to the Romans. In it there are stately palaces altogether destitute of inhabitants, notwithstanding it abounds with great store of provisions.

From here, travelling through many countries, at length I came to the land of Job named Hus, which is full of all kinds of victuals, and very pleasantly situated. Near by are certain mountains having good pastures for cattle. Here also manna is found in great abundance. Four partridges are sold for less than a Venetian groat. In this country there are most comely old men. Here also the men spir and knit, and not the women. This land borders upon the north part of Chaldæa.

Chapter 2

OF THE MANNERS OF THE CHALDÆANS *AND OF INDIA

DEPARTING from here, I travelled into Chaldæa, which is a great kingdom, and I passed by the tower of Babel. This region has a language peculiar to itself, and there are beautiful men, and deformed women. The men of this country have their hair combed and trimmed like our women, and they wear golden turbans upon their heads richly set with pearl, and precious stones. The women are clad in a coarse smock only reaching to their knees, with long sleeves hanging down to the ground. And they go barefooted, wearing drawers that reach to the ground. They wear no attire upon their heads, but their hair hangs dishevelled about their ears; and there are many other strange things also.

From here I came into the lower India, which the Tartars overran and wasted. In this country the people eat dates for the most part. Forty-two pounds are sold for less than a groat.

I passed further, also many days' journey, to the ocean sea [Persian Gulf], and the first city where I arrived is called Ormes, being well fortified, and having great store of merchandise and treasure. So extreme is the heat in this country, that the privates of men come out of their bodies and hang down even unto their mid-legs. And, therefore, the inhabitants of the same place, to preserve their own lives, do make a certain ointment, and anointing their privy members therewith, do tie them up in certain bags fastened to their bodies, for otherwise they must needs die.

Here also they use a kind of barque or ship called *iase* being made only with hemp. And I went on board one of them, wherein I could not find any iron at all, and in the space of twenty-eight days I arrived at the city of Tana, where four of our friars were martyred for the faith of Christ. This country is well situated, having abundance of bread and wine, and of other victuals. This kingdom in old time was very large and under the dominion of King Porus, who fought a great battle with Alexander the Great. The people of this country are idolaters worshipping fire, serpents, and trees. Over all this land the Saracens rule, having taken it by main force, and they themselves are now subject to King Dili. Here are many kinds of beasts, namely, black lions in great abundance, and apes also, and monkeys, and bats as big as doves. Also there are mice as big as our country dogs, and therefore they are hunted with dogs, because cats are not able to encounter them. Moreover, in the same country every man has a bundle of great branches standing in a water-pot before his door, which bundle is as great as a pillar, and it will not wither, so long as water is applied. There are many other novelties and strange things which would bring great delight to hear tell.

Chapter 3

HOW PEPPER IS HAD ❦ AND WHERE IT GROWS

MOREOVER, that it may be learnt how pepper is had, it is to be understood that it grows in a certain kingdom where I myself arrived, being called Malabar, and it is not so plentiful in any other part of the world as it is there. The forest in which it grows extends for a good eighteen days' journey. And in this forest there are two cities, one called Flandrina and the other Cyncilim [Cranganor]. In Flandrina both Jews and Christians live, between whom there is often contention and war; however, the Christians overcome the Jews at all times.

In this country pepper is obtained in this manner: First it grows in leaves like ivy, which they plant near great trees as we do our vines, and they bring forth pepper in clusters, as our vines yield grapes. Being ripe, they are of a green colour, and are gathered as we gather grapes, and then the grains are laid in the sun to be dried, and being dried are put into earthen vessels. Thus is pepper made and kept.

Now, in the same wood there are many rivers, containing great store of crocodiles, and of other serpents, which the inhabitants burn up with straw and with other dry fuel, and so they go to gather their pepper without danger.

At the south end of the forests stands the city of Polumbum, which abounds with merchandise of all kinds. All the inhabitants of that country worship a living ox, as their god, whom they put to labour for six years, and in the seventh year they cause him to rest from all his work, placing him in a solemn and public place, and calling him a holy beast. Moreover, they use this foolish ceremony. Every morning they take two basins, either of silver, or of gold, and with one they receive the urine of the ox, and with the other his dung. With the urine they wash their face, their eyes, and all their five senses. Of the dung they put into both their eyes, then they anoint the balls of their cheeks therewith, and thirdly their breast. Then they say that they are sanctified for all that day. And as the people do, even so do their king and queen.

These people worship also a dead idol, which, from the navel upward, resembles a man, and from the navel downward an ox. The very same idol delivers oracles, and sometimes requires the blood of forty virgins to be given to it. And, therefore, the men of that region do consecrate their daughters and their sons to their idols, even as Christians do their children to some religion or saint in heaven. Likewise they sacrifice their sons and their daughters, and many persons are put to death before the said idol by reason of that accursed ceremony.

Also many other heinous and abominable villainies do these brutish beastly people commit, and I saw many strange things among them which I do not mean here to insert. Another most vile custom this nation retains. When any man dies they burn his dead corpse to ashes, and if his wife survives him, they burn her also, because, say they, she shall accompany her husband when he is come to a new world. However, if the wife has children by her husband, she may if she will, remain still alive with them, without shame or reproach, but, for the most part, they all of them make choice to be burnt with their husbands. Now, if the wife dies before her husband, that law binds not the husband to such inconvenience, but he may marry another wife.

Likewise, the nation has another strange custom, in that their women drink wine, but their men do not. Also the women have the lids and brows of their eyes, and beards shaven, but their men have not; with many other base and filthy fashions which the said women do use contrary to the nature of their sex. From that kingdom I travelled ten days' journey to another kingdom called Mobar,[1] which contains many cities. Within a certain church of the same country, the body of St. Thomas the apostle is interred, the very same church being full of idols; and in fifteen houses round about this church, there dwell certain priests who are Nestorians, that is to say, false, and bad Christians, and schismatics.

Chapter 4

OF A STRANGE AND UNCOUTH IDOL ✥ AND OF CERTAIN CUSTOMS AND CEREMONIES

In this kingdom of Mobar there is a wonderful strange idol, being made after the shape and resemblance of a man, as big as the image of our Christopher, and consisting all of pure and glittering gold. About the neck of this image hangs a collar, full of most rich and precious stones, some of which are of more value than a whole kingdom. The church containing this idol is all of beaten gold, the roof, the pavement, and the ceiling of the walls within and without. To this idol the Indians go on pilgrimage, as we do to St. Peter's. Some go with halters about their necks, some with their hands bound behind them, some with a knife sticking in their arm or leg; and if, after they remove it, the flesh of their wounded arm festers, they esteem their limb to be holy, and think that their god is well pleased with them.

Near the temple of that idol is a lake made by the hands of men in an open and common place, where the pilgrims cast gold, silver, and precious stones, for the honour of the

---

1 "In this province of Maabar is the body of the glorious martyr, Saint Thomas the Apostle, who there suffered martyrdom." *Marco Polo*, p. 295.

idol and the repairing of his temple. Therefore when anything is to be adorned or mended, they go to this lake, taking up the treasure which was cast in. Moreover, at every yearly feast of the making or repairing of the idol, the king and queen, with the whole multitude of the people and all the pilgrims, assemble themselves, and placing the idol in a most stately and rich chariot, they carry him out of their temple with songs, and with all kinds of musical harmony. And a great company of virgins go procession-wise two and two in file singing before him.

Many pilgrims also put themselves under the chariot wheels, to the end that their false god may go over them. All they over whom the chariot rides are crushed in pieces, and divided in sunder, and slain right out. In doing this, they think themselves most holy to die in the service of their god. And by this means every year there die under the idol more than five hundred persons, whose carcases are burned, and their ashes are kept for relics, because they died in that manner for their god.

They have another detestable ceremony. For when any man offers to die in the service of his false god, his parents and all his friends assemble themselves together with a consort of musicians, making him a great and solemn feast. This feast being ended, they hang five sharp knives about his neck and carry him before the idol, and so soon as he has arrived he takes one of his knives, crying with a loud voice: "For the worship of my god do I cut this my flesh." And then he casts the morsel which is cut, at the face of his idol. But at the very last wound when he murders himself, he utters these words: "Now do I yield myself to death in the behalf of my god." Being dead, his body is burned, and is esteemed by all men to be holy.

The king of this region is most rich in gold, silver, and

precious stones, and there are the fairest pearls in all the world.

Travelling from here by the ocean sea fifty days' journey southward, I came to a certain land named Lammori [Sumatra, Marco Polo's Lamori], where, in regard of extreme heat, the people both men and women go stark-naked from top to toe. Seeing me apparelled, they scoffed at me, saying that God made Adam and Eve naked. In this country all women are held in common, so that no man can say, this is my wife. Also when any of the said women bears a son or a daughter, she bestows it upon any one that hath consorted with her. Likewise all the land of this region is possessed in common, so that there is not mine and thine, or any propriety of possession in the division of lands. However, every man has his own house.

Man's flesh, if it be fat, is eaten as ordinarily there as beef in our country. And although the people are most vile, yet the country is exceedingly good, abounding with all commodities, as flesh, corn, rice, silver, gold, wood of aloes, camphor, and many other things. Merchants coming to this region for traffic do usually bring with them fat people, selling them to the inhabitants as we sell hogs, who immediately kill and eat them.

In this island towards the south there is another kingdom called Simoltra [Sumatra], where both men and women mark themselves with red-hot irons in twelve different spots on their faces. This nation is at continual war with certain naked people in another region.

Then I travelled further unto another island called Java, the compass of which by sea is three thousand miles. The king of this island has seven other crowned kings under his jurisdiction. The island is thoroughly inhabited, and is thought to be one of the principal islands of the whole world.

In the same island there grows great plenty of cloves, camphor, and nutmegs, and in a word all kinds of spices are
there to be had, and great abundance of all victuals except
wine.

The king of this land of Java has a most brave and sumptuous palace, the most loftily built that ever I saw. It has
most high staircases leading up to the rooms, of silver and
of gold alternately, throughout the whole building. Also
the lower rooms were paved all over with one square plate
of silver, and another of gold. All the walls upon the inner
side were covered over with plates of beaten gold, whereupon were engraven the pictures of knights, each having
around his head a wreath of gold, adorned with precious
stones. The ceiling of the palace was of pure gold. With
this king of Java the great Khan of Cathay had many conflicts in war; whom the said king of Java has always overcome and vanquished.

Chapter 5

OF CERTAIN TREES YIELDING MEAL ❧ HONEY ❧ AND POISON

NEAR this island is another called Panten, or Tathala-
masin. And the king of the same country has many islands
[the Archipelago] under his dominion. In this land there
are trees yielding meal, honey, and wine, and the most
deadly poison in all the whole world. Against this poison
there is but one remedy, and that is: if any man has taken of
the poison, and would be delivered of the danger thereof,
let him temper the dung of a man in water, and so drink a
good quantity thereof. It expels the poison immediately.

Meal is produced out of trees after this manner. They
are mighty huge trees, and when they are cut with an axe
at the ground, there issues out of the stock a certain liquor

like gum, which they take and put into bags made of leaves, laying them for fifteen days in the sun. At the end of these fifteen days, when the said liquor is thoroughly parched, it becomes meal. Then they steep it first in sea water, washing it afterward with fresh water, and so it is made into a very good and savoury paste, from which they make either meat or bread, as they think good. Of this bread I myself did eat, and it is white outside and somewhat brown within.

By this country is the sea called the Dead Sea [Antarctic], which runs continually southward, and whoever falls into it is never seen again. In this country also are found canes of an incredible length, namely, of sixty paces high or more, and they are as big as trees. Other canes there are called *cassan*, which overspread the earth like grass, and out of every root of them spring forth certain branches, which run along the ground almost for the space of a mile. In the said canes there are found certain stones, one of which, if worn by a person, he cannot be wounded with any iron. Therefore the men of this country for the most part carry such stones with them wherever they go. Many also cause one of the arms of their children, while they are young, to be lanced, putting one of these stones into the wound, and closing it up with the powder of a certain fish, which powder does immediately cure the wound.

And by the virtue of these stones, the people do for the most part triumph both on sea and land. However, there is one kind of stratagem which the enemies of this nation, knowing the virtue of the said stones, do practise against them: they provide themselves with arrows and weapons poisoned with the poison of trees, and they carry in their hands wooden stakes most sharp and hard-pointed, as if they were iron. Likewise they shoot arrows without iron heads, and so they confound and slay some of their unarmed foes who trust too securely to the virtue of their stones.

Of these canes called *cassan* they make sails for their ships, and little houses, and many other necessaries.

From here after many days' travel, I arrived at another kingdom called Zampa [Japan], a most beautiful and rich country, and abounding with all kinds of victuals. The king had so many wives and concubines that he had three hundred sons and daughters by them. This king hath ten thousand and four tame elephants, which are kept even as we keep droves of oxen, or flocks of sheep in pasture.

Chapter 6

OF THE ABUNDANCE OF FISHES ❧ WHICH CAST THEMSELVES UPON THE SHORE

IN this country there is one strange thing to be observed. Many kinds of fishes in those seas come swimming towards the said country in such abundance that, for a great distance into the sea, nothing can be seen but the backs of fishes. They cast themselves upon the shore when they come near it, and allow men, for the space of three days, to come and to take as many of them as they please, and then they return again to the sea. After one kind of fish comes another kind, offering itself after the same manner, and so in like sort all other kinds; however, they do this but once in a year. I demanded of the inhabitants there how, or by what means, this strange accident could come to pass. They answered, that fishes were taught, even by nature, to come and to do homage to their emperor. There are tortoises also as big as an oven. Many other things I saw which seem incredible, unless a man should see them with his own eyes.

In this country also dead men are burned, and their wives

are burned alive with them. The men of the country say that she goes to accompany him in another world, that he should take none other wife in marriage.

Moreover I travelled on further by the ocean sea towards the south, and passed through many countries and islands. One is called Nicoveran [Nicobar], and it contains in compass two thousand miles, wherein men and women have dogs' faces, and worship an ox for their god; and therefore all of them carry the image of an ox of gold or silver upon their foreheads. The men and women of this country go all naked, saving that they hang a linen cloth before their privates. The men of that country are very tall and mighty, and by reason that they go naked, when they are to make battle, they carry iron or steel shields before them, which cover and defend their bodies from top to toe. Whomsoever they take in battle they devour, if he is not able to ransom himself. But if he is able to redeem himself for money, they let him go free.

Their king wears about his neck three hundred great and most beautiful pearls, and says every day three hundred prayers to his god. He wears upon his finger also a stone called a ruby of a span long, which seems to be a flame of fire, and therefore when he wears it, no man dares approach him. They say that there is no other stone in the whole world of more value than it. Neither could at any time the great Tartarian emperor of Cathay either by force, money, or policy obtain it, in spite of the fact that he has done the utmost of his endeavour for this purpose.

Chapter 7

OF THE ISLAND OF CEYLON ❧ AND OF THE MOUNTAIN WHERE ADAM MOURNED FOR HIS SON ABEL

I PASSED also by another island called Ceylon, which contains in compass above two thousand miles; wherein are an infinite number of serpents, and great store of lions, bears, and all kinds of raving wild beasts, and especially elephants. In this country there is a huge mountain, where, the inhabitants of that region report, Adam mourned for his son Abel the space of five hundred years. In the midst of this mountain there is a most beautiful plain, wherein is a little lake containing a great amount of water, which the inhabitants report to have come from the tears of Adam and Eve. However, I proved that to be false, because I saw the water flow into the lake.

This water is full of horse-leeches, and blood suckers, and of precious stones also; these precious stones the king takes not for his own use, but once or twice every year he permits certain poor people to dive under the water for the stones, and all that they can get he bestows upon them, to the end that they may pray for his soul. That they may, with less danger, dive under the water, they take lemons which they peel, anointing themselves thoroughly with the juice thereof, and so they may dive naked under the water, the horse-leeches not being able to hurt them. From this lake the water runs into the sea, and at a low ebb, the inhabitants dig rubies, diamonds, pearls, and other precious stones out of the shore. Wherefore it is thought that the king of this island has greater abundance of precious stones than any other monarch in the whole earth.

In this island there are all kinds of beasts and fowls, and the people told me that these beasts would not invade nor hurt any stranger, but only the natural inhabitants. I saw in this island fowls as big as our country geese, having two heads,[1] and other miraculous things, which I will not here write of.

Travelling on further toward the south, I arrived at a certain island called Bodin, which in our language means unclean. In this island there live most wicked persons, who devour and eat raw flesh, committing all kinds of uncleanness and abominations. For the father eats his son, and the son his father, the husband his own wife, and the wife her husband, and this they do in the following manner. If any man's father be sick, the son straightway goes to the soothsayer, or prognosticating priest, requesting him to demand of his god, whether his father shall recover of that infirmity or not. Then both of them go to an idol of gold or of silver, making their prayers to it in manner following: "Lord, thou art our god, and thee we do adore, beseeching thee to resolve us, whether such a man must die, or recover of such an infirmity or no." Then the devil answers out of the idol. If he says he shall live, then his son returns and ministers things necessary to him, till he has attained his former health. But if he says he shall die, then the priest goes to him, and putting a cloth to his mouth, strangles him therewith. This being done, he cuts his dead body into pieces, and all his friends and kinsfolks are invited to the eating thereof, with music and all kinds of mirth. But his bones are solemnly buried.

When I found fault with this custom, demanding a reason for it, one of them gave me this answer: "This we do, lest the worms should eat his flesh, for then his soul should suffer great torments." I could by no means remove from

---

[1] The Rhinoceros Hornbill, a bird with two bills. "How easy here to call Odoric a liar! but how unjust, when the matter has been explained." Yule in *Cathay and the Way Thither*, Vol. II.

them this belief. Many other novelties and strange things there are in this country, which no man would credit, unless he saw them with his own eyes.

However, I—before almighty God—do here make record of nothing but of that only of which I am as sure as a man may be sure. Concerning these islands I inquired of various well-experienced persons, who all of them, as it were with one consent, answered me, saying, that this India contained forty-four hundred islands under it, or within it, in which islands there are sixty-four crowned kings. And they say, moreover, that the greater part of those islands are well inhabited. And here I conclude concerning that part of India.

Chapter 8

OF THE UPPER INDIA ❦ AND OF THE PROVINCE OF MANCY

First of all, therefore, having travelled many days' journey upon the ocean sea toward the east, at length I arrived at a certain great province called Mancy, being in Latin named India. Concerning this India I inquired of Christians, of Saracens, and of idolaters, and of all such as bear any office under the great Khan. All of them with one consent answered, that this province of Mancy has more than two thousand great cities within the precincts thereof, and that it abounds with plenty of victuals, as bread, wine, rice, flesh, and fish. All the men of this province are craftsmen and merchants, who, though they be in extreme poverty, so long as they can help themselves by the labour of their hands, will never beg alms of any man.

The men of this province are of a fair and comely personage, but somewhat pale, having their heads shaven but a little. But the women are the most beautiful under the sun.

The first city of India which I came to is called Ceuskalon [Canton], a day's journey distant from the sea. It stands upon a river, the water whereof, near the mouth where it empties itself into the sea, overflows the land for the space of twelve days' journey. All the inhabitants of this India are worshippers of idols. The city of Ceuskalon has such a huge navy belonging to it that no man would believe it unless he should see it. In this city I saw three hundred pounds of good and new ginger sold for less than a groat. There are the greatest and the fairest geese, and most plenty of them to be sold in all the whole world, as I suppose. They are as white as milk [the Guinea goose], and have a bone upon the crown of their heads as big as an egg, being of the colour of blood; under their throat they have a skin or bag hanging down half a foot. They are exceeding fat, and sold cheaply. Also they have ducks and hens in this country, each as big as two of ours.

There be monstrous great serpents likewise, which are taken by the inhabitants and eaten. A solemn feast among them without serpents is thought nothing of. To be brief, in this city there are all kinds of victuals in great abundance.

From here I passed by many cities, and at length I came to a city named Zayton, wherein the Friars Minorites have two places of abode, to which I transported the bones of the dead friars, who had suffered martyrdom for the faith of Christ, as is above mentioned. In this city there is abundance of all kind of victuals and very cheap. The city is as big as two of Bologna, and in it are many monasteries of religious persons, all which worship idols. I myself was in one of those monasteries, and it was told me that there were in it three thousand religious men, having eleven thousand idols; and one of these idols, which seemed to me but little in regard of the rest, was as big as our Christopher.

These religious men every day feed their idol gods; whereupon at a certain time I went to behold the banquet and indeed those things which they brought to them were good to eat, and fuming hot, and when the steam ascended up to their idols they said that their gods were refreshed. Howbeit, all the meat they conveyed away, eating it up themselves, and so they fed their dumb gods with the smoke only.

Chapter 9

OF THE CITY FUZO

TRAVELLING more eastward, I came unto a city named Fuzo [Fu-chow], which contains thirty miles in circuit, wherein are exceeding great and fair cocks, and all their hens are as white as the very snow, having wool instead of feathers, like unto sheep.[1] It is a most stately and beautiful city and stands upon the sea.

Then I went eighteen days' journey on further, and passed by many provinces and cities, and in the way I went over a certain great mountain, upon the one side I beheld all living creatures to be as black as a coal, and the men and women on that side differed somewhat in manner of living from others. On the other side of the said hill every living thing was snow-white, and the inhabitants in their manner of living were altogether unlike the others. There, all married women carry in token that they have husbands, a great trunk of horn upon their heads.

From here I travelled eighteen days' journey further, and came to a certain great river, and entered also a city, which had a mighty bridge across the river. My host with whom I sojourned, being desirous to show me some sport, said to me: "Sir, if you would see any fish being caught, go

---

[1] These birds are called the *Fleecy Persian* by poultry-fanciers, but the Chinese call them "velvet-hair fowls."

with me." Then he led me to the bridge, carrying in his arms with him certain dive-doppers or water-fowls, bound to perches, and about every one of their necks he tied a thread, lest they should eat the fish as fast as they took them. He carried three great baskets with him also. Then he loosened the dive-doppers from the poles, which presently went into the water, and within less than the space of one hour, caught as many fish as filled the three baskets; which being full, my host untied the threads from about their necks, and entering the second time into the river they fed themselves with fish, and being satisfied they returned and allowed themselves to be bound to their perches as they were before. And when I did eat of those fish, I thought they were exceedingly good.

Travelling on for many days, at length I arrived at another city called Canasia [the modern Hang-chow], which signifies in our language the city of heaven. Never in my life did I see so great a city. It contains in circuit a hundred miles. Neither saw I any plot thereof, which was not thoroughly inhabited. I saw many houses of ten or twelve stories high, one above another. It has mighty large suburbs containing more people than the city itself. Also it has twelve principal gates; and about the distance of eight miles, in the highway to every one of these gates stands a city as big by estimation as Venice, or Padua.

The city of Canasia is situated in waters, or marshes, which always stand still, neither ebbing nor flowing; however, it has a defence for the wind like Venice. In this city there are more than eleven thousand bridges, many of which I counted and passed over them. Upon every one of these bridges stand certain watchmen of the city, keeping continual watch and ward about the city, for the great Khan the Emperor of Cathay. The people of this country say, that they have one duty that they must pay their lord. For every fire one *balis* of tax is paid tribute; and each *balis* is five papers like pieces of silk, which are worth one florin and a half of our coin. Ten or twelve households have one fire between them, and so pay tribute but for one fire only. All those tributary fires amount to the number of eighty-five *thuman*, with other four *thuman* of the Saracens, which make eighty-nine in all. Each *thuman* equals ten thousand.

The residue of the people of the city are some of them Christians, some merchants, and some travellers through the country, whereupon I marvelled much how such an infinite number of persons could inhabit and live together. There is great abundance of victuals in this city, as bread and wine, and especially of hogs' flesh, with other necessaries.

Chapter 10

OF A MONASTERY WHERE MANY STRANGE BEASTS OF MANY SPECIES DO LIVE UPON A HILL

IN the above-mentioned city four of our friars had converted a mighty and rich man to the faith of Christ, at whose house I continually abode, for as long as I remained in the city. Who upon a certain time said to me: "Ara," that is to say, father, "will you go and behold the city?" And I said, "Yes." Then we embarked, and directed our course to a certain great monastery; when we arrived, he called a religious person with whom he was acquainted, saying to him concerning me: "This Raban Francus," that is to say, this religious Frenchman, "comes from the western parts of the world, and is now going to the city of Kanbalu [Peking] to pray for the life of the great Khan, and therefore you must show him some rare thing, that when he returns to his own country he may speak of this strange sight or novelty seen in the city of Canasia." Then the religious man took two great baskets full of scraps from the table, and led me into a little walled park, the door of which he unlocked with his key, and there appeared before us a pleasant fair green plot, which we entered. In the green stands a little mount in form of a steeple, replenished with fragrant herbs, and fine shady trees. And while we stood there, he took a cymbal, or bell, and rang, as they use to ring to dinner or bevoir in cloisters, at the sound of which many creatures of divers kinds came down from the mount, some like apes, some like cats, some like monkeys, and some having faces like men. And while I stood beholding of them, they gathered themselves together about him, to the number of forty-two hundred of those creatures, putting themselves in good order, before whom he set a platter, and gave them the fragments to eat. And when they had eaten he rang upon his cymbal the second time, and they all returned to their former places. Then, wondering greatly at the matter, I demanded what kind of creatures those might be. "They are," said he, "the souls of noble men which we do here feed, for the love of God who governeth the world; and as a man was honourable or noble in this life, so his soul after death, enters into the body of some excellent beast or other, but the souls of simple and rustic people do possess the bodies of more vile and brutish creatures." Then I began to refute that foul belief; but my speech did not at all prevail with him, for he could not be persuaded that any soul might remain without a body.

From here I departed unto a certain city named Chilenso [Nanking], the walls of which were forty miles in circuit. In this city there are three hundred and sixty bridges of stone, the fairest that ever I saw; and it is well inhabited, having a great navy belonging to it, and abounding with all kind of victuals and other commodities. And then I went to a certain river called Thalay [Ta-kiang], which, where it is most narrow, is seven miles broad; and it runs through the midst of the land of pygmies, whose chief city is called Cathan, and is one of the goodliest cities in the world. These pygmies are three of my spans high, and they make larger and better cloth of cotton and silk than any other nation under the sun.

Coasting along by this river, I came unto a certain city named Janzu [Yamzai], in which there is one house for the friars of our order, and there are also three churches of the Nestorians.

This Janzu is a noble and great city, containing forty-eight *thuman* of tributary fires, and in it are all kinds of victuals, and great plenty of such beasts, owls and fish as Christians do usually live upon. The lord of the same city has in yearly revenues for salt only, fifty *thuman* of *balis*, and one *balis* is worth a florin and a half of our coin. Insomuch that one *thuman* of *balis* amounts to the value of fifteen thousand florins. However, the lord favours his people in one respect, for sometimes he forgives them freely two hundred *thuman*, lest there should be any scarcity or dearth among them.

There is a custom in this city that when any man is determined to banquet his friends, going about to certain taverns or cooks' houses appointed for the same purpose, he says to every particular host, you shall have such, and such of my friends, whom you must entertain in my name, for so much I will bestow upon the banquet. And by that means his friends are better feasted than they should have been at his own home.

Ten miles from this city, about the head of the river of Thalay, there is a certain other city called Montu, which has the greatest navy that I saw in the whole world. All their ships are as white as snow, and they have banqueting houses in them, and many other rare things also, which no man would believe, unless he had seen them with his own eyes.

Chapter 11

OF THE CITY OF KANBALU

TRAVELLING eight days' journey further by many territories and cities, at length I came by fresh water to a certain city named Lencyn, standing upon the river of Karauoran [Yellow River], which runs through the midst of Cathay, and does great harm in the country when it overflows the banks, or breaks the channel. From there passing along the river eastward, after many days, and the sight of divers cities, I arrived at a city called Sumakoto [Shan-tung], which contains more silk than any other city of the world. When there is great scarcity of silk, forty pounds are sold for less than eight groats.

In this city there is abundance of merchandise, and of all kinds of victuals also, as of bread, wine, flesh, fish, with all choice and delicate spices.

Then travelling on still towards the east by many cities, I came to the noble and renowned city of Kanbalu, which is of great antiquity, being situated in the province of Cathay. This city the Tartars took, and near to it within the space of half a mile they built another city called Taydo. The city of Taydo has twelve gates, each of them two miles distant from another. Also the space lying in the midst between these two cities is very well and thoroughly inhabited, so that they make as it were but one city between them. The whole compass or circuit of both cities together is forty miles.

In this city the great emperor Khan has his principal seat, and his imperial palace, the walls of which palace contain four miles in circuit. Near to his palace are many other palaces and houses of his nobles which belong to his court. Within the precincts of the imperial palace there is a most beautiful mount, set and replenished with trees, which is called the Green Mount, having a most royal and sumptuous palace standing thereupon, in which, for the most part, the great Khan resides.

Upon one side of the mount there is a great lake, whereupon a most stately bridge is built, in which lake is great abundance of geese, ducks, and all kinds of water-fowls. In the wood growing upon the mount there is great store of all birds, and wild beasts. And, therefore, when the great Khan will solace himself with hunting or hawking, he needs not so much as once to step forth of his palace. Moreover, the principal palace, wherein he makes his abode, is very large, having within it fourteen pillars of gold, and all the walls are hung with red skins, which are said to be the most costly skins in all the world. In the midst of the palace stands a jar of two yards high, which consists of a precious stone called *merdochas* [jade] and is wreathed about with gold, and at each corner is the golden image of a serpent, as it were, furiously shaking and casting forth his head. This jar also has a kind of network of pearl wrought about it. Likewise into the jar wine is conveyed through certain pipes and conduits, such as is drunk in the emperor's court. Upon this there also hang many vessels of gold for those who desire to drink of the liquor.

In the palace there are many peacocks of gold. When any Tartar makes a banquet for his lord, if the guests chance to clap their hands for joy and mirth, the golden peacocks also will spread abroad their wings, and lift up their trains, and make as if they would dance. This I suppose is done by art magic or by some secret engine under the ground.

Chapter 12

OF THE GLORY AND MAGNIFICENCE OF THE GREAT KHAN

MOREOVER, when the great Emperor Khan sits on his imperial throne of estate, on his left side sits his queen, or empress, and upon another inferior seat there sit two other women, which are to accompany the emperor, when his spouse is absent, but in the lowest place of all, there sit all the ladies of his kindred. All the married women wear upon their heads a kind of ornament in shape like a man's foot, of a cubit and a half in length, and the lower part of the foot is adorned with cranes' feathers, and is all over thick set with great and Oriental pearls.

Upon the right hand of the great Khan sits his first-begotten son and heir apparent to his empire, and under him sit all the nobles of the blood royal. There are also four secretaries, which put all things in writing that the emperor speaks. In his presence likewise stand his barons and others of his nobility, with great trains of followers after them, of whom none dare speak so much as one word, unless they have obtained license of the emperor so to do, except his jesters and stage-players, who are appointed of purpose to solace their lord.

Neither dare they attempt to do aught, but only according to the pleasure of their emperor. About the palace gate stand certain barons to keep all men from treading upon the threshold of the gate.

When it pleases the great Khan to solemnize a feast, he has about him fourteen thousand barons, carrying wreaths and little crowns upon their heads, and giving attendance upon their lord, and every one of them wears a garment of gold and precious stones, which is worth ten thousand florins. His court is kept in very good order, by governors of tens, governors of hundreds, and governors of thousands, insomuch that every one in his place performs his duty, neither is there any defect to be found.

I, Friar Odoric, was present in person for the space of three years, and was often at the banquets, for we Minor Friars have a place of abode appointed out for us in the emperor's court, and are enjoined to go and bestow our blessing upon him. And I inquired of certain courtiers concerning the number of persons pertaining to the emperor's court. They answered me, that of stage-players, musicians, and such like, there were eighteen *thuman* at the least, and that the keepers of dogs, beasts, and fowls were fifteen *thuman*, and the physicians for the emperor's body, were four hundred. The Christians also were eight in number, together with one Saracen. At my being there, all these persons had all kinds of necessaries both for apparel and victuals out of the emperor's court.

Moreover, when he desires to journey from one country to another, he has four troops of horsemen, one being appointed to go a day's journey before, and another to come a day's journey after him, the third to march on his right hand, and the fourth on his left, in the manner of a cross, he himself being in the midst. And so every particular troop have their daily journeys limited to them, to the end they may provide sufficient victuals without defect.

Now the great Khan himself is carried in manner following: He rides in a chariot with two wheels, upon which a majestic throne is built of the wood of aloe, being adorned with gold and great pearls, and precious stones, and four elephants bravely furnished do draw the chariot, before which elephants are four great horses richly trapped and covered to lead the way. Hard by the chariot, on both sides, are four barons laying hold and attending thereupon, to keep all persons from approaching their emperor. Upon the chariot also two milk-white gerfalcons do sit, and seeing any game which he would take, he lets them fly, and so they take it, and after this manner does he solace himself as he rides.

Moreover, no man dare come within a stone's cast of the chariot, but such as are appointed. The number of his own followers, of his wives' attendants, and of the train of his first-begotten son and heir apparent, would seem incredible to any man, unless he had seen it with his own eyes. The great Khan has divided his empire into twelve parts or provinces, and one of the provinces has two thousand great cities within its precincts. Whereupon his empire is of that length and breadth that to whatsoever part thereof he intends his journey, he has space enough for six months' continual progress, except his islands which are at the least five thousand.

Chapter 13

OF CERTAIN INNS OR HOSPITALS APPOINTED FOR TRAVELLERS THROUGHOUT THE WHOLE EMPIRE

THE emperor, so that travellers may have all things necessary throughout his whole empire, has caused certain inns to be provided in sundry places upon the highways, where all things pertaining unto victuals are in a continual readiness. And when any news happen in any part of his empire, if he chance to be far absent from that part, his messengers upon horses or dromedaries ride post to him, and when they and their beasts are weary, they blow their horn, and at the noise of it, the next inn likewise provides a horse and a man who takes the letter of him that is weary, and runs to another inn. And so by many inns, and many posts, the report, which ordinarily could scarce come in thirty days, is in one natural day brought to the emperor. Therefore no happening of any moment can be done in his empire, but straightway he has intelligence thereof.

Moreover, when the great Khan himself will go hunting, he uses this custom. Some twenty days' journey from the city of Kanbalu there is a forest six days' journey in circuit, in which forest there so many kinds of beasts and birds that it would sound incredible to report. To this forest, at the end of every third or fourth year, he resorts with his whole train, and they all of them together surround the forest, sending dogs into the same, which by hunting do chase the beasts, lions and stags, and other creatures, to a most beautiful plain in the midst of the forest, because all the beasts of the forest tremble, especially at the cry of the hounds. Then comes the great Khan himself, being carried upon three elephants, and shoots five arrows into the whole herd of beasts, and after him all his barons, and after them the rest of his courtiers and family do all in like manner discharge their arrows also, and every man's arrow has a special mark. Then they all go to the beasts which are slain, suffering the living beasts to return into the wood that they may have more sport with them another time, and every man enjoys that beast as his own wherein he finds his arrow has stuck.

Chapter 14

OF THE FOUR FEASTS WHICH THE GREAT KHAN CELEBRATES EVERY YEAR IN HIS COURT

FOUR great feasts in a year does the Emperor Khan celebrate; namely, the feast of his birth, the feast of his circumcision, the feast of his coronation, and the feast of his marriage. And to these feasts he invites all his barons, his stage-players, and all such as are of his kindred. Then the great Khan sitting on his throne, all his barons present themselves before him, with wreaths and crowns upon their heads, being variously attired, for some of them are in green, namely, the principal; the second are in red, and the third in yellow, and they hold each man in his hand a little ivory table of elephant's tooth, and they are girt with golden girdles half a foot broad, and they stand upon their feet keeping silence.

About them stand the stage-players or musicians with their instruments. And in one of the corners of a certain great palace, all the philosophers or magicians remain for certain hours, and do attend upon points or characters. When the time which the philosophers awaited is come, a certain crier calls out with a loud voice, saying, "Bow yourselves before your Emperor." With that all the barons fall flat upon the earth. Then he cries out again: "Arise all." And immediately they all arise. Likewise the philosophers wait for another suitable moment, and when it comes, the crier calls out: "Put your fingers in your ears." And again he cries, "Pluck them out." Again, at the third point he calls: "Bolt this meal."

Many other circumstances also do they perform, all which they say have some certain signification. But neither would I write them, or give any heed to them, because they are vain and ridiculous. And when the musicians' hour is come, then the philosophers say, "Solemnize a feast unto your lord." With that all of them sound their instruments, making a great and clamorous noise. And immediately another cries, "Peace, peace!" And they all cease. Then come the women musicians and sing sweetly before the emperor, which music was more delightful to me. After them come in the lions and do their obeisance unto the great Khan. Then the jugglers cause golden cups full of wine to fly up and down in the air, and to apply themselves to men's mouths that they may drink of them. These and many other strange things I saw in the court of the great Khan, which no man would believe unless he had seen them, and therefore I omit to speak of them.

I was informed also by certain credible persons, of another miraculous thing, namely, that in a certain kingdom of the great Khan, wherein stand the mountains called Caspian, the kingdom's name is Kalor, there grow great melons, which when ripe do open at the tops, and within them is found a little beast like a young lamb. I myself have heard reported that there stand certain trees upon the shore of the Irish Sea, bearing fruit like a melon, which, at a certain time of the year do fall into the water, and become birds.

Chapter 15

OF VARIOUS PROVINCES AND CITIES

AFTER three years I departed out of the empire of Cathay, travelling fifty days' journey towards the west. And at length I came to the empire of Prester John, whose principal city is Kosan, which has many other cities under it. From there passing many days' travel, I came to a province called Casan, which is for good commodities one of the only provinces under the sun, and is very well inhabited, for when we depart out of the gates of one city we may behold the gates of another city, as I myself saw in many of them.

The breadth of the province is fifty days' journey, and the length about sixty. In it there is great plenty of all victuals, and especially of chestnuts, and it is one of the twelve provinces of the great Khan. Going on further, I came to a certain kingdom called Tibet, which is in subjection to the great Khan also, wherein I think there is more bread and wine than in any other part of the world. The people of this country do, for the most part, live in tents made of black felt. Their principal city [Lhasa] is surrounded with fair and beautiful walls, being built of white and black stones, which are disposed chequerwise one by another, and curiously put together. Likewise all the highways in this country are exceedingly well paved. In this city none dare shed the blood of a man, or of any beast, for the reverence they bear a certain idol. In this city their Abassi, that is to say, their Pope, is resident, being the head and prince of all idolaters, upon whom he bestows and distributes gifts after his manner, even as our Pope of Rome accounts himself to be the head of all Christians.

The women of this country wear their hair plaited in over a hundred tresses, and they have two teeth in their mouths as long as the tusks of a boar. When a man's father dies among them, his son assembles together all the priests and musicians that he can get, saying that he is determined to honour his father. Then they carry the body to a field, all his kinsfolk, friends and neighbours accompanying them. Here the priests with great solemnity cut off the father's head, giving it to his son, which being done, they divide the whole body into morsels, and so leave it behind them, returning home with prayers in the company of the son. So soon as they are departed, certain vultures, which are accustomed to such banquets, come flying from the mountains, and carry away all the morsels of flesh; and from thenceforth a fame is spread abroad that the said party deceased was holy, because the angels of God carried him into paradise. This is the greatest and highest honour that the son can devise to perform for his deceased father. Then the son takes his father's head and, first cooking it and eating the flesh, he makes of the skull a drinking cup, from which himself with all his family and kindred do drink with great solemnity and mirth, in the remembrance of his dead father. Many other vile and abominable things does this nation commit, which I mean not to write, because men neither can nor will believe, except they should have sight of them.

Chapter 16

OF A CERTAIN RICH MAN ❦ WHO IS FED AND NOURISHED BY FIFTY VIRGINS

WHILE I was in the province of Mancy, I passed by the palace of a certain famous man, who has fifty virgin damsels continually attending upon him, feeding him every meal, as a bird feeds her young ones. Also he has sundry kinds of meat served at his table, and three dishes of each kind. And when the virgins feed him, they sing most sweetly. This man has in yearly revenues thirty *thuman* of *tagars* of rice, every *thuman* equals ten thousand *tagars,* and one *tagar* [about 140 pounds] is the burden of an ass. His palace is two miles in circuit, the pavement is one place of gold, and another of silver. Near the wall of the palace there is a mount artificially wrought with gold and silver, whereupon stand turrets and steeples in miniature and other things for the amusement and recreation of the great man. And it was told me that there were four such men in that kingdom.

It is accounted a great grace for the men of that country to have long nails upon their fingers, and especially upon their thumbs, which nails they may fold about their hands. But the grace and beauty of their women is to have small and slender feet; and therefore the mothers, when their daughters are young, do bind up their feet, that they may not grow great.

Travelling on further towards the south, I arrived at a certain country called Melistorte, which is a very pleasant and fertile place. And in this country there was a certain aged man called the Old Man of the Mountain, who round about two mountains had built a wall to enclose them. Within this wall there were the fairest and most crystal fountains in the whole world: and about the fountains there were most beautiful virgins in great number, and goodly horses also, and in a word, everything that could be devised for bodily pleasure and delight, and therefore the inhabitants of the country call the same place by the name of Paradise. The Old Man, when he saw any proper and valiant young man, would admit him into his paradise. Moreover, by certain conduits he makes wine and milk to flow abundantly. This Old Man when he has a mind to revenge himself or to slay any king or baron, commands him that is governor of the said paradise, to bring there one of the youths, permitting him a while to take his pleasure therein, and then to give him a certain drug of sufficient force to cast him into such a slumber as should make him quite void of all sense, and so being in a profound sleep to convey him out of his paradise; who being awaked, and seeing himself thrust out of the paradise would become so sorrowful that he could not in the world devise what to do, or whither to turn. Then would he go to the Old Man, beseeching him that he might be admitted again into his paradise, who says to him: "You cannot be admitted, unless you will slay such or such a man for my sake, and if you will give the attempt only, whether you kill him or no, I will place you again in paradise, that there you may remain always." Then would the youth without fail put the same in execution, endeavouring to murder all those against whom the Old Man had conceived any hatred. And therefore all the kings of the East stood in awe of the Old Man, and gave him great tribute.

Chapter 17
OF THE DEATH OF THE OLD MAN OF THE MOUNTAIN

WHEN the Tartars had subdued a great part of the world, they came to the Old Man, and took from him the custody of his paradise, who being incensed by this, sent abroad many desperate and resolute persons and caused many of the Tartar nobles to be slain. The Tartars, seeing this, went and besieged the city where the Old Man was, took him, and put him to a most cruel and miserable death.

The friars in that place have this special gift; namely, that by the virtue of the name of Christ, and in the virtue of his precious blood, which he shed upon the cross for the salvation of mankind, they do cast forth devils out of them that are possessed. And because there are many possessed men in those parts, they are bound and brought ten days' journey to the friars. When they are freed of the unclean spirits, they do presently believe in Christ who delivered them, accounting him for their God, being baptized in his name, and also delivering immediately to the friars all their idols, and the idols of their cattle, which are commonly made of felt or of women's hair. Then the friars kindle a fire in a public place, where the people resort, that they may see the false gods of their neighbours burnt, and cast the idols into the flame, but they jump out of the fire again. Then the friars sprinkle the fire with holy water, casting the idols into it the second time, and with that the devils flee in the likeness of black smoke, and the idols still remain till they are consumed unto ashes. Afterward, this noise and outcry from the devil is heard in the air: "Behold and see how I am expelled out of my habitation." And by these means the friars do baptize great multitudes.

There was another terrible thing which I saw there. Passing by a certain valley, which is beside a pleasant river, I saw many dead bodies, and in the valley also I heard divers sweet sounds and harmonies of music, especially the noise of citherns. I was greatly amazed. This desert valley is in length seven or eight miles at the least, into which any one who enters dies presently, and can by no means pass alive through it. Moreover, I was tempted to go in, and to see what it was. At length making my prayers, and recommending myself to God in the name of Jesus, I entered, and saw such swarms of dead bodies there as no man would believe unless he were an eye-witness thereof. At the one side of the valley in a certain rock, I saw the face of a man, which beheld me with such a terrible aspect that I thought verily I should have died in the same place. But always this sentence, "The Word became Flesh, and Dwelt amongst us," I began to pronounce, making the sign of the cross, and nearer than seven or eight paces I dared not approach to the face in the rocks. But I departed and fled to another place in the valley, ascending up to a little sandy mountain, where looking round about, I saw nothing but heard the citherns, which continued sounding and playing by themselves without the help of musicians. And being upon the top of the mountain, I found silver there like the scales of fishes in great abundance; and I gathered some into my bosom to show for a wonder, but my conscience rebuking me, I cast it up. And so, by God's grace, I departed without danger. And when the men of the country knew that I was returned out of the valley alive, they reverenced me, saying that I was baptized and holy, and that the bodies were men subject to the devils infernal, who used to play upon cithern, to the end they might allure people to enter, and so murder them. Thus much concerning those things which I beheld most certainly with mine eyes, I, Friar Odoric, have here written. Many strange things also I have of purpose omitted, because men will not believe them unless they see them.

Chapter 18

OF THE HONOUR AND REVERENCE DONE TO THE GREAT KHAN

I WILL report one thing more, which I saw, concerning the great Khan. It is a usual custom in those parts, that when the Khan travels through any country, his subjects kindle fires before their doors, casting spices therein to make a perfume, that their lord passing by may smell the sweet odours thereof, and much people come forth to meet him. Upon a certain time when he was coming towards Kanbalu, the fame of his approach being published, a bishop of ours, with certain of our Minorite Friars and myself, went two days' journey to meet him; and being come close to him, we put a cross upon wood, I myself having a censer in my hand, and began to sing with a loud voice: *"Veni, creator spiritus."* And as we were singing, he caused us to be called, commanding us to come to him; notwithstanding that no man dare approach within a stone's cast of his chariot, unless he be called, but such only as keep his chariot. And when we came near to him, he veiled his hat, or bonnet, being of an inestimable price, doing reverence to the cross. And immediately I put incense into the censer, and our bishop taking the censer perfumed him, and gave him his benediction.

Moreover, they that come before the Khan do always bring some oblation to present to him, observing the ancient law, "Thou shalt not appear in my presence with an empty hand." And for that reason we carried apples with us, and offered them in a platter with reverence to him. Taking out two of them, he did eat some part of one. And then he signalled to us, that we should go, lest the horse coming on might injure us. With that we departed from him, and turned aside, going to certain of his barons, which had been converted to the faith by friars of our order, being at the same time in his army. We offered them the apples, and they received them at our hands with great joy, seeming to us to be as glad as if we had given them some great gift.

I, Friar Odoric of Friuli, of a certain territory called Portius Vahonis, and of the Order of the Minorites, do testify and bear witness to the Reverend Father Guidotus, minister of the province of St. Anthony, in the marquisate of Treviso, in accordance with my vow of obedience, that all the things herein written, either I saw with mine own eyes, or heard the same reported by credible and substantial persons. The common report also of the countries where I was, testifieth those things which I saw, to be true. Many other things I have omitted, because I beheld them not with mine own eyes. But from day to day I prepare myself to travel countries or lands, in which action I dispose myself to die or to live, as it shall please my God.

All the things above were faithfully taken down in writing by Friar William de Solanga just as Friar Odoric uttered them by word of mouth, in the year of our Lord 1330, in the month of May, and in the place of St. Anthony of Padua. Neither did he trouble to write them in difficult Latin or in an eloquent style, but just as Odoric himself told them, to the end that men might the more easily understand the things reported.

THE TRAVELS OF
RABBI BENJAMIN OF TUDELA
1160–1173

RABBI BENJAMIN OF TUDELA

Rabbi Benjamin began his travels from Saragossa, Spain, in 1160, long before Carpini, Rubruck and Marco Polo. He went through Italy, Greece and Constantinople to Syria and Jerusalem. From Jerusalem he went to Damascus and Bagdad. He visited Egypt, Assyria, Persia and reached the frontiers of China. His journeys covered a space of about thirteen years.

We have in the record of Rabbi Benjamin, first-hand descriptions of Damascus, Jerusalem, Bagdad, and of the ruins of the Tower of Babel. He tells of the discovery at Mount Sion of the underground tomb of David, with its sepulchres of Solomon and all the kings of Judæa, of its pillars of marble encrusted with gold and silver and of a table upon which rested a golden sceptre and crown. He tells of the tombs of Abraham, Isaac, Jacob, Samuel, Sarah, Rebecca and Leah. He marks the spot where the ark of Noah landed and he measures for us the spiral stone steps of the fallen Tower of Babel. He speaks of the palace of the Calif of Bagdad, of the treasures, customs, of charities to the sick and poor, of the Jewish Prince of the Captivity, and how the Rabbis in the East receive consecration. He also tells us why the glass coffin of Daniel was suspended by heavy chains from the middle of a bridge.

We know from Rabbi Benjamin that the Jews in the East were noted for the arts of dyeing and glass-making. The geographical information that he presents agrees in general with the records of contemporary Arabian geographers. A Latin translation of his Hebrew text was made as early as 1575.

THE TRAVELS OF
RABBI BENJAMIN OF TUDELA

1160—1173

Hebrew Preface

This book contains the reports of Rabbi Benjamin, the son of Jonah, of blessed memory, of Tudela, in the kingdom of Navarre. This man travelled through many and distant countries, as related in the following account, and took down in writing in each place what he saw or what was told him by men of integrity, whose names were known in Spain. Rabbi Benjamin also mentions some of the principal men in the places he visited; and when he returned, he brought this report along with him to the country of Castile in the year A. D. 1173. The above-mentioned Rabbi Benjamin was a man of wisdom and understanding, and of much information; and after strict inquiry his words were found to be true and correct, for he was a true man.

Travels of RABBI BENJAMIN *of Blessed Memory*

THUS SAYS RABBI BENJAMIN, son of Jonah, of blessed memory. I first set out from the city of Saragossa, and proceeded down the river Ebro to Tortosa. Two days' journey brought me to the ancient city of Tarragona, which contains many ancient remains of masonry, and similar buildings are found nowhere else in the whole kingdom of Spain. This city stands on the coast. Two days thence is Barcelona, in which place there is a congregation of wise, learned, and princely men, such as Shesheth,

Shealthiel, and Solomon, son of Abraham, son of Chisdai of blessed memory. The city is handsome, though small, and is situated on the sea-shore. Its trade attracts merchants from all parts of the world: from Greece, from Pisa, Genoa, and Sicily, from Alexandria in Egypt, from Palestine and the adjacent countries.

A day's journey and a half brings you to Gerona, which city contains a small congregation of Jews. From thence it is three days to Narbonne, eminent for its university, from which the study of the law spreads over all countries. The city contains many wise and noble men, especially Calonymos, son of the great and noble Theodoros of blessed memory, a descendant of the house of David, as proved by his pedigree. This man holds landed property from the sovereigns of the country, and nobody can deprive him of it by force. There is also Abraham, the president of the university, Makhir, Juda, and others of much merit and learning. Altogether the number of Jews amounts to about three hundred. It is four parasangs [each parasang being equal to 3¼ miles] thence to the city of Beziers, which contains a congregation of learned men, the principals of which are Solomon Chalaphtha and Joseph, son of Nathaniel of blessed memory.

From thence it is two days to Har Gáash, or Montpellier, a city conveniently situated for trade, being within two parasangs from the coast. You here meet with Christian and Mahometan merchants from all parts: from Algarve [Portugal], Lombardy, the Roman Empire, Egypt, Palestine, Greece, France, Spain, and England. People of all tongues meet here, chiefly in consequence of the traffic of the Genoese and Pisans. The Jews of this city are among the wisest and most esteemed of the present generation. Reuben, son of Theodoros, Nathan, son of Zacharias,

Samuel, their rabbi, Shelemiah, and Mordecai of blessed memory, are the principal among them. Others are very rich, and benevolent towards all who apply to them for assistance. It is four parasangs hence to Lunel, a city containing also a holy congregation of Jews, who employ all their time in the study of the law. This town is the place of residence of the celebrated rabbi Meshullam and his five sons, Joseph, Isaac, Jacob, Aaron, and Asher, all of whom are eminent scholars and rich men. The latter is an ascetic, who does not attend to any worldly business, but studies day and night, keeps fasts, and never eats meat. He possesses an extraordinary degree of knowledge of everything relating to Talmudic learning. Moses, his brother-in-law, Samuel, the minister, Solomon Cohen, and the physician Juda, son of Thibbon, of Spanish origin, are also inhabitants of Lunel.

All foreign students who resort hither to study the law, are supplied with food and raiment at the public expense during the whole time of their stay in the university. The Jews of this city, amounting to about three hundred, are wise, holy, and benevolent men, who support their poor brethren near and far. The town stands within two parasangs of the coast.

It is two parasangs hence to Beaucaire, a large town, containing about four hundred Jews, and a great university under the presidency of the great rabbi, Abraham, son of David of blessed memory, a scholar of the first eminence in Scriptural and Talmudic learning. He attracts students from distant countries, who are lodged in his own house and are taught by him; he, moreover, provides them with all necessaries of life from his own means and private property, which is very considerable. Joseph, son of Menachem, Benbenast, Benjamin, Abraham, and Isaac, son of Moses of blessed memory of this city, are also very great scholars and wise men.

It is three parasangs further to Nogres, or Bourg de St. Gilles. The chief of the Jewish inhabitants, of which there are about one hundred, are Isaac, son of Jacob, Abraham, son of Juda, Eliasar, Isaac, Moses, and Jacob, son of the late rabbi Levi of blessed memory. This town is a place of pilgrimage, visited by the inhabitants of distant countries and islands. It is situated within three parasangs of the sea, on the very banks of the large river Rhone, which traverses the whole of Provence. It is the place of residence of Abba Mari, son of Isaac of blessed memory, who holds the office of steward to Count Raymond.

To Arles, three parasangs. The chief of its two hundred Israelites are Moses, Tobi, Isaiah, Solomon the rabbi, Nathan, and Abba Mari of blessed memory. It is three days hence to Marseilles, a city containing many eminent and wise men. Its three hundred Jews form two congregations, one of which resides in the lower town on the shore of the Mediterranean, and the other in the upper part, near the fortress. The latter supports a great university and boasts of many learned scholars. Simeon, son of Antoli, his brother, Jacob, and Levaro, are the chief of the upper synagogue; Jacob Perpiano, a rich man, Abraham, and his son-in-law, Meir, Isaac, and another Meir, preside over the lower congregation. An extensive trade is carried on in this city, which stands on the coast. And here people take ship for Genoa, which also stands on the coast, and is reached in about four days.

Two Jews from Ceuta, Samuel, son of Khilam, and his brother, reside there. The city is surrounded by a wall; no king governs over it, but senators chosen by the citizens out of their own body. Every house is provided with a tower, and in times of civil commotion war is carried on from the tops of these towers. The Genoese are masters of the sea, and build vessels called galleys, by means of which they carry on war in many places and bring home much plunder and booty. They are now at war with the Pisans.

From their city it is a distance of two days' journey to Pisa, which is a place of very great extent, containing about ten thousand fortified houses, from which war is carried on in times of civil commotion. All the inhabitants are brave; no king or prince governs over them, the supreme authority being vested in senators chosen by the people. The principal of the twenty Jews resident at Pisa are Moses, Chaim and Joseph. The city has no walls, and stands about four miles from the sea, the navigation being carried on by means of vessels which ply on the Arno, a river that runs through the city. From here it is four parasangs to Lucca, a large city, which contains about forty Jews, the principal of whom are David, Samuel, and Jacob.

A journey of six days from here brings you to the large city of Rome, the metropolis of all Christendom. Two hundred Jews live there, who are very much respected, and pay tribute to no one. Some of them are officers in the service of Pope Alexander [III], who is the chief ecclesiastic and head of the Christian church. The principal of the many eminent Jews resident here are Daniel and Jechiel. The latter is one of the Pope's officers, a handsome, prudent, and wise man, who frequents the Pope's palace, being the steward of his household and minister of his private property. Jechiel is a descendant of Nathan, the author of the book Aruch [a celebrated dictionary] and its comments. There are likewise at Rome, Joab, son of the rabbi Solomon, Menachem, the president of the university, Jechiel, who

resides in Trastevere, and Benjamin, son of Shabthai of
blessed memory.

The city of Rome is divided into two parts by the river
Tiber, which runs through it.   In the first of these divisions
you see the large place of worship called St. Peter's of Rome,
on the site of the extensive palace of Julius Cæsar.   The
city contains numerous buildings and structures entirely different from all other buildings upon the face of the earth.
The extent of ground covered by the ruined and inhabited
parts of Rome amounts to twenty-four miles.   You there
find eighty halls of the eighty eminent kings who were all
called Imperator, from King Tarquin to King Pepin, the
father of Charles [Charlemagne], who first conquered Spain
and wrested it from the Mahometans.

In the outskirts of Rome is the palace of Titus, who was
rejected by three hundred senators in consequence of his
having wasted three years in the conquest of Jerusalem,
which, according to their opinion, he ought to have accomplished in two years.   There is likewise the hall of the palace
of Vespasian, a very large and strong building; also
the hall of Galba, containing three hundred and sixty
windows, equal in number to the days of the year.   The circumference of this palace is nearly three miles.   A battle
was fought here in times of yore, and in the palace fell more
than a hundred thousand, whose bones are hung up there
even to the present day.   The king caused a representation of
the battle to be drawn, army against army, the men, the
horses, and all their accoutrements being sculptured in marble, in order to preserve a memorial of the wars of antiquity.
You there find also a cave under ground containing the king
and his queen upon their thrones, surrcunded by about one
hundred nobles of their court, all embalmed by physicians
and in good preservation to this day.

Another remarkable object is St. Giovanni *in porta Latina*, in which place of worship there are two copper pillars constructed by King Solomon of blessed memory, whose name, "Solomon, son of David," is engraved upon each. The Jews in Rome told Benjamin that every year, about the time of the ninth of Ab [commemorating the destruction of both temples at Jerusalem], these pillars sweat so much that the water runs down from them. You see also there the cave in which Titus, the son of Vespasian, hid the vessels of the temple, which he brought from Jerusalem; and in another cave on the banks of the Tiber, you find the sepulchres of those holy men of blessed memory, the ten martyrs of the kingdom [the ancient teachers of Mishna].

Opposite St. Giovanni de Laterano, there is a statue of Samson, with a lance of stone in his hand; also that of Absalom, the son of David, and of Constantine, who built Constantinople, which city is called after his name; his statue is cast in copper, the man and horse being gilt. Rome contains many other remarkable buildings and works the whole of which nobody can enumerate.

Four days from Rome is Capua, a large city, built by King Capys. The town is elegant, but the water is bad, and the country unhealthy. Among the three hundred Jews who reside at Capua are many very wise men of universal fame, such as Konpasso and his brother, Samuel, Saken, and the rabbi David, who bears the title of Principalo.

From thence to Puzzuolo, or Sorrento, a large city built by Tsintsan Hadareser, who fled in fear of King David of blessed memory. This city has been inundated in two spots by the sea; and even to this day you may see the streets and towers of the submerged city. A hot spring, which issues forth from under ground, produces the oil called Petroleum, which is collected upon the surface of the water and used in medicine. There are likewise hot baths, proceeding from hot subterranean springs, which here issue from under ground. Two of these baths are situated on the sea-shore, and whoever is afflicted with any disease generally experiences great relief, if not certain cure, from the use of these waters. During the summer season all persons afflicted with diseases crowd hither from the whole of Lombardy.

From this place a man may travel fifteen miles by a causeway under the mountains, constructed by Romulus, the founder of Rome, who feared David, king of Israel, and Joab, his general, and constructed buildings both upon and under the mountains. The city of Naples is very strongly fortified; it is situated on the coast, and was originally built by the Greeks. The principal of the five hundred Jews who live here are Chiskiah, Shalom, Eliah Cohen, and Isaac, from Mount Hor.

One day's journey brings you to Salerno, the chief medical university of Christendom. The number of Jews living here amounts to about six hundred, among whom Juda, son of Isaac, Melchisedek, the grand rabbi, originally from Siponte, Solomon Cohen, Elija Hajevani, the Greek, Abraham Narboni and Thamon deserve particular notice as wise and learned men. The city is surrounded by a wall towards the land; one part of it, however, stands on the shore of the sea. The fort on the summit of the hill is very strong. Half a day to Amalfi, among the inhabitants of which city are twenty Jews, the chief being Chananel, the physician, Elisha, and the benevolent noble Abu-al-Gid. The Christian population of this country is chiefly occupied with trade; they do not till the ground, but buy everything for money, because they reside on high mountains and upon rocky hills; fruit, however, abounds; the land being covered with vineyards, olive-groves, gardens, and orchards. Nobody ventures to make war upon them.

One day to Bavento, a large city between the coast and a high mountain. The congregation of Jews is about two hundred, of which the principals are Calonymos, Sarach, and Abraham of blessed memory. From hence two days to Melfi in Apulia, with about two hundred Jews, of which Achimaats, Nathan, and Sadok are the principal. One day's journey hence to Ascoli; the principal of the forty Jews who live there are Kontilo, Semach, his son-in-law, and Joseph. Two days to Trani, on the coast. All the pilgrims who travel to Jerusalem assemble here, on account of the convenience of its port. This city contains about two hundred Israelites, the chief of whom are Elijah, Nathan the lecturer, and Jacob. Trani is a large and elegant town.

One day's journey to St. Nicholas di Bari, formerly a large city, but it was destroyed by William, king of Sicily. It still lies in ruins, and contains neither Jewish nor Christian inhabitants. One day's journey and a half to Taranto, the frontier town of Calabria, the inhabitants of which are Greeks. It is a large city, and the principal of the three hundred Jews who live there are Mali, Nathan and Israel. One day's journey to Brindisi, on the sea-coast, containing about ten Jews, who are dyers. Two days to Otranto, on the coast of the Grecian sea; the principal of its five hundred Jewish inhabitants are Menachem, Khaleb, Meier and Mali.

From thence you cross over in two days to the island of Corfu, containing but one Jew, a dyer, of the name of Joseph. Unto this place reaches the kingdom of Sicily.

Two days' voyage by sea brings you to the coast of Arta, the confines of the empire of Manuel, king of Greece. On this coast lies a village with about a hundred Jewish inhabitants, the principal of whom are Shelachiah and Hercules.

Two days to Achelous, containing ten Jews, of whom the principal is Shabthai. Half a day to Anatolica on the gulf. One day by sea to Patras. This is the city of Antipatros, king of Greece, one of the four kings who rose after Alexander. It contains large and ancient buildings, and about fifty Jews reside there, of whom Isaac, Jacob and Samuel are the principal. Half a day by sea to Lepanto, on the coast. The principal of the hundred Jews who reside there are Gisri, Shalom and Abraham. One day's journey and a half to Crissa. Two hundred Jews live there by themselves on Mount Parnassus, and carry on agriculture upon their own land and property; of these, Solomon, Chaim and Jedaiah are the principal. Three days to the city of Corinth, which contains about three hundred Jews, of whom the chief are Leon, Jacob and Ezekias.

Three days to the large city of Thebes, containing about two thousand Jewish inhabitants. These are the most eminent manufacturers of silk and purple cloth in all Greece. Among them are many eminent Talmudic scholars and men as famous as any of the present generation. The principal of them are, the great rabbi Aaron Koti, his brother, Moses; Chija, Elijah Tareteno and Joktan. No scholars like them are to be found in the whole Grecian Empire, except at Constantinople.

A journey of three days brings you to Negropont, a large city on the coast, to which merchants resort from all parts. Of the two hundred Jews who reside there, the principal are Elijah Psalteri, Emanuel and Khaleb. From thence to Jabustrisa is one day's journey. This city stands on the coast, and contains about one hundred Jews, the principal of whom are Joseph, Samuel and Nethaniah. Rabenica is distant one day's journey, and contains about one hundred Jews, of whom Joseph, Eleasar and Isaac are the principal. Sinon

Potamo or Zeitun, is one day's journey further; Solomon and Jacob are the principal of its fifty Jewish inhabitants.

Here we reach the confines of Wallachia, the inhabitants of which country are called Vlachi. They are as nimble as deer, and descend from their mountains into the plains of Greece, committing robberies and making booty. Nobody ventures to make war upon them, nor can any king bring them to submission, and they do not profess the Christian faith. Their names are of Jewish origin, and some even say that they have been Jews, which nation they call brethren. Whenever they meet an Israelite, they rob, but never kill him, as they do the Greeks. They profess no religious creed.

From thence it is two days to Gardiki, a ruined place, containing but few Jewish or Grecian inhabitants. Two days further, on the coast, stands the large commercial city of Armiro, which is frequented by the Venetians, the Pisans, the Genoese, and many other merchants. It is a large city, and contains about four hundred Jewish inhabitants; of whom the chief are Shiloh, Joseph the elder, and Solomon, the president. One day to Bissina; the principal of the hundred Jews who reside here are the rabbi Shabtha, Solomon and Jacob. The town of Saloniki is distant two days by sea; it was built by King Seleucus, one of the four Greek nobles who rose after Alexander, is a very large city, and contains about five hundred Jewish inhabitants. The rabbi, Samuel, and his sons are eminent scholars, and he is appointed provost of the resident Jews by the king's command. His son-in-law Shabthai, Elijah and Michael, also reside there. The Jews are much oppressed in this place, and live by the exercise of handicraft.

Mitrizzi, distant two days' journey, contains about twenty Jews. Isaiah, Makhir and Eliab are the principal of them. Drama, distant from hence two days' journey, contains about one hundred and forty Jews, of whom the chief are Michael and Joseph. From thence one day's journey to Christopoli, which contains about twenty Jewish inhabitants. Three days from thence by sea stands Abydos, on the coast.

It is five days' journey through the mountains to the large city of Constantinople, the metropolis of the whole Grecian Empire, and the residence of the Emperor, King Manuel [Manuel Comnenus, 1143 to 1180]. Twelve princely officers govern the whole empire by his command, each of them inhabiting a palace at Constantinople, and possessing fortresses and cities of his own. The first of these nobles bears the title of Præpositus magnus; the second is called Megas Domesticus, the third Dominus, the fourth Megas Ducas, the fifth Œconomus magnus, and the names of the others are similar to these.

The circumference of the city of Constantinople is eighteen miles; one-half of the city being bounded by the continent, the other by the sea, two arms of which meet here; the one a branch or outlet of the Russian, the other of the Spanish sea. Great stir and bustle prevails at Constantinople in consequence of the conflux of many merchants, who resort thither, both by land and by sea, from all parts of the world for purposes of trade, including merchants from Babylon and from Mesopotamia, from Media and Persia, from Egypt and Palestine, as well as from Russia, Hungary, Patzinakia, Budia, Lombardy and Spain. In this respect the city is equalled only by Bagdad, the metropolis of the Mahometans.

At Constantinople is the place of worship called St. Sophia, and the metropolitan seat of the Pope of the Greeks, who are at variance with the Pope of Rome. It contains as many altars as there are days of the year, and possesses innumerable riches, which are augmented every year by the contributions of the two islands and of the adjacent towns and villages. All the other places of worship in the whole world do not equal St. Sophia in riches. It is ornamented with pillars of gold and silver, and with innumerable lamps of the same precious materials.

The Hippodrome is a public place near the wall of the palace, set aside for the king's sports. Every year the birthday of Jesus the Nazarene is celebrated there with public rejoicings. On these occasions you may see there representations of all the nations who inhabit the different parts of the world, with surprising feats of jugglery. Lions, bears, leopards, and wild asses, as well as birds, which have been trained to fight each other, are also exhibited. All this sport, the equal of which is nowhere to be met with, is carried on in the presence of the king and the queen.

King Manuel has built a large palace for his residence on the sea-shore, near the palace built by his predecessors; and to this edifice is given the name of Blachernes. The pillars and walls are covered with pure gold, and all the wars of the ancients, as well as his own wars, are represented in pictures. The throne in this palace is of gold, and ornamented with precious stones; a golden crown hangs over it, suspended on a chain of the same material, the length of which exactly admits the emperor to sit under it. This crown is ornamented with precious stones of inestimable value. Such is the lustre of these diamonds, that, even without any other light, they illumine the room in which they are kept. Other objects of curiosity are met with here which it would be impossible to describe adequately.

The tribute, which is brought to Constantinople every year from all parts of Greece, consisting of silks, and purple cloths, and gold, fills many towers. These riches and buildings are equalled nowhere in the world. They say that the tribute of the city alone amounts every day to twenty thousand florins, arising from rents of hostelries and bazaars, and from the duties paid by merchants who arrive by sea and by land. The Greeks who inhabit the country are extremely rich, and possess great wealth in gold and precious stones. They dress in garments of silk, ornamented with gold and other valuable materials. They ride upon horses, and in their appearance they are like princes. The country is rich, producing all sorts of delicacies, as well as abundance of bread, meat, and wine. They are well skilled in the Greek sciences, and live comfortably, "every man under his vine and his fig tree." The Greeks hire soldiers of all nations, whom they call barbarians, for the purpose of carrying on their wars with the sultan of the Thogarmim, who are called Turks. They have no martial spirit themselves, and, like women, are unfit for warlike enterprises. . . .

No Jews dwell in the city with them; they are obliged to reside beyond the one arm of the sea, where they are shut in by the channel of Sophia on one side, and they can reach the city by water only, when they want to visit it for purposes of trade. The number of Jews at Constantinople amounts to two thousand Rabbanites and five hundred Caraites, who live on one spot, but divided by a wall. The principal of the Rabbanites, who are learned in the law, are the rabbi Abtalion, Obadiah, Aaron Khuspo, Joseph Sargeno and Eliakim the elder. Many of them are manufacturers of silk cloth, many others are merchants, some being extremely rich; but no Jew is allowed to ride upon a horse, except Solomon Hamitsri, who is the king's physician, and by whose influence the Jews enjoy many advantages even in their state of oppression, which is very severely felt by them; and the hatred against them is increased by the practise of the tanners, who pour out their filthy water in the streets and even before the very doors of the Jews, who, being thus defiled, become objects of contempt to the Greeks.

Their yoke is severely felt by the Jews, both good and bad; for they are exposed to be beaten in the streets, and must submit to all sorts of bad treatment. Still the Jews are rich, good, benevolent, and religious men, who bear the misfortunes of their exile with humility. The quarter inhabited by the Jews is called Pera.

Two days from Constantinople stands Rodosto, containing a congregation of about four hundred Jews, the principal of whom are Moses, Abijah and Jacob. From hence it is two days to Gallipoli. Of the two hundred Jews of this city the principal are Elijah Kapid, Shabthai the little, and Isaac Megas; this latter term in the Greek language means tall.

To Kilia, two days. The principal of the fifty Jews who inhabit this place are Juda, Jacob and Shemaiah. It is hence two days to Mitilene, one of the islands of the sea. Ten places in this island contain Jewish congregations. Three days from thence is situated the island of Chio, containing about four hundred Jews, the principal of whom are Elijah, Theman and Shabthai. The trees which yield mastic are found here. Two days bring us to the island of Samos, which contains about three hundred Jews, the chief of whom are Shemaria, Obadiah and Joel. These islands contain many congregations of Jews.

It is three days hence by sea to Rhodes. The principal of the four hundred Jews who reside here are Aba, Chananel and Elijah. From here it is four days to Cyprus. Besides the Rabbanitic Jews in this island, there is a community of heretic Jews called Kaphrosein, or Cyprians. They are Epicureans, and the orthodox Jews excommunicate them.

These sectarians profane the evening of the Sabbath and keep holy that of the Sunday.

We next come in two days to Corycus, the frontier of Aram, which is called Armenia. Here are the confines of the empire of Toros, king of the mountains, sovereign of Armenia, whose rule extends to the city of Dhuchia and the country of the Thogarmim, or Turks. Two days further is Malmistras, which is Thersoos, situated on the coast. Thus far reaches the empire of the Javanites, who are called Greeks.

The large city of Antioch is distant two days hence. It stands on the banks of the Makloub, which river flows down from Mount Lebanon, from the country of Hamah. The city was founded by King Antiochus, and is overlooked by a very high mountain. A wall surrounds this height, on the summit of which is situated a well. The inspector of the well distributes the water by subterranean aqueducts, and thus provides the houses of the principal inhabitants of the city. The other side of the city is surrounded by the river. This place is very strongly fortified, and in the possession of Prince Boemond Poitevin, surnamed le Baube [Boemond III]. It contains about ten Jews, who are glass manufacturers, and the principal of whom are Mordecai, Chaiim and Ishmael.

Two days bring us from thence to Lega, which is Latachia, and contains about two hundred Jews, the principal of whom are Chiia and Joseph. Then it is two days to Jebilee, the Baal Gad of Scripture, under Mount Lebanon.

In this vicinity reside the people called Assassins, who do not believe in the tenets of Mahometanism, but in those of one whom they consider like unto the prophet Kharmath. They fulfil whatever he commands them, whether it be a matter of life or death. He goes by the name of Sheikh-al-

Hashishin, or their Old Man, by whose commands all the acts of these mountaineers are regulated. His residence is in the city of Kadmus, the Kedemoth of Scripture, in the land of Sichon. The Assassins are faithful to one another by the command of their Old Man, and make themselves the dread of every one, because their devotion leads them gladly to risk their lives, and to kill even kings when commanded.[1] The extent of their country is eight days' journey. They are at war with the Christians, called Franks, and with the Count of Tripoli, which is Tarablous el Sham. Some time ago Tripoli was visited by an earthquake, which destroyed many Jews and Gentiles, numbers of the inhabitants being killed by the falling houses and walls, under the ruins of which they were buried. More than twenty thousand persons were killed in Palestine by this earthquake.

One day's journey to the other Jebail, which was the Gebal of the children of Ammon; it contains about one hundred and fifty Jews, and is governed by seven Genoese, the supreme command being vested in one of them named Julianus Embriaco. You there find the ancient place of worship of the children of Ammon. The idol of this people is seated on a cathedra, or throne, constructed of stone and richly gilt; two female figures occupy the seats on his side, one being on the right, the other on the left, and before it stands an altar, upon which the children of Ammon anciently offered sacrifices and burned incense. The city contains about two hundred Jews, the principal of whom are Meir, Jacob and Szimchah. It stands on the coast of the sea of the Holy Land. Two days hence is Beyrut, which is Beeroth. The principal of its fifty Jewish inhabitants are Solomon, Obadiah and Joseph. It is hence one day's jour-

1 The Old Man of the Mountains and his "paradise" are described in *Marco Polo*, p. 53.

ney to Saida, which is Sidon of Scripture, a large city, with about twenty Jewish inhabitants.

Within twenty miles of this place reside a people who are at war with the inhabitants of Sidon, and who are called Druses. They are called heathens and unbelievers, because they confess no religion. Their dwellings are on the summits of the mountains and in the ridges of the rocks, and they are subject to no king or prince. Mount Hermon, a distance of three days' journey, is the boundary of their territory. This people live incestuously; a father cohabits with his own daughter, and once every year all men and women assemble to celebrate a festival, upon which occasion, after eating and drinking, they hold promiscuous intercourse. They say that the soul of a virtuous man is transferred to the body of a new-born child; whereas that of the wicked transmigrates into a dog or some other animal. This their way is their folly.

Jews have no permanent residence among them, although some tradesmen and a few dyers travel through the country occasionally, to carry on their trades or sell goods, and return home when their business is done. The Druses are friendly towards the Jews; they are so nimble in climbing hills and mountains that nobody can successfully carry on war against them.

One day's journey to New Sur, a very beautiful city the port of which is in the town itself, and is guarded by two towers, within which the vessels ride at anchor. The officers of the customs draw an iron chain from tower to tower every night, thus effectually preventing any thieves or robbers from escape by boats or by other means. There is no port in the world equal to this. About four hundred Jews reside here, the principal of whom are the judge Ephraim Mitsri, Meier of Carcasson, and Abraham, the elder of the community. The Jews of Sur are shipowners and manufacturers of the celebrated Tyrian glass; the purple dye is also found in this vicinity. If you mount the walls of New Sur, you may see the remains of "Tyre the crowning," which was inundated by the sea; it is about the distance of a stone's throw from the new town, and whoever embarks may observe the towers, the markets, the streets, and the halls at the bottom of the sea. The city of New Sur is very commercial, and one to which traders resort from all parts.

It is one day hence to Acre, the Acco of Scripture, on the confines of the tribe of Asher. It is the frontier town of Palestine; and, in consequence of its situation on the shore of the Mediterranean and of its large port, it is the principal place of disembarkation of all pilgrims who visit Jerusalem by sea. A river called Kishon runs near the city. There are here about two hundred Jewish inhabitants, of whom Zadok, Jepheth and Jona are the principal.

Three parasangs further is Kaiffa, which is Gath Hachepher. One side of this city is situated on the coast, on the other it is overlooked by Mount Carmel. Under the mountain are many Jewish sepulchres, and near the summit is the cavern of Elija, upon whom be peace. Two Christians have built a place of worship near this site, which they call St. Elias. On the summit of the hill you may still trace the site of the altar which was rebuilt by Elija of blessed memory, in the time of King Ahab, and the circumference of which is about four yards. The river Mukattua runs down the mountain and along its base. It is four parasangs to Khephar Thanchum, which is Capernaum, identical with Meon, the place of abode of Nabal the Carmelite.

Six parasangs brings us to Cæsarea, the Gath of the Philistines of Scripture, inhabited by about ten Jews and two hundred Cutheans. The latter are Samaritan Jews, commonly called Samaritans. This city is very elegant and beautiful, situated on the sea-shore, and was built by King Herod, who called it Cæsarea in honour of the emperor, or Cæsar. To Kakun, the Keilah of Scripture, half a day's journey; in this place are no Jews. To St. George, the ancient Luz, half a day's journey. One Jew only, a dyer, lives here. To Sebaste, one day's journey. This is the ancient Shomron, where you may still trace the site of the palace of Ahab, king of Israel. It was formerly a very strong city, and is situated on a mount, in a fine country, richly watered, and surrounded with gardens, orchards, vineyards, and olive-groves. No Jews live here.

It is two parasangs further to Nablous, the ancient Sichem, on Mount Ephraim. This place contains no Jewish inhabitants, and is situated in the valley between Mount Gerizim and Mount Ebal. It is the abode of about one hundred Cutheans, who observe the Mosaic law only, and are called Samaritans. They have priests, descendants of Aaron the priest of blessed memory, whom they call Aaronim. These do not intermarry with any other but priestly families; but they are priests only of their own law, who offer sacrifices and burnt-offerings in their synagogue on Mount Gerizim. They do this in accordance with the words of Scripture, "Thou shalt put the blessing on Mount Gerizim," and they pretend that this is the holy temple. On Passover and holidays they offer burnt-offerings on the altar which they have erected on Mount Gerizim, from the stones put up by the children of Israel after they had crossed the Jordan. They pretend to be of the tribe of Ephraim, and are in possession of the tomb of Joseph the righteous, the son of our father Jacob, upon whom be peace, as is proved by the following passage of Scripture, "The bones of Joseph, which the children of Israel brought up with them from Egypt, they buried in Sichem."

The Samaritans do not possess the three letters He, Cheth, and Ain; the He of the name of our father Abraham, and they have no glory; the Cheth of the name of our father Isaac, in consequence of which they are devoid of piety; the Ain of the name of Jacob, for they want humility. Instead of these letters, they always put an Aleph, by which you may know that they are not of Jewish origin, because, in their knowledge of the law of Moses they are deficient in three letters. This sect carefully avoid being defiled by touching corpses, bones, those killed by accident, or graves; and they change their daily garments whenever they visit their synagogue, upon which occasion they wash their body and put on other clothes. These are their daily habits.

Mount Gerizim is rich in wells and orchards, whereas Mount Ebal is dry like stone and rock. The city of Nablous lies in the valley between these two hills. Four parasangs from there is situated Mount Gilboa, which Christians call Monto Jelbon. The country in this part is very barren. Five parasangs further is the valley of Ajalon, called by the Christians Val de Luna. One parasang to Gran David, formerly the large city of Gibeon. It contains no Jewish inhabitants.

From thence it is three parasangs to Jerusalem, a small city strongly fortified with three walls. It contains a numerous population, composed of Jacobites, Armenians, Greeks, Georgians, Franks, and indeed of people of all tongues. The dyeing-house is rented by the year, and the exclusive privilege of dyeing is purchased from the king by the Jews of Jerusalem, two hundred of whom dwell in one corner of the city, under the tower of David. About ten yards of the base of this building are very ancient, having been con-

structed by our ancestors; the remaining part was added by
the Mahometans. The city contains no building stronger
than the tower of David.

There are at Jerusalem two hospitals, which support four
hundred knights, and afford shelter to the sick; these are
provided with everything they may want, both during life
and in death; the second is called the hospital of Solomon,
being the palace originally built by King Solomon. This
hospital also harbours and furnishes four hundred knights,
who are ever ready to wage war, over and above those knights
who arrive from the country of the Franks and other parts
of Christendom. These generally have taken a vow upon
themselves to stay a year or two, and they remain until the
period of their vow is expired. The large place of worship,
called Sepulchre, and containing the sepulchre of that man
[Jesus], is visited by all pilgrims.

Jerusalem has four gates, called the gates of Abraham,
David, Sion, and Jehoshaphat. The latter stands opposite
the place of the holy temple, which is occupied at present
by a building called Templo Domino. Omar Ben Al-Khataab erected a large and handsome cupola over it, and nobody
is allowed to introduce any image or painting into this place,
it being set aside for prayers only. In front of it you see
the western wall, one of the walls which formed the Holy of
Holies of the ancient temple; it is called the Gate of Mercy,
and all Jews resort thither to say their prayers near the wall
of the courtyard. At Jerusalem you also see the stables
erected by Solomon, and which formed part of his house.
Immense stones have been employed in this building, the
like of which are nowhere else to be met with. You further
see to this day vestiges of the canal near which the sacrifices
were slaughtered in ancient times; and all Jews inscribe their
names upon an adjacent wall. If you leave the city by the

gate of Jehoshaphat, you may see the pillar erected on Absalom's place, and the sepulchre of King Uzziah, and the great spring of Shiloah, which runs into the brook Kedron. Over this spring is a large building erected in the times of our forefathers. Very little water is found at Jerusalem; the inhabitants generally drink rain water, which they collect in their houses.

From the Valley of Jehoshaphat the traveller immediately ascends the Mount of Olives, as this valley only intervenes between the city and the mount. From here the Dead Sea is distinctly visible. Two parasangs from the sea stands the salt pillar into which Lot's wife was metamorphosed; and although the sheep continually lick it, the pillar grows again, and retains its original state. You also have a prospect over the whole valley of the Dead Sea, and of the brook of Shittim, even as far as Mount Nebo. Mount Sion is also near Jerusalem, upon the acclivity of which stands no building except a place of worship of the Nazarenes. The traveller further sees there three Jewish cemeteries, where formerly the dead were buried; some of the sepulchres had stones with inscriptions upon them, but the Christians destroy these monuments, and use the stones in building their houses.

Jerusalem is surrounded by high mountains. On Mount Sion are the sepulchres of the house of David, and those of the kings who reigned after him. In consequence of the following circumstance, however, this place is at present hardly to be recognized. Fifteen years ago, one of the walls of the place of worship on Mount Sion fell down, and the patriarch commanded the priest to repair it. He ordered stones to be taken from the original wall of Sion for that purpose, and twenty workmen were hired at stated wages, who broke stones from the very foundation of the walls of Sion.

Two of these labourers, who were intimate friends, upon a certain day treated one another, and repaired to their work after their friendly meal. The overseer accused them of dilatoriness, but they answered that they would still perform their day's work, and would employ thereupon the time while their fellow labourers were at meals. They then continued to break out stones, until, happening to meet with one which formed the mouth of a cavern, they agreed to enter it in search of treasure, and they proceeded until they reached a large hall, supported by pillars of marble, encrusted with gold and silver, and before which stood a table, with a golden sceptre and crown. This was the sepulchre of David, king of Israel, to the left of which they saw that of Solomon in a similar state, and so on the sepulchres of all the kings of Juda, who were buried there. They further saw chests locked up, the contents of which nobody knew, and were on the point of entering the hall, when a blast of wind like a storm issued forth from the mouth of the cavern so strong that it threw them down almost lifeless on the ground.

There they lay until evening, when another wind rushed forth, from which they heard a voice like that of a man calling aloud, "Get up, and go forth from this place." The men rushed out full of fear, and proceeded to the patriarch to report what happened to them. This ecclesiastic summoned into his presence Abraham el-Constantini, a pious ascetic, one of the mourners of the downfall of Jerusalem, and caused the two labourers to repeat what they had previously reported. Abraham thereupon informed the patriarch that they had discovered the sepulchres of the house of David and of the kings of Juda.

The following morning the labourers were sent for again, but they were found stretched on their beds and still full of fear; they declared that they would not attempt to go again to the cave, as it was not God's will to discover it to any one. The patriarch ordered the place to be walled up, so as to hide it effectually from every one unto the present day. The above-mentioned Abraham told me all this.

Two parasangs from Jerusalem is Bethlehem of Judæa, called Beth-lehem; and within half a mile of it, where several roads meet, stands the monument which points out the grave of Rachel. This monument is constructed of eleven stones, equal to the number of the children of Jacob. It is covered by a cupola, which rests upon four pillars; and every Jew who passes there inscribes his name on the stones of the monument.

Twelve Jews, dyers by profession, live at Bethlehem. The country abounds with rivulets, wells, and springs of water. Six parasangs further is Hebron. The ancient city of that name was situated on the hill, and lies in ruins at present; whereas the modern town stands in the valley, even in the field of Machpelah. Here is the large place of worship called St. Abraham, which during the time of the Mahometans was a synagogue. The Gentiles have erected six sepulchres in this place, which they pretend to be those of Abraham and Sarah, of Isaac and Rebecca, and of Jacob and Leah; the pilgrims are told that they are the sepulchres of the fathers, and money is extorted from them. But if any Jew come, who gives an additional fee to the keeper of the cave, an iron door is opened, which dates from the times of our forefathers who rest in peace, and with a burning candle in his hands, the visitor descends into a first cave, which is empty, traverses a second in the same state, and at last reaches a third, which contains six sepulchres, those of Abraham, Isaac, and Jacob, and of Sarah, Rebecca, and Leah, one opposite the other.

All these sepulchres bear inscriptions, the letters being

engraved: thus, upon that of Abraham, we read, "This is the sepulchre of our father Abraham, upon whom be peace"; and so on that of Isaac and upon all the other sepulchres. A lamp burns in the cave and upon the sepulchres continually, both night and day; and you there see tubs filled with the bones of Israelites, for unto this day it is a custom of the house of Israel to bring thither the bones of their relicts and of their forefathers, and to leave them there. On the confines of the field of Machpelah stands the house of our father Abraham, who rests in peace; before which house there is a spring, and, out of respect to Abraham, nobody is allowed to construct any building on that site.

It is five parasangs hence to Beit Jaberim, the ancient Mareshah, where there are but three Jewish inhabitants. Five parasangs further bring us to Toron de los Caballeros, which is Shunem, inhabited by three hundred Jews. We then proceed three parasangs to St. Samuel of Shiloh, the ancient Shiloh, within two parasangs of Jerusalem. When the Christians took Ramleh, which is Ramah, from the Mahometans, they discovered the sepulchre of Samuel the Ramathi near the Jewish synagogue, and removed his remains to Shiloh, where they erected a large place of worship over them, called St. Samuel of Shiloh to the present day. It is three parasangs to Pesipua, which is Gibeah of Saul, or Geba of Benjamin; it contains no Jews. Three parasangs to Beith Nubi, which is Nob, the city of the priests. In the middle of the road are the two rocks of Jonathan, the name of one of which is Botsets, and of the other Séné. The two Jews who live here are dyers.

It is three parasangs from here to Ramleh, which is Harama, where you still find walls erected by our forefathers, as is evident from the inscriptions upon the stones. The city

contains about three Jews; but it was formerly very considerable, for a Jewish cemetery in its vicinity is two miles in
extent. Five parasangs hence to Jaffa, the Japho of Scripture, on the coast; one Jew only, a dyer by profession, lives
here. Three parasangs to Ibelin, the ancient Jabneh, where
the site of the schools may still be traced; it contains no Jews.
Here was the frontier of the tribe of Ephraim. Two parasangs to Palmis, or Asdoud, formerly a city of the Philistines, at present in ruins, and containing no Jews. Two
parasangs to Ascalon, which is in fact the New Ascalon, built
on the coast by Ezra the priest, of blessed memory, and
originally called Benebra, distant about four parasangs from
ancient Ascalon, which lies in ruins. This city is very large
and handsome; and merchants from all parts resort to it,
on account of its convenient situation on the confines of
Egypt. There are here about two hundred Rabbanite Jews,
of whom the principal are Tsemach, Aaron and Solomon,
besides about forty Caraites, and about three hundred
Cutheans, or Samaritans. In the city is a fountain called Bir
Ibrahim-al-Khahil, which was dug in the time of the Philistines.

From here to St. George, which is Lydda, and in one day
and a half to Serain, the Jezreel of Scripture, a city containing a remarkably large fountain. It has one Jewish
inhabitant, a dyer. Three parasangs to Sufurieh, the Tsip-
pori of antiquity. The sepulchres of Rabenu Hakkadosh,
of Chija, who came back from Babylon, and of Jonah the
son of Amittai the prophet, are shown here; they are buried
in the mountain, which also contains numerous other sepulchres.

From hence it is five parasangs to Tiberias, a city situated
on the Jordan, which here bears the name of the Sea of
Chinnereth, or Lake of Tiberias. Here are the falls of the

Jordan, in consequence of which the place bears also the name of Ashdoth-Pisga, which means "the place where the rapid rivers have their fall." The Jordan afterwards empties itself into Lake Asphaltes, or the Dead Sea. Tiberias contains about fifty Jews, the principal of whom are Abraham the astronomer, Muchthar and Isaac. The hot waters, which spout forth from underground, are called the warm baths of Tiberias. In the vicinity is the synagogue of Khaleb, son of Jepuneh; and among numerous other Jewish sepulchres are those of Jochanan, son of Zakhai, and of Jonathan, son of Levi. These are all in Lower Galilee.

Two parasangs bring us to Tebnin, the Thimnatha of Scripture, where you find the sepulchre of Samuel [Simeon] the Just, and many other sepulchres of Israelites. It is then one day to Gish, which is Gush Chaleb, and contains about twenty Jewish inhabitants. We go six parasangs to Meroon, which is Maron; in a cave near this place are the sepulchres of Hillel and Shamai, and of twenty of their disciples, as well as those of Benjamin, son of Jephet, and of Juda, son of Bethera. Six parasangs to Alma, which contains fifty Jewish inhabitants, and a large cemetery of the Israelites. Half a day brings you to Kades, which is Kadesh Naphthali, on the banks of the Jordan. Here are the sepulchres of Eleasar, son of Arach, of Eleasar, son of Asariah, of Chuni Hamaagal, of Simeon, son of Gamaliel, of Jose Hagelili, and of Barak the son of Abinoam. This place contains no Jews.

A day's journey brings us to Belinas, the ancient Dan, where the traveller may see a cave, from which the Jordan issues, and three miles on this river unites its waters with those of the Arnon, a rivulet of the ancient land of Moab. In front of the cave you may still trace vestiges of the altar of the image of Micha, which was adored by the children of

Dan in ancient times. Here also is the site of the altar erected by Jeroboam, son of Nebat, in honour of the golden calf; and here were the confines of the land of Israel toward the uttermost sea.

Two days from this place brings you to Damascus, a large city and the frontier town of the empire of Noureddin, king of the Thogarmim, or Turks. This city is very large and handsome, and is inclosed with a wall and surrounded by a beautiful country, which in a circuit of fifteen miles presents the richest gardens and orchards, in such numbers and beauty as to be without equal upon earth. The rivers Amana and Parpar, the sources of which are on Mount Hermon, on which the city leans, run down here. The Amana follows its course through Damascus, and its waters are carried by means of pipes into the houses of the principal inhabitants, as well as into the streets and markets. A considerable trade is carried on here by merchants of all countries. The Parpar runs between the gardens and orchards in the outskirts, and supplies them copiously with water.

Damascus contains a Mahometan mosque, called "the Synagogue of Damascus," a building of unequalled magnificence. They say that it was the palace of Ben-Hadad, and that one wall of it is framed of glass by enchantment. This wall contains as many openings as there are days in the solar year, and the sun in gradual succession throws its light into the openings, which are divided into twelve degrees, equal to the number of the hours of the day, so that by this contrivance everybody may know what time it is.

The palace contains vessels richly ornamented with gold and silver, formed like tubs, and of a size to allow three persons to bathe in them at once. In this building is also preserved the rib of a giant, which measures nine spans in length, and two in breadth, and which belonged to an ancient

giant king named Abchamas, whose name was found engraved upon a stone of his tomb, and it was further stated
in the inscription that he reigned over the whole world.

This city contains three thousand Jews, many of whom are
learned and rich men; it is the residence of the president of
the university of Palestine, named Ezra, whose brother, Sar
Shalom, is the principal of the Jewish court of law. The
other distinguished Jews are Joseph, who ranges fifth in
the university, Matsliach, the lecturer and master of the
schools, Meir, a flower of the learned, Joseph Ibn Pilath,
who may be called the prop of the university, Heman the
elder, and Zadok the physician. The city contains also two
hundred Caraites and about four hundred Samaritans, sects
which here live upon friendly terms, but they do not intermarry.

It is one day's journey thence to Jelaad, which is Gilead;
it contains about sixty Jews, the principal of whom is Zadok.
The city is large, well watered, and surrounded by gardens
and orchards. Half a day's journey further stands Salkhat,
the city of Salcah of Scripture.

From thence to Baalbec is half a day's journey. This is
the city mentioned in Scripture as Baalath in the valley of
Lebanon, which Solomon built for the daughter of Pharaoh.
The palace is constructed of stones of enormous size, measuring twenty spans in length and twelve in breadth; no binding
material holds these stones together, and people pretend that
the building could have been erected only by the help of
Ashmodai. A copious spring takes its rise at the upper side
of the city, through which its waters rush like those of a
considerable river. They are employed in the working of
several mills within the city, which also incloses numerous
gardens and orchards.

Tadmor in the desert was also built by Solomon of equally

large stones; this city is surrounded by a wall, and stands in the desert, far from any inhabited place, being four days' journey distant from the above-mentioned Baalath. It contains two thousand warlike Jews, who are at war with the Christians and with the Arabian subjects of Noureddin, and assist their neighbours the Mahometans. Their chiefs are Isaac Hajevani, Nathan and Usiel.

Half a day brings us to Cariyatin, which is Kirjathaim; one Jew only, a dyer by profession, lives there. One day hence is Hamah, the Hamath of Scripture, on the Orontes, under Mount Lebanon. Some time ago this city was visited by an earthquake, in consequence of which fifteen thousand men died in one day, leaving only seventy survivors. The principals of the Jews here are Ulah Hacohen, the sheikh Abu al Galeb, and Muktar. Half a day to Reiha, which is Hazor.

Three pasarangs to Lamdin, from whence it is a journey of two days to Aleppo, the Aram Zoba of Scripture. This city is the residence of King Noureddin, and contains his palace, a building fortified by an extraordinarily high wall. There being neither spring nor river, the inhabitants are obliged to drink rain water, which is collected in every house in a cistern called in Arabic, *algub*. The principal of the fifteen hundred Jews who live in Aleppo are Moses el-Constandini, Israel and Seth.

To Bales, which is Pethor on the Euphrates, two days. Even at this day you there still find remains of the tower of Balaam the son of Beor—may the name of the wicked rot!—which he built in accordance with the hours of the day. This place contains about ten Jews. Half a day hence we come to Kala Jiaber, which is Sela Midbarah. This city remained in the power of the Arabs even at the time when the Thogarmim took their country and dispersed them in the desert.

It contains about two thousand Jews, of whom Zedekiah, Chia and Solomon are the principal.

One day brings us to Racca, which is Calneh of Scripture, on the confines of Mesopotamia, being the frontier town between that country and the empire of the Thogarmim; it contains about seven hundred Jewish inhabitants, the principal of whom are Sakhai, Nadib, who is blind, and Joseph. One of the synagogues was built by Ezra the scribe, when he returned to Jerusalem from Babylon.

It is one day hence to the ancient place of Haran, which contains twenty Jewish inhabitants, who also possess a synagogue erected by Ezra. Nobody is allowed to construct any building on the spot where the house of our father Abraham was situated; even the Mahometans pay respect to the place, and resort thither to pray.

Two days' journey from there to the mouth of the El-Khabur, the Habor of Scripture. This river takes its course through Media, and loses itself in the Kizil Ozein. About two hundred Jews dwell near this place. Two days to Nisibin, a large city plentifully watered, and containing about one thousand Jews. Two days to Jezireh Ben Omar, an island in the Tigris, at the foot of Mount Ararat, and four miles distant from the spot where the ark of Noah rested. Omar Ben Al-Khataab removed the ark from the summit of the two mountains and made a mosque of it.

There still exists in the vicinity of the ark a synagogue of Ezra the scribe, which is visited by the Jews of the city on the ninth of Ab [the day which marks the destruction of the temples in Jerusalem]. The city of Jezireh Omar Ben Al-Khataab contains about four thousand Jews, the principals of whom are Mubchar, Joseph and Chiia.

Two days from thence stands Mosul, mentioned in Scripture as Ashur the great, which contains about seven thousand

Jews, the principal of whom are Sakhai, the prince, a descendant of King David, and Joseph, surnamed Borhan-al-Jhulkh, who is astronomer of Seifeddin, the brother of Noureddin, king of Damascus. This city, situated on the confines of Persia, is of great extent and very ancient; it stands on the banks of the Tigris, and is joined by a bridge to Nineveh. Although the latter lies in ruins, there are numerous inhabited villages and small towns on its site.

Nineveh is on the Tigris, distant one parasang from the town of Arbil [Erbela]. Mosul contains the synagogues of Obadiah, of Jonah, son of Amittai, and of Nahum the Elkoshite. It is three days to Rahabah, which is Rehoboth, by the river Euphrates, and contains about two thousand Jews, the principal of whom are Ezekiah, Ehud and Isaac. The city is surrounded by a wall, it is very handsome, large, and well fortified; and the environs abound with gardens and orchards. One day to Karkisia, the Carchemish of Scripture, on the banks of the Euphrates, containing about five hundred Jewish inhabitants, of whom the principal are Isaac and Elchanan.

Two days to Juba, which is Pumbeditha, in Nehardea; it contains about two thousand Jews, some of them eminent scholars. The rabbi Chen, Moses and Eliakim are the principal. Here the traveller may see the sepulchres of Juda and Samuel, opposite two synagogues which they erected during their lives; as well as the sepulchres of Bosthenai, the prince of the captivity, of Nathan, and of Nachman, the son of Papa.

Five days to Hardah, or Hadrah, containing fifteen thousand Jews, of whom Saken, Joseph and Nathaniel are the principal. Two days to Akbara, the city which was built by Jeconiah, king of Juda; it contains about ten thousand Jews, the principal of whom are Joshua and Nathan.

Two days from thence stands Bagdad, the large metropolis of the Calif Emir-al-Mumenin al Abassi, of the family of their prophet, who is the chief of the Mahometan religion. All Mahometan kings acknowledge him, and he holds the same dignity over them which the Pope enjoys over the Christians. The palace of the Calif at Bagdad is three miles in extent. It contains a large park filled with all sorts of trees, both useful and ornamental, and all kinds of beasts, as well as a pond of water carried thither from the river Tigris; and whenever the calif desires to enjoy himself and to sport and carouse, birds, beasts, and fishes are prepared for him and for his courtiers, whom he invites to his palace.

This great Abasside is extremely friendly towards the Jews, many of his officers being of that nation; he understands all languages, is well versed in the Mosaic law, and reads and writes the Hebrew tongue. He enjoys nothing but what he earns by the labour of his own hands, and therefore manufactures coverlets, which he stamps with his seal, and which his officers sell in the public market. These articles are purchased by the nobles of the land, and from their profit his necessaries are provided. The calif is an excellent man, trustworthy and kind-hearted towards every one, but generally invisible to the Mahometans.

The pilgrims, who come hither from distant countries on their way to Mecca in Yemen, desire to be presented to him, and thus address him from the palace: "Our lord, light of the Mahometans and splendour of our religion, show us the brightness of thy countenance"; but he does not heed their words. His servants and officers then approach and pray: "O lord, manifest thy peace to these men who come from distant lands and desire shelter in the shadow of thy glory."

After this petition, he rises and puts one corner of his garment out of the window, which the pilgrims eagerly kiss.

One of the lords then addresses them thus: "Go in peace, for our lord, the light of the Mahometans, is well pleased and gives you his blessing." This prince being esteemed by them equal to their prophet, they proceed on their way, full of joy at the words addressed to them by the lord who communicated the message of peace.

All the brothers and other members of the calif's family are accustomed to kiss his garments. Every one of them possesses a palace within that of the calif, but they are all bound with chains of iron, and a special officer is appointed over each household to prevent their rising in rebellion against the great king. These measures are taken in consequence of what occurred some time ago, when the brothers rebelled and elected a king among themselves; to prevent this in future, it was decreed that all the members of the calif's family should be chained, in order to prevent their rebellious intentions. Every one of them, however, resides in his palace, and is there much honoured; and they possess villages and towns, the rents of which are collected for them by their stewards. They eat and drink, and lead a merry life. The palace of the great king contains large buildings, pillars of gold and silver, and treasures of precious stones.

The calif leaves his palace but once every year, namely, at the time of the feast called Ramadan; on which occasion many visitors assemble from distant parts, in order to have an opportunity of beholding his countenance. He then bestrides the royal mule, dressed in kingly robes, which are composed of gold and silver cloth. On his head he wears a turban, ornamented with precious stones of inestimable value; but over this turban is thrown a black veil, as a sign of humility, and as much as to say: "See all this worldly honour will be converted into darkness on the day of death."

He is accompanied by a numerous retinue of Mahometan

nobles, arrayed in rich dresses and riding upon horses, princes of Arabia, of Media, of Persia, and even of Tibet, a country distant three months' journey from Arabia. The procession goes from the palace to the mosque at the Bozra gate, which is the metropolitan mosque. All who walk in procession, both men and women, are dressed in silk and purple. The streets and squares are enlivened with singing and rejoicing, and by parties who dance before the great calif. He is saluted loudly by the assembled crowd, who cry: "Blessed art thou, our lord and king." He thereupon kisses his garment, and by holding it in his hand, acknowledges and returns the compliment.

The procession moves on into the court of the mosque, where the calif mounts a wooden pulpit and expounds their law unto them. The learned Mahometans rise, pray for him, and praise his great kindness and piety; upon which the whole assembly answer, "Amen!" The calif then pronounces his blessing, and kills a camel, which is led thither for that purpose, and this is their offering. It is distributed to the nobles, who send portions of it to their friends who are eager to taste of the meat killed by the hands of their holy king, and are much rejoiced therewith.

The calif, after this ceremony, leaves the mosque, and returns alone, along the banks of the Tigris, to his palace; the noble Mahometans accompanying him in boats, until he enters this building. He never returns by the way he came; and the path on the bank of the river is carefully guarded all the year round, so as to prevent any one treading in his footsteps. The calif never leaves his palace again for a whole year. He is a pious and benevolent man, and has erected buildings on the other side of the river, on the banks of an arm of the Euphrates, which runs on one side of the city. These buildings include many large houses, streets, and hostelries for the sick poor, who resort thither in order to be cured. There are about sixty medical warehouses here, all well provided from the king's stores with spices and other necessaries; and every patient who claims assistance is fed at the king's expense, until his cure is completed.

There is further a large building, called Dar-al-Maraphtan, in which are confined all the insane persons who are met with, particularly during the hot season, every one of whom is secured by iron chains until his reason returns, when he is allowed to return to his home. For this purpose they are regularly examined once a month by officers appointed by the king for that purpose; and when they are found to be possessed of reason they are immediately liberated. All this is done by the king in pure charity towards all who come to Bagdad, either ill or insane; for the king is a pious man, and his intention is excellent in this respect.

Bagdad contains about one thousand Jews, who enjoy peace, comfort, and much honour under the government of the great king. Among them are very wise men and presidents of the colleges, whose occupation is the study of the Mosaic law. The city contains ten colleges. The principal of the great college is the rabbi Samuel, the son of Eli, principal of the college Geon Jacob; the provost of the Levites is the president of the second; Daniel, the master of the third college; Eleasar, the fellow, presides over the fourth; Eleasar, the son of Tsemach, is chief of the fifth college; he is master of the studies, and possesses a pedigree of his descent from the prophet Samuel, who rests in peace, and he and his brothers know the melodies that were sung in the temple during its existence. Chasadiah, principal fellow, is the master of the sixth; Chagai, the prince, the principal of the seventh, and Ezra, the president of the eighth college; Abraham, called Abu Tahir, presides over the ninth, and

Zakhai, son of Bosthenai, master of the studies, is president of the tenth college. All these are called Batlanim, which means, the Idle: because their sole occupation consists in the discharge of public business. During every day of the week they dispense justice to all the Jewish inhabitants of the country, except Monday, which is set aside for assemblies under the presidency of the rabbi Samuel, master of the college Geon Jacob, who on that day dispenses justice to every applicant, and is assisted therein by the other Batlanim, presidents of the colleges.

The principal of all these, however, is Daniel, the son of Chisdai, who bears the titles of Prince of the Captivity and Lord, and who possesses a pedigree which proves his descent from King David. The Jews call him "Lord, Prince of the Captivity," and the Mahometans entitle him Saidna Ben Daoud, noble descendant of David. He holds great command over all Jewish congregations under the authority of the Emir-al-Mumenin, the lord of the Mahometans, who has commanded that he shall be respected, and has confirmed his power by granting him a seal of office.

Every one of his subjects, whether he be Jew or Mahometan or of any other faith, is commanded to rise in the presence of the prince of the captivity, and to salute him respectfully, under a penalty of one hundred stripes. Whenever he pays a visit to the king, he is escorted by numerous horsemen, both Jews and Gentiles, and a crier proclaims aloud: "Make way before our lord the son of David, as becomes his dignity"; in Arabic, *Amilu tarik la-saidna ben-Daud*. Upon these occasions he rides upon a horse, and his dress is composed of embroidered silk; on his head he wears a large turban covered with a white cloth, and surmounted by a chain, or diadem. The authority of the prince of the captivity extends over the countries of Mesopotamia, Persia,

Khorassan, Seba, which is Yemen, Diarbekh, all Armenia and the land of Kota near Mount Ararat, over the country of the Alans, which is shut in by mountains, and has no outlet except by the Iron Gate which was made by Alexander. Also over Sikbia and all the provinces of the Turks unto the Caspian mountains, over the country of the Georgians unto the river Oxus—these are the Girgasim of Scripture, and believe in Christianity—and as far as the frontiers of the provinces and cities of Tibet and India.

All the Jewish congregations of these different countries receive authority from the prince of the captivity to elect rabbis and ministers, all of whom appear before him in order to receive consecration and the permission to officiate, upon which occasions presents and valuable gifts are offered to him, even from the remotest countries. The prince of the captivity possesses hostelries, gardens, and orchards in Babylonia, and extensive landed property inherited from his forefathers, of which nobody can deprive him. He enjoys a certain yearly income from the Jewish hostelries, the markets, and the merchandise of the country, which is levied in form of a tax, over and above what is presented to him from foreign countries. He is very rich, an excellent scholar, and so hospitable that numerous Israelites dine at his table every day.

At the time of the installation of the prince of the captivity he expends considerable sums in presents to the calif, and to his princes and nobles. This ceremony is performed by the calif, who lays his hands on the prince, after which the latter rides home from the king's abode to his own house, seated in a royal state carriage, and accompanied with the sound of various musical instruments; he afterwards lays his hands on the gentlemen of the university, to reinstall them.

Many of the Jews of Bagdad are good scholars and very

rich. The city contains twenty-eight Jewish synagogues, situated partly in Bagdad and partly in Al-Khorkh, on the other side of the river Tigris, which runs through and divides the city. The metropolitan synagogue of the prince of the captivity is ornamented with pillars of richly coloured marble, plated with gold and silver; on the pillars are inscribed verses of the Psalms in letters of gold. The ascent to the holy ark is composed of ten marble steps, on the uppermost of which are the stalls set apart for the prince of the captivity and the other princes of the house of David.

The city of Bagdad is three miles in circumference; the country in which it is situated is rich in palm-trees, gardens, and orchards, so that nothing equals it in Mesopotamia. Merchants of all countries resort thither for purposes of trade, and it contains many wise philosophers, well skilled in sciences, and magicians proficient in all sorts of enchantment.

Two days from here stands Gihiagin, or Ras-al-Ain, which is Ressaina, "the great city"; it contains about five thousand Jews and a large synagogue. In a house near the synagogue is a sepulchre . . . and, in a cave below it, those of twelve disciples.

From here it is one day to Babylon. This is the ancient Babel, and now lies in ruins; but the streets still extend thirty miles. The ruins of the palace of Nebuchadnezzar are still to be seen; but people are afraid to venture among them on account of the serpents and scorpions with which they are infested. Twenty thousand Jews live within about twenty miles from this place, and perform their worship in the synagogue of Daniel, who rests in peace. This synagogue is of remote antiquity, having been built by Daniel himself; it is constructed of solid stones and bricks. Here the traveller may also behold the palace of Nebuchadnezzar, with the burning fiery furnace into which were thrown Hananiah, Mishael and Azariah; it is a valley well known to every one.

Hillah, at a distance of five miles, contains about ten thousand Jews and four synagogues, one of which is that of Meier, whose sepulchre is in front of it; another is that of Seiri, son of Hama, and Miri. Public worship is performed daily in these synagogues. Four miles away is the tower built by the dispersed generation. It is constructed of bricks called *al-ajurr;* the base measures two miles, the breadth two hundred and forty yards, and the height about one hundred *canna* [over 400 feet!]. A spiral passage, built into the tower, in stages of ten yards each, leads up to the summit, from which we have a prospect of twenty miles, the country being one wide plain and quite level. The heavenly fire, which struck the tower, split it to its very foundation.

Half a day farther on, at Napacha, which contains two hundred Jews, is the synagogue of Isaac Napacha, in front of which is his sepulchre. Three parasangs away, on the banks of the Euphrates, stands the synagogue of the prophet Ezekiel, who rests in peace. The place of the synagogue is fronted by sixty towers, the space between every two of which is also occupied by a synagogue; in the court of the largest stands the ark, and behind it is the sepulchre of Ezekiel, the son of Buzi the priest. This monument is covered with a large cupola, and the building is very handsome; it was erected by Jechoniah, king of Juda, and the thirty-five thousand Jews who went along with him, when Evil-Merodach released him from the prison, which was situated between the river Chaboras and another river.

The names of Jechoniah and of all those who came with him are inscribed on the wall, the king's name first, that of Ezekiel last. This place is considered holy even to the present day, and is one of those to which people resort from

remote countries in order to pray, particularly at the season
of new year and Atonement day. There are great rejoicings
here at that time, which are attended even by the prince of
the captivity and the presidents of the colleges of Bagdad.
The assembly is so large that their temporary abodes cover
twenty-two miles of open ground, and attract many Arabian
merchants, who keep a market or fair.

On the day of Atonement the proper lesson of the day is
read from a very large manuscript Pentateuch in Ezekiel's
own handwriting. A lamp burns night and day on the
sepulchre of the prophet, and has always been kept burning
since the day he lighted it himself; the oil and wicks are
renewed as often as necessary. A large house belonging to
the sanctuary contains a very numerous collection of books,
some of them as ancient as the second, some even of the time
of the first temple, it being the custom that whoever dies
childless bequeaths his books to this sanctuary.

The inhabitants of the country lead to the sepulchre all
foreign Jews, who come from Media and Persia to visit it in
fulfilment of vows. The noble Mahometans also resort
thither to pray, because they hold the prophet Ezekiel—on
whom be peace!—in great veneration, and they call this place
Dar Melicha, the agreeable abode. The sepulchre is also
visited by all devout Arabs. Within half a mile of the synagogue are the sepulchres of Hananiah, Mishael and Azariah, each covered with a large cupola. Even in times of
war, neither Jew nor Mahometan ventures to despoil and
profane the sepulchre of Ezekiel.

Three miles from hence stands the city of Al-Kotsonaath,
containing three hundred Jewish inhabitants and the sepulchres of Papa, Huna, Joseph Sinai, and Joseph, the son of
Hama, in front of each of which is a synagogue in which
Jews daily pray. Three parasangs to Ain Japhata, which

contains the sepulchre of the prophet Nahum the Elkoshite, who rests in peace. In a Persian village, a day from there, are the sepulchres of Chisdai, Akiba and Dossa; and in another village, half a day's distance in the desert, are those of David, Juda, Kubreh, Sechora and Aba; and on the river Lega, a distance of one day, that of king Zedekiah, who rests in peace; the latter is ornamented by a large cupola.

It is one day hence to the city of Kufa, which contains about seventy thousand Jews; and in it is the sepulchre of King Jechoniah, which consists of a large building with a synagogue in front. One day and a half to Sura, the place called in the Talmud Matha-Mechasia, formerly the residence of the princes of the captivity and of the principals of the colleges. At Sura are the sepulchres of Shrira and his son Rabenu Hai, Rabenu Sadiah-al-Fajumi, Samuel, the son of Chophni the priest, and Zephaniah, the son of Khushi, the son of Gedaliah the prophet, and of many other princes of the captivity, descendants of the house of David, who formerly resided there before the city was ruined. Two days distant is Shafjathib, where there is a synagogue, which the Israelites erected with earth and stones brought from Jerusalem, and which they called "the transplanted of Nehardea." One day and a half away is El Jubar, or Pumbeditha, on the river Euphrates, containing about three thousand Jews, and the synagogues, sepulchres, and colleges of Rab and Samuel.

At twenty-one days' journey through the desert of Sheba, or Al-Yemen, from which Mesopotamia lies in a northerly direction, are the abodes of the Jews who are called Beni [children of] Rechab, men of Thema. The seat of their government is at Thema, or Tehama, where their prince and governor rabbi Chanan resides. This city is large, and the extent of their country is sixteen days' journey towards the northern mountain range. They possess large and strong cities and are not subject to any of the Gentiles, but undertake warlike expeditions into distant provinces with the Arabians, their neighbours and allies, to take the spoil and the prey.

These Arabians are Bedouins, who live in tents in the deserts and have no fixed abode; they are in the habit of undertaking marauding expeditions into the province of Yemen. The Jews are a terror to their neighbours. Their country being very extensive, some of them cultivate the land and rear cattle. A number of studious and learned men, who spend their lives in the study of the law, are maintained by the tithes of all produce, part of which is also employed towards sustaining the poor and the ascetics, called "Mourners of Sion" and "Mourners of Jerusalem." These eat no meat and abstain from wine, dress always in black, and live in caves or in low houses, and keep fasts all their lives except on Sabbaths and holy days.

They continually implore the mercy of God for the Jews in exile, and devoutly pray that he may have compassion on them for the sake of his own great name; and they also include in their prayers all the Jews of Tehama and of Telmas. The latter contains about one hundred thousand Jews, who are governed by prince Salomon, who, as well as his brother, prince Chanan, are descendants of the royal house of David, who rests in peace, which is proved by their pedigrees. In doubtful cases they solicit the decisions of the prince of the captivity, and set aside forty days of every year, during which they go in rent clothes, and keep fasts, and pray for all the Jews who live in exile.

The province of which Thanaejm is the metropolis contains forty cities, two hundred villages, and one hundred small towns, and is inhabited by about three hundred thousand Jews. Thanaejm is a very strong city, fifteen square miles in extent, and large enough to allow agriculture to be carried on within its boundaries; within it are also situated the palace of prince Salomon, and many gardens and orchards. Telmas is also a city of considerable magnitude; it contains about one hundred thousand Jews, is strongly fortified, and situated between two very high mountains. Many of its inhabitants are well informed, wise, and rich.

The distance from Telmas to Chaibar is three days' journey. It is reported that these Jews are of the tribes of Reuben, Gad, and half the tribe of Manasseh, who were led away captives by Shalmaneser, king of Ashur, and who repaired into these mountainous regions, where they erected the above-named large and strong cities. They carry on war with many kingdoms, and are not easily to be reached because of their situation, which requires a march of eighteen days through uninhabited deserts, and thus renders them difficult of access.

Chaibar is also a very large city, and contains among its fifty thousand Jewish inhabitants many learned scholars. The people of this city are valiant, and engaged in wars with the inhabitants of Mesopotamia, with those of the northern districts, and with those of Yemen, who live near them; the latter province borders on India.

It is a distance of twenty-five days' journey from the country of these Jews to a city on the river Virah, in Yemen, which place contains about three thousand Jews. Waset [the ancient Cybate] is distant seven days, and contains about ten thousand Jews, among whom is Nedain. Five days hence bring us to Bassora on the Tigris, which contains two thousand Israelites, many of whom are learned and wealthy. From hence it is two days to the river Samarra, or Shat-el-Arab. This is the frontier of Persia, and [the city here] contains fifteen hundred Jews. The sepulchre of Ezra the priest and scribe is in this place, where he died on his journey from Jerusalem to King Artaxerxes. In front of the sepulchre a large synagogue and a Mahometan mosque have been erected, the latter as a mark of the veneration in which Ezra is held by the Mahometans, who are very friendly towards the Jews, and resort thither to pray.

Four miles from thence begins Khuzistan, the Elam of Scripture, a large province, which, however, is but partially inhabited, a portion of it lying in ruins. Among the latter are the remains of Shushan [Susa], the metropolis and palace of King Ahasuerus, which still contains very large and handsome buildings of ancient date. It has seven thousand Jewish inhabitants, with fourteen synagogues; in front of one of which is the sepulchre of Daniel, who rests in peace.

The river Ulai divides the city into two parts, which are connected by a bridge; that portion of it which is inhabited by the Jews contains the markets, to which all trade is confined, and there all the rich dwell; on the other side of the river they are poor, because they are deprived of the above-named advantages, and have even no gardens or orchards. These circumstances gave rise to jealousy, which was fostered by the belief that all honour and riches originated in the possession of the remains of the prophet Daniel, who rests in peace, and who was buried on the favoured side of the river. A request was made by the poor for permission to remove the sepulchre to the other side, but it was rejected; upon which a war arose, and was carried on between the two parties for a long time. This strife lasted until "their souls become loath," and they came to a mutual agreement, by which it was arranged that the coffin which contained Daniel's bones should be deposited alternately every year on either side. Both parties faithfully adhered to this arrangement, until it was interrupted by the interference of Sanjar Shah ben Shah, who governs all Persia [and conquered Samarkand in 1140], and holds supreme power over forty-five of its kings. This prince is called in Arabic Sultan-al-Fars-al-Khabir, Supreme Commander of Persia, and his empire extends from the banks of the Shat-el-Arab to the city of Samarkand and the Kizil Ozein, inclosing the city of Nishapur, the cities of Media, and the Chaphton mountains, and reaches as far as Tibet, in the forests of which country that animal is found which yields the musk. The extent of his empire is four months and four days' journey.

When this great emperor, Sanjar king of Persia, came to Shushan and saw that the coffin of Daniel was removed from one side to the other, he crossed the bridge with a very numerous retinue, accompanied by Jews and Mahometans, and inquired into the reason of those proceedings. Upon being told what we have related, he declared it to be derogatory to the honour of Daniel, and commanded that the distance between the two banks should be exactly measured, that Daniel's coffin should be deposited in another coffin, made of glass, and that it should be suspended from the centre of the bridge by chains of iron. A place of public worship was erected on the spot, open to every one who desired to say his prayers, whether he be Jew or Gentile; and the coffin of Daniel is suspended from the bridge unto this very day. The king commanded that, in honour of Daniel, nobody should be allowed to fish in the river one mile on each side of the coffin.

It is three days to Rudbar, which contains twenty thousand Jews, among whom are many scholars and rich men, but they generally live under great oppression. Two days bring us to the river Holwan, near which you find the abodes of about four thousand Jews.

Four days to the district of Mulidet, possessed by a sect who do not believe in the tenets of Mahomet, but live on the summit of high mountains, and pay obedience to the commands of the Old Man in the country of the Assassins. Four congregations of Jews dwell among them, and combine with them in their wars. They do not acknowledge the authority of the kings of Persia, but live on their mountains, whence they occasionally descend to make booty and to take spoil, with which they retire to their mountain fortresses, beyond the reach of their assailants. Some of the Jews who live in this country are excellent scholars, and all acknowledge the authority of the prince of the captivity, who resides at Bagdad in Babylonia.

Five days farther is Amaria, which contains twenty-five thousand Jews. This congregation forms part of those who live in the mountains of Chaphton, and which amount to more than a hundred, extending to the frontiers of Media. These Jews are descendants of those who were originally led into captivity by King Shalmaneser; they speak the Syriac language, and among them are many excellent Talmudic scholars; they are neighbours to those of the city of Amaria, which is situated within one day's journey of the empire of Persia, to the king of which they are tributary. This tribute is collected by a deputy, and amounts here, as well as in all Mahometan countries, to one *amiri* of gold, equal to one golden *maravedi* and one-third [about one pound sterling], for each male inhabitant of the age of fifteen and upwards.

Ten years ago there rose a man of the name of David El-Roy, of the city of Amaria, who had studied under the prince of the captivity, Chisdai, and under Eli, the president of the college of Geon Jacob in the city of Bagdad, and who became an excellent scholar, being well versed in the Mosaic law, in the decisions of the rabbis, and in the Talmud; understanding also the profane sciences, the language and the writings of the Mahometans, and the scriptures of the magicians and enchanters. He made up his mind to rise in rebellion against the king of Persia, to unite and collect the Jews who live in the mountains of Chaphton, and with them to engage in war with all Gentiles, making the conquest of Jerusalem his final object. He gave signs to the Jews by false miracles, and assured them, "the Lord has sent me to conquer Jerusalem, and to deliver you from the yoke of the Gentiles." Some of the Jews did believe in him, and called him Messiah.

When the king of Persia became acquainted with these circumstances, he sent and summoned David into his presence. The latter went without fear, and when brought before the court he was asked, "Art thou the king of the Jews?" to which he made answer and said, "I am." Upon this the king immediately commanded that he should be secured and put into the prison where are kept the captives who are imprisoned for life, situated in the city of Dabaristan, on the banks of the Kizil Ozein, which is a broad river. After a lapse of three days, when the king sat in council to take the advice of his nobles and officers respecting the Jews who had rebelled against his authority, David appeared among them, having liberated himself from prison without human aid. When the king beheld him, he inquired, "Who has brought thee hither, or who has set thee at liberty?" To which David made answer, "My own wisdom and subtlety; for verily I fear neither thee nor thy servants."

The king immediately commanded that he should be seized, but his servants answered and said, "We see him not, and are aware of his presence only by hearing the sound of his voice." The king was very much astonished at David's exceeding subtlety, who thus addressed him: "I now go my own way"; and he went out, followed by the king and all his nobles and servants to the banks of the river, where he took his shawl, spread it upon the water, and crossed thereon. At that moment he became visible, and all the servants of the king saw him cross the river on his shawl. He was pursued by them in boats, but without success, and they all confessed that no magician upon earth could equal him. He that very day travelled to Amaria, a distance of ten days' journey, by the help of the Shem Hamphorash [knowledge of the secret letters of the name of Jehovah], and related to the astonished Jews all that had happened to him.

The king of Persia afterwards sent to the Emir-el-Mumenin, the calif of Bagdad, principal of the Mahometans, to solicit the influence of the prince of the captivity, and of the presidents of the colleges, in order to check the proceedings of David El-Roy, and threatening to put to death all Jews who inhabited his empire. The congregations of Persia were very severely dealt with about that time, and sent letters to the prince of the captivity and the presidents of the colleges at Bagdad to the following purpose: "Why will you allow us to die, and all the congregations of this empire? Restrain the deeds of this man, and prevent thereby the shedding of innocent blood."

The prince of the captivity and the president of the colleges then addressed David in letters which run thus: "Be it known unto thee that the time of our redemption has not yet arrived, and that we have not yet seen the signs by which it is to manifest itself, and that by strength no man shall prevail. We therefore command thee to discontinue the course thou hast adopted, on pain of being excommunicated from all Israel."

Copies of these letters were sent to Sakhai, the prince of the Jews in Mosul, and to Joseph the astronomer, who is called Borhan-al-Fulkh, and also resides there, with the request to forward them to David El-Roy. The last-mentioned prince and the astronomer added letters of their own, in which they advised and exhorted him; but he, nevertheless, continued in his criminal career. This he carried on until a certain prince of the name of Sin-el-Din, a vassal of the king of Persia, and a Turk by birth, cut it short by sending for the father-in-law of David El-Roy, to whom he offered ten thousand florins if he would secretly kill David El-Roy. This agreement being concluded, he went to David's house while he slept, and killed him on his bed, thus destroying his plans and evil designs.

Notwithstanding this, the wrath of the king of Persia still continued against the Jews who lived in the mountains and in his country, who in their turn craved the influence of the prince of the captivity with the king of Persia. Their petitions and humble prayers were supported by a present of one hundred talents of gold, in consideration of which the anger of the king of Persia was subdued, and the land was tranquillized.

From that mountain to Hamadan is a journey of ten days; this was the metropolis of Media, and contains about fifty thousand Jews. In front of one of the synagogues is the sepulchre of Mordecai and Esther. Four days from these stands Dabaristan, on the river Kizil Ozein; it contains about four thousand Jewish inhabitants. The city of Ispahan is distant seven days' journey; it is the metropolis of Persia, and residence of the king, being twelve miles in extent, and containing about fifteen thousand Jews. Sar Shalom, the rabbi of this city and of all other towns of the Persian empire, has been promoted to the dignity by the prince of the captivity.

Four days distant stands Shiraz, or Mars, a large city,

containing about ten thousand Jews. It is seven days thence to Giva [Khiva], a large city on the banks of the Oxus, containing about eight thousand Jews. Very extensive commerce is carried on in this place, to which traders of all countries and languages resort; the country about it is very flat.

Five days away, on the frontiers of the kingdom, stands Samarkand, a city of considerable magnitude, which contains about fifty thousand Jews. The prince-rabbi Obadiah is the governor of the community, which includes many wise and learned men. Four days distant is the province of Tibet, in the forests of which country that beast is found which yields the musk.

To the mountains of Khazvin, on the river Kizil Ozein, it is a journey of eight and twenty days. Jews of those parts, who live in Persia at present, report that the city of Nishapur is inhabited by four tribes of Israel; the tribe of Dan, that of Zebulon, and that of Naphthali, being part of the first exiles who were carried into captivity by Shalmaneser, king of Ashur, as reported in Scripture. He banished them to Halah and Habor, the mountains of Gozan, and the mountains of Media. The extent of their country is twenty days' journey, and they possess many towns and cities in the mountains. The river Kizil Ozein forms their boundary on one side, and they are subject to no nation, but are governed by their own prince, who bears the name of rabbi Joseph Amarkhela Halevi.

Some of these Jews are excellent scholars; others carry on agriculture; and many of them are engaged in war with the country of Cuth, by way of the desert. They are in alliance with the Caphar Tarac, or infidel Turks, who adore the wind and live in the desert. This is a people who eat no bread and drink no wine, but devour the meat raw and quite unprepared; they have no noses, but draw breath through two small holes, and eat all sorts of meat, whether from clean or unclean beasts. They are on very friendly terms with the Jews.

About eighteen years ago this nation invaded Persia with a numerous host, and took the city of Rai, which they smote with the edge of the sword, carrying off the spoil to their deserts. Nothing similar had been seen before in the king-dom of Persia; and when the king of that country was made acquainted with this occurrence, his wrath was kindled, for, said he, "In the time of my predecessors no host like this ever issued from the desert; I will go and will extinguish their name from the earth."

He raised the war-cry in the whole empire, collected all his troops, and made inquiry whether he could find any guide that would show him the place where his enemies pitched their tents. A man was met with, who spoke thus to the king: "I will show thee the place of their retreat, for I am one of them." The king promised to enrich him if he would fulfil his promise, and show him the way. Upon inquiry how many provisions would be necessary for this long march through the desert, the spy answered: "Take with you bread and water for fifteen days, as you will find no provisions whatever before you reach their country."

This advice being acted upon, they travelled fifteen days in the desert, and as they met with nothing that could serve for sustenance, they became extremely short of provisions, and men and beasts began to die. The king sent for the spy, and thus spoke to him: "What is become of thy promise to show us our enemy?" No other reply being made than, "I have mistaken my way," the head of the spy was cut off by the king's command.

Orders were issued that every one who had any provisions

left should share them with his companion; but everything
eatable was consumed, even the beasts, and after travelling
thirteen additional days in the desert, they at last reached
the mountains of Khazvin, where the Jews dwell. They
encamped in the gardens and orchards, and near the springs,
which are in the vicinity of the river Kizil Ozein. It being
the fruit season, they made free with it and destroyed much,
but no living being came forward. They saw, however,
cities and many towers on the mountains, and the king commanded two of his servants to go and inquire the name of
the nation which inhabited these mountains, and to cross
over to them, either in boats or by swimming the river. They
at last discovered a large bridge, fortified by towers, and
secured by a gate which was locked, and on the other side of
the bridge a considerable city. They shouted on their side of
the bridge until at last a man came forth to inquire what they
wanted or to whom they belonged. They could not, however, make themselves understood, but brought an interpreter who spoke both languages; the questions being repeated,
they replied: "We are the servants of the king of Persia,
and have come to inquire who you are and whose subjects."
The answer was: "We are Jews, we acknowledge no king or
prince of the Gentiles, but are subjects of a Jewish prince."
Upon inquiries after the Ghuzi, the Caphar Tarac, or infidel
Turks, the Jews made answer: "Verily they are our allies,
and whoever seeks to harm them we consider our own
enemy."

The two men returned and reported this to the king of
Persia, who became much afraid, and particularly so when,
after a lapse of two days, the Jews sent a herald to offer him
battle. The king said, "I am not come to make war against
you, but against the Caphar Tarac, or infidel Turks, who are
my enemies; and if you attack me I will certainly take my

vengeance, and will destroy all the Jews in my own kingdom, for I am well aware of your superiority over me in
my present position; but I entreat you to act kindly and not
to harass me, but allow me to fight with the Caphar Tarac,
my enemy, and also to sell me as much provision as I want
for the maintenance of my host."

The Jews took counsel among themselves, and determined
to comply with the request of the king of Persia for the sake
of his Jewish subjects. The king and all his host were
consequently admitted into the country of the Jews, and
during his stay of fifteen days he was treated with most
honourable distinction and respect. The Jews, however,
meanwhile sent information to their allies, the Caphar Tarac,
and made them acquainted with the above-mentioned circumstances; these took possession of all the mountain passes,
and assembled a considerable host, consisting of all the
inhabitants of that desert, and when the king of Persia
went forth to give them battle, the Caphar Tarac conquered,
killing and slaying so many of the Persians that the king
escaped to his country with only very few followers. One
of the horsemen of the retinue of the king enticed a Jew of
that country, named Moses, to go along with him; he carried this man with him into Persia, and there made him a
slave. Upon a certain day, when the king was the spectator
of sports carried on for his amusement, and consisting principally of the exercise of handling the bow, among all competi-
tors none excelled this Moses.

The king inquired after this man by means of an interpreter, and was told what had happened to him, and how
he had been forcibly carried away from his country by the
horseman; upon learning this the king not only immediately
granted him his liberty, but gave him a dress of honour,
composed of silk and fine linen, and many other presents.

A proposal was also made to Moses, that, if he would renounce his religion for that of the Persians, he should be treated with the utmost kindness, should gain considerable riches, and be made the king's steward; but he refused, and said, "I cannot make up my mind to any such step." The king, however, placed him in the house of the rabbi Sar Shalom, of the Ispahan congregation, who in the course of time became his father-in-law. This very Moses related all these things unto me.

From thence I returned to the country of Khuzistan, which lies on the Tigris. This river runs downward and falls into the Indian Sea [Persian Gulf], in the vicinity of an island called Kish. The extent of this island is six miles, and the inhabitants do not carry on any agriculture, for they have no rivers, nor more than one spring in the whole island, and are consequently obliged to drink rain water. It is, however, a considerable market, being the spot to which the Indian merchants and those of the islands bring their commodities. While the traders of Mesopotamia, Yemen, and Persia import all silk and purple cloths, flax, cotton, hemp, mash, wheat, barley, millet, rye, and all other sorts of comestibles and pulse, which articles form objects of exchange, those from India import great quantities of spices, and the inhabitants of the island live by what they gain in their capacity of brokers to both parties. The island contains about five hundred Jews.

It is ten days' passage by sea to El-Katif, a city with about five thousand Israelites. In this vicinity the pearls are found. About the twenty-fourth of the month of Nisan [April], large drops of rain are observed upon the surface of the water, which are swallowed by the reptiles, which then close their shells and fall to the bottom of the sea; about the middle of the month of Thishri [October], people dive with the assistance of ropes, collect these reptiles from the bottom, and bring them up, after which they are opened and the pearls taken out.

Seven days distant is Chulam [Marco Polo's Koulam], on the confines of the country of the sun-worshippers, who are descendants of Kush, are addicted to astrology, and are all black. This nation is very trustworthy in matters of trade; and whenever foreign merchants enter their port, three secretaries of the king immediately repair on board their vessels, write down their names, and report them to him. The king grants them security for their property, which they may even leave in the open fields without any guard. One of the king's officers sits in the market, and receives goods that may have been found anywhere, and which he returns to those applicants who can minutely describe them. This custom is observed in the whole empire of the king.

From Easter to new year [October], during the whole of the summer, the heat is extreme. From the third hour of the day [9:00 A. M.], people shut themselves up in their houses until the evening, at which time everybody goes out. The streets and markets are lighted up, and the inhabitants employ all the night upon their business, which they are prevented from doing in the daytime by the excessive heat.

Pepper grows in this country; the trees which bear this fruit are planted in the fields, which surround the towns, and every one knows his plantation. The trees are small, and the pepper is originally white, but when they collect it they put it into basins and pour hot water upon it; it is then exposed to the heat of the sun, and dried, in order to make it hard and more substantial, in the course of which process it becomes of a black colour. Cinnamon, ginger, and many other kinds of spices also grow in this country.

The inhabitants do not bury their dead, but embalm them with certain spices, put them upon stools, and cover them with cloths, every family keeping apart. The flesh dries upon the bones; and as these corpses resemble living beings, everybody recognizes his parents and all the members of his family for many years to come. These people worship the sun. About half a mile from every town they have large places of worship, and every morning they run towards the rising sun; every place of worship contains a representation of that luminary, so constructed by enchantment that upon the rising of the sun it turns round with a great noise, at which moment both men and women take up their censers and burn incense in honour of this their deity. "This their way is their folly."

All the cities and countries inhabited by these people contain only about one hundred Jews, who are of black colour, as well as the other inhabitants. The Jews are good men, observers of the law, and possess the Pentateuch, the prophets, and some little knowledge of the Talmud and its decisions.

The island of Khandy [Ceylon], is distant twenty-two days' journey. The inhabitants are fire worshippers called Druses, and twenty-three thousand Jews live among them. These Druses have priests everywhere in the houses consecrated to their idols, and these priests are expert necromancers, the like of whom are to be met with nowhere. In front of the altar of their house of prayer is a deep ditch, in which a large fire is continually kept burning; this they call Elahuta, Deity. They pass their children through it, and into this ditch they also throw their dead.

Some of the great of this country take a vow to burn themselves alive; and if any such devotee declares to his children and kindred his intention to do so, they all applaud him and say, "Happy shalt thou be, and it shall be well with thee." When the appointed day arrives, they prepare a sumptuous feast, place the devotee upon his horse, if he be rich, or lead him on foot, if he be poor, to the brink of the ditch. He then throws himself into the fire, and all his kindred manifest their joy by the playing of instruments until he is entirely consumed. Within three days of this ceremony two of the principal priests repair to his house, and thus address his children: "Prepare the house, for to-day you will be visited by your father, who will manifest his wishes unto you." Witnesses are selected among the inhabitants of the town, and lo! the devil appears in the image of the dead. The wife and children inquire after his state in the other world, and he answers: "I have met my companions, but they will not admit me into their company, before I have discharged my debts to my friends and neighbours." He then makes a will, divides his goods among his children, and commands them to discharge all debts he owes and to receive what people owe him; this will is written down by the witnesses. In consequence of this falsehood and deceit, which the priests pass off by magic, they retain a strong hold upon the people, and make them believe that their equal is not to be met with upon earth.

From here the passage to China is effected in forty days. This country lies eastward, and some say that the star Orion predominates in the sea which bounds it, and which is called the Sea of Nikpha. Sometimes this sea is so stormy that no mariner can conduct his vessel; and whenever a storm throws a ship into this sea, it is impossible to govern it; the crew and the passengers consume their provisions, and then die miserably. Many vessels have been lost in this way; but people have learned how to save themselves from this fate by the following contrivance: they take bullocks' hides along with them, and whenever this storm arises and throws them into the Sea of Nikpha, they sew themselves up in the hides, taking care to have a knife in their hand, and being secured against the sea-water, they throw themselves into the ocean. Here they are soon perceived by a large eagle called a griffin, which takes them for cattle, darts down, seizes them in his grip, and carries them upon dry land, where he deposits his burden on a hill or in a dale, there to consume his prey. The man, however, now makes use of his knife to kill the bird, creeps forth from the hide, and tries to reach an inhabited country. Many people have been saved by this stratagem.

Gingaleh is but three days distant by land, although it requires a journey of fifteen days to reach it by sea; this place contains about one thousand Israelites. To Khulan, seven days by sea; no Jews live there. Twelve days to Sebid, which contains but few Jews.

Eight days away is Middle India, which is called Aden, and in Scripture Eden in Thelasar. This country is very mountainous, and contains many independent Jews, who are not subject to the power of the Gentiles, but possess cities and fortresses on the summits of the mountains; from whence they descend into the country of Maatum, with which they are at war. Maatum, also called Nubia, is a Christian kingdom, and the inhabitants are called Nubians. The Jews generally take spoil and plunder from them, which they carry into their mountain fastnesses, the possession of which makes them almost unconquerable. Many of the Jews of Aden visit Egypt and Persia.

To the country of Assuan is twenty days' journey, through the desert of Sheba, on the banks of the Nile [Pison], which comes down here from the country of the blacks. This country is governed by a king, whom they call Sultan-al-

Habash, and some of the inhabitants resemble beasts in every respect. They eat the herbs which grow on the banks of the Nile, go naked in the fields, and have no notions like other men; for instance, they cohabit with their own sisters and with anybody they find. The country is excessively hot; and when the people of Assuan invade their country, they carry wheat, raisins, and figs, which they throw out like bait, thereby alluring the natives. These are made captive, and sold in Egypt and in the adjoining countries, where they are known as black slaves, being the descendants of Ham.

From Assuan to Chaluah it is twelve days. This place contains about three hundred Jews, and is the starting-point of the caravans which traverse the desert Al-Zahara in fifty days on their way to Zavila, the Havilah of Scripture, which is in the country of Ganah. This desert contains mountains of sand; and, whenever a storm arises, the caravans are exposed to the imminent danger of being buried alive by the sand; those which escape, however, carry iron, copper, different sorts of fruits, pulse, and salt. Gold and precious stones are brought back in exchange. This country lies westward of Kush, or Abyssinia.

Thirteen days' journey from Chaluah stands Kuts, a city on the frontiers of Egypt, containing thirty thousand Jewish inhabitants. To Fayuhm five days; this is Pithom; it contains about twenty Jews, and has, even to this day, some remains of the buildings erected by our forefathers.

Four days from thence brings us to Mizraim, or Memphis, commonly called Old Cairo. This large city stands on the banks of the Nile, called Al-Nil, and contains about two thousand Jews. Here are two synagogues, one of the congregation of Palestine, called the Syrian, the other of the Babylonian Jews, or those of Irac. They follow different customs regarding the division of the Pentateuch into Parashioth and Sedarim. The Babylonians read one Parasha every week, as is the custom throughout Spain, and finish the whole of the Pentateuch every year, whereas the Syrians have the custom of dividing every Parasha into three Sedarim, and concluding the lecture of the whole once in three years. They keep, however, the long-established custom of assembling both congregations to perform public service together, as well on the day of the joy of the law as on that of the dispensation of the law. Rabbi Nathaniel, the lord of lords, is the president of the Jewish university, and, in his capacity of primate of all the Jewish congregations of Egypt, exercises the right of electing Rabanim and ministers. He is one of the officers of the great king, who resides in the fortress of Zoan in the city of Mizraim, which is the metropolis of all those Arabians who obey the Emir-al-Mumenin of the sect of Ali ben Abitaleb. All the inhabitants of his country are called rebels, because they rebelled against the Emir-al-Mumenin al-Abassi who resides at Bagdad, and there is continual hatred between them.

The residence of Zoan was selected for its convenience. The prince appears in public twice every year; once at the time of their great holiday, and the second time at the moment of the inundation of the Nile. Zoan is inclosed by a wall, whereas Mizraim is open, and the Nile washes one portion of it. The city is large, containing many markets and bazaars, and very wealthy Jewish inhabitants.

Rain, frost, and snow are almost unknown here, the climate being very warm. The river overflows once every year, in the month of Elul [August] and, inundating the whole country, irrigates it to the extent of fifteen days' journey. The water remains standing on the land during that and the following month, whereby it is moistened and made fit for agriculture. A marble pillar, constructed with great skill, has been erected in front of an island. Twelve yards of this pillar protrude above the level of the river; and whenever the water rises to a height sufficient to cover the pillar, people know that it has inundated the whole land of Egypt to the extent of fifteen days' journey; if one-half only of the pillar be covered, it shows that one-half of the country is yet dry. A certain officer measures the rise of the river every day, and makes proclamation in Zoan and in Mizraim in these words: "Praise God, for the river has risen so and so much!"

The measurement and the proclamation is repeated every day. Whenever the water submerges the whole pillar, it produces great plenty in the whole land of Egypt. The proprietors of land cause ditches to be dug along their fields, into which the fishes are swept with the rising waters; and when the river retires into its bed, the fish remaining in the trenches are collected by the proprietors and used for food. Others sell them to merchants, by whom they are cured, and sold in this state all over the country. The fat of these fishes, with which they abound, is used by the rich of the land instead of oil, and they light their lamps with it. Those who eat of the fish, and drink Nile water after it, need not fear any bad consequences, the water being an excellent preventive.

Persons who inquire the reason of the rise of the Nile are told by the Egyptians that it is caused by the heavy rains which fall in the country of Abyssinia, the Havilah of Scripture, which is elevated above the level of Egypt. This forces the river out of its bed, and inundates the whole country. Whenever the overflowing of the Nile is suspended, they can neither sow nor reap, "and the famine is sore in the land." The time for sowing in Egypt is the month of

Marcheshvan [November], after the river has retired into its usual bed; in Adar [March] they cut barley, and in Nisan [April] the wheat. In the same month the following fruits are ripe: a kind of acid plum called cherry, nuts, cucumbers, gourds, St. John's bread, beans, spelt-corn, chick-pease, as well as all sorts of herbs, such as purslane, asparagus, or fennel, grapes, lettuce, coriander, succory, cabbage, and wine. Upon the whole the country abounds with good things. The gardens and orchards are watered partly from wells and partly from the Nile.

Above Mizraim the Nile is divided into four arms, one of which proceeds to Damietta, which is Caphtor of Scripture, and there falls into the sea; a second flows towards Rashid, or Rosetta, which is near Alexandria, and there falls into the sea; the third takes the direction of Ashmun, the large city on the frontier of Egypt. The banks of these four arms are lined on both sides with cities, towns, and villages; and are enlivened by numerous travellers who journey both by river and by land. In fact, upon the whole earth there is no country so populous and well cultivated as Egypt, which is of ample territory and full of all sorts of good things.

From New to Old Mizraim is a distance of two parasangs. The latter lies in ruins, but the sites of the walls and the houses may still be traced at this day, as also the granaries of Joseph, of which there is a large number. The pyramids, which are seen here, are constructed by magic; and in no other country or other place is anything equal to them. They are composed of stones and cement, and are very substantial. In the outskirts of the city is the very ancient synagogue of our great master Moses, upon whom be peace. An old and very learned man is the overseer and clerk of this place of public worship; he is called Al-Sheikh Abunasar. Old Mizraim is three miles in extent.

From thence to the land of Goshen is eight parasangs. It is called Belbeis, is a large city, and contains about three thousand Jewish inhabitants. Half a day to Iskiil Ain-al-Shems, the ancient Raamses, which is in ruins. Here are remains of the buildings erected by our forefathers, and tower-like buildings constructed of bricks. One day's journey to Al-Boutidg; about two hundred Jews live here. Half a day to Sefita, which contains about two hundred Jews. To Damira, four parasangs; this place contains about seven hundred Jews. Five days to Mahaleh, which contains about five hundred Israelites.

Two days from thence stands Alexandria, which Alexander the Macedonian, who built this extremely strong and handsome city, called after his own name. In the outskirts of the city was the school of Aristotle, the preceptor of Alexander. The building is still very handsome and large, and is divided into many apartments by marble pillars. There are about twenty schools, to which people flocked from all parts of the world in order to study the Aristotelian philosophy. The city is built upon arches, which are hollow below. The streets are straight, and some of them are of such extent that the eye cannot overlook them at once; that which runs from the Rosetta to the sea-gate is a full mile in lengh.

The port of Alexandria is formed partly by a pier, which extends a mile into the sea. Here is also a high tower, called lighthouse, in Arabic, Minar of Alexandria, on the summit of which was placed a glass mirror. All vessels which approached with hostile intentions, from Greece and from the western side, could be observed at fifty days' distance by means of this glass mirror, and precautions were taken against them.

Many years after the death of Alexander there arrived a

Grecian vessel commanded by a man of the name of Theodoros, who was extremely cunning. The Grecians were subject to the Egyptians at the time, and the above-named shipper brought a valuable present to the king of Egypt, consisting of silver, gold, and silk garments. He rode at anchor in view of the mirror, the customary station of all merchantmen who arrived, and the keeper of the lighthouse, as well as his servants, were invited every day by him, until they became very intimate and paid one another frequent visits. Upon a certain day the keeper and all his servants were invited to a sumptuous meal, and were plied so much with wine that both he and his servants became drunk and fell into a sound sleep. This opportunity was seized by the shipper and his crew to break the mirror, after which exploit they left the port the same night.

From that time the Christians began to visit Alexandria with small and large vessels, and took the large island of Crete, as well as Cyprus, which are in possession of the Greeks to this day; and the Egyptians have not been able to withstand the Greeks ever since. The lighthouse is still a mark to all seafaring men. It is observed at the distance of one hundred miles by day, and at night bears a light which serves as a guide to all mariners.

The city is mercantile, and affords an excellent market to all nations. People from all Christian kingdoms resort to Alexandria, from Valentia, Tuscany, Lombardy, Apulia, Amalfi, Sicily, Rakuvia, Catalonia, Spain, Roussillon, Germany, Saxony, Denmark, England, Flanders, Hainaut, Normandy, France, Poitou, Anjou, Burgundy, Mediana, Provence, Genoa, Pisa, Gascony, Aragon, and Navarre. From the west you meet Mahometans from Andalusia, Algarve, Africa, and Arabia, as well as from the countries towards India, Savila, Abyssinia, Nubia, Yemen, Mesopotamia and

Syria, besides Greeks and Turks. From India they import all sorts of spices, which are bought by Christian merchants. The city is full of bustle, and every nation has its own *fonteccho*, or hostelry, there.

On the sea-shore is a marble sepulchre, upon which are depicted all sorts of birds and beasts, all in very ancient characters, which nobody can decipher; but it is supposed that it is the tomb of a king of very ancient date, who reigned even before the flood. The length of the tomb is fifteen spans by six in breadth.

Alexandria contains about three thousand Jews.

From here we reach Damietta in two days; this place contains about two hundred Jews. Half a day from thence to Sunbat, the inhabitants of which sow flax and weave fine linen, which forms a very considerable article of exportation. Four days to Ailah, which is Elim of Scripture; it belongs to the Bedouin Arabs. Two days to Rephidim, which is inhabited by Arabians, and contains no Jews. One day to Mount Sinai, on the summit of which the Syrian monks possess a place of worship. At the base of the mountain is a large village; the inhabitants, who speak the Chaldæan language, call it Tour Sinai. The mountain is small, is in possession of the Egyptians, and is distant five days from Mizraim. The Red Sea is one day's journey from Mount Sinai; this sea is an arm of the Indian Sea.

Back to Damietta, from whence by sea to Tennis, the Chanes of Scripture, an island of the sea, containing about forty Israelites; here is the boundary of the Empire of Egypt. From there we go, in twenty days, by sea to Messina, on the coast of the island of Sicily, situated on the strait called Lunir, an arm of the sea which divides Calabria from Sicily. This city contains about two hundred Jews, and is beautifully situated in a country abounding with gardens and orchards, and full of good things. Most of the pilgrims who embark for Jerusalem assemble here, because this city affords the best opportunity for a good passage.

Two days from thence stands Palermo, a large city, two square miles in extent. It contains the extensive palace of King William [William II of Sicily], and is inhabited by about fifteen hundred Jews and many Christians and Mahometans. The country is rich in wells and springs, grows wheat and barley, and is covered with gardens and orchards; it is, in fact, the best in the whole island of Sicily. This city is the seat of the viceroy, whose palace is called Al-Hacina, and contains all sorts of fruit-trees, as also a great spring, surrounded by a wall, and a reservoir called Al-Behira, in which abundance of fish are preserved. The king's vessels are ornamented with silver and gold, and are ever ready for the amusement of himself and his women. There is also a large palace, the walls of which are richly ornamented with paintings and with gold and silver. The pavement is of marble and rich mosaic, representing all sorts of figures; in the whole country there is no building equal to this.

The island begins at Messina, where many pilgrims meet, and extends to Catania, Syracuse, Masara, Pantaleone, and Trapani, being six days in circumference. Near Trapani is found the stone called coral. From thence you cross over and reach Rome in three days; from Rome by land in five days to Lucca, and from there you get in twelve days to Bardin, by Mount Maurienne, and over the passes of Italy.

Here are the confines of Germany, a country full of hills and mountains. The Jewish congregations of Germany inhabit the banks of the great river Rhine, from Cologne, where the empire commences, to Cassanburg, the frontier of Germany, which is fifteen days' journey, and is called

Ashkenas by the Jews. These are the cities of Germany which contain congregations of Israelites, all situated on the river Moselle—Coblence, Andernach, Kaub, Kartania, Bingen, Worms, and Mistran. In fact, the Jews are dispersed over all countries, and whoever hinders Israel from being collected, shall never see any good sign, and shall not live with Israel. And at the time which the Lord has appointed to be a limit of our captivity and to exalt the horn of his anointed, every one shall come forth and shall say, "I will lead the Jews and I will assemble them."

These cities contain many eminent scholars; the congregations are on the best terms with one another, and are friendly towards strangers. Whenever a traveller visits them they rejoice and hospitably receive him. They are full of hopes, and say: "Be of good spirit, dear brethren, for the salvation of the Lord will be quick, like the twinkling of an eye; and, indeed, were it not that we had doubted hitherto that the end of our captivity had not yet arrived, we should have assembled long ago; but this is impossible before the time of song arrives, and the sound of the cooing turtle gives warning; then will the message arrive, and we will say, The name of the Lord be exalted!" They send letters to one another, by which they exhort to hold firm in the Mosaic law. Those that spend their time as mourners of the downfall of Sion and the destruction of Jerusalem are always dressed in black clothes, and pray for mercy before the Lord, for the sake of their brethren.

Besides the cities which we have already mentioned as being in Germany, there are, further, Astransburg, Duisburg, Mantern, Pisingas, Bamberg, Zor, and Regensburg, on the confines of the empire; all these cities contain many rich and learned Jews. Further on is the country of Bohemia, called Prague. Here begins Sclavonia, called by the Jews who inhabit it Khenaan, because the inhabitants sell their children to all nations, which is also applicable to the people of Russia. The latter country is very extensive, reaching from the gates of Prague to those of Kiev, a large city on the borders of the empire. The country is very mountainous and full of forests; in the latter the beasts called vaiverges [white squirrel] are met, which yield the sable fur or ermine. In winter the cold is so intense that nobody ventures to leave his house. So far the kingdom of Russia.

The kingdom of France, called by the Jews Tsarphat, reaches from the town of Alsodo to Paris, the metropolis, and is six days in extent. This city, situated on the river Seine, belongs to King Louis, and contains many learned men, the equal of which are to be met with at present nowhere upon earth. They employ all their time upon the study of the law, are hospitable to all travellers, and on friendly terms with all their Jewish brethren.

May the Lord in his mercy be full of compassion towards them and us, and may he fulfil towards both the words of his Holy Scripture: "Then the Lord thy God will turn thy captivity, and have compassion upon thee, and will return and gather thee from all the nations, whither the Lord thy God hath scattered thee."—Amen, Amen, Amen.

BIBLIOGRAPHY

BIBLIOGRAPHY

ABEL-RÉMUSAT, *Memoires de l' Institut Royal.* Inscriptions and belles lettres. Vol. VI, Paris, 1822. Contains records of correspondence between the European princes and the Mongols.

ADLER, M. N., *The Travels of Rabbi Benjamin of Tudela,* with critical Hebrew text. London, 1907. 8vo.

Anecdotes of the Chinese. Contains a chapter on Marco Polo. 1845. 32mo.

BABER, E. COLBORNE, *Travels and Researches in Western China.* London, 1882. 8vo.

BACKER, LOUIS DE, *Guillaume de Rubrouck,* Ambassadeur de Saint Louis en Orient. A fairly complete and good text. Paris, 1877. 16mo.

——, *Guillaume de Rubrouck,* Ambassadeur de Saint Louis en Orient. Récit de son voyage traduit de l'original Latin et annoté. Paris, 1877. 18mo.

BACON, ROGER, *Opus Majus.* Edited by John Henry Bridges. Oxford, 1897. 2 vols. 8vo.

BADGER, GEORGE PERCY, *The Nestorians and Their Rituals.* London, 1852. 2 vols. 8vo.

BALL, J. DYER, *Things Chinese,* or Notes connected with China. History, Government, Literature, Religion, Customs, etc. 5th edition revised by E. Chalmers Werner. London, 1925. 8vo.

BARBARO, JOSAFA, *Travels to Tana and Persia.* Thomas' translation, edited by Lord Stanley of Alderley. Hakluyt Society. London, 1873. 8vo.

BEAL, SAMUEL, *Buddhist Records of the Western World.* Translated from the Chinese of Hiuen Tsiang (A. D. 629). London, 1906. 2 vols. 8vo.

BEAZLEY, CHARLES RAYMOND, *The Dawn of Modern Geography.* Vol. III deals with *A History of Exploration and Geographical Science from the middle of the 13th to the early years of the 15th centuries.* Oxford, 1897-1906. 8vo.

——, *The Texts and Versions of John de Plano Carpini and William de Rubruquis,* as printed for the first time by Hakluyt in 1598 together with some shorter pieces. Hakluyt Society. London, 1903. 8vo.

——, *On a hitherto unexamined manuscript of John de Plano Carpini.* London, 1903. 8vo.

BOULGER, C. D., *A Short History of China.* London, 1893. 8vo.

BRUCE, MAJOR CLARENCE D., *In the Footsteps of Marco Polo,* Being an Account of a Journey Overland from Simla to Pekin. Edinburgh, 1907. 8vo.

——, *In the Footsteps of Marco Polo.* An Account of a Journey Overland to Pekin. London, 1907. 8vo.

BRETSCHNEIDER, DR. E., *Notes on Chinese Mediæval Travellers to the West.* Shanghai, 1875. 8vo.

——, *On the Knowledge.* Possessed by the Ancient Chinese on the Arabs and Arabian Colonies and other western countries mentioned in Chinese Records. London, 1871. 8vo.

——, *Notes on Chinese Mediæval Travellers to the West.* Shanghai, 1875. 8vo.

——, *Archæological and Historical Researches on Peking and Its Environs.* Shanghai, 1876. 8vo.

——, *Mediæval Researches* from Eastern Asiatic Sources. London, 1910. 2 vols. 8vo.

Buddhist Birth Stories, or *Jātaka Tales.* Translated by T. W. Rhys Davids. The oldest collection of folk-lore known. London, 1880. 8vo.

China and the English. The first chapter deals with Marco Polo and his journey. London, 1836. 32mo.

Chinese Classics, The. Translation and critical notes by James Legge. Hongkong-London, 1861-73. 8vo.

CLAVIJO, RUY GONZALEZ DE, *Narrative of the Embassy to the Court of Timour at Samarcand,* A. D. *1403-6.* Translated by Clements R. Markham. Hakluyt Society. London, 1859. 8vo.

CONTARINI, AMBROSIO, *The Travels.* To the Great Lord Ussuncassan, King of Persia, in 1473. Edited by Lord Stanley of Alderley. Hakluyt Society. London, 1873. 8vo.

CONTI, *Travels of Nicolo.* In India in the 15th century. Hakluyt Society. London, 1857. 8vo.

COOLEY, W. D., *History of Maritime and Inland Discovery.* London, 1831.

CORDIER, HENRI, *Mélanges d'Histoire et de Géographie Orientales.* Paris. 4 vols. 8vo. Volume II contains chapters on Church Missions and Tartar Invasions.

——, *Histoire Générale de la Chine et de ses Relations avec les Pays Etrangers depuis le temps les plus anciens jusqu'a la Chute de la Dynastie Mandchoue.* Paris, 1920. 4 vols. 8vo.

——, *Les Voyages en Asie au 14° siècle du bienheureux frère Odoric de Pordenone, Religieux de Saint François.* Paris, 1891. 4to.

——, *Le Christianisme en Chine et en Asie sous les Mongols.* Paris, 1918. 8vo.

COULING, S., *The Encyclopædia Sinica.* A valuable one-volume encyclopædia of China and things Chinese. London, 1917. 4to.

CURTIN, JEREMIAH, *The Mongols.* Boston, 1908. 8vo.

D'OHSSON, LE BARRON C., *Histoire des Mongols, depuis Tchinguiz Khan jusqu'à Timour Bey ou Tamerlan.* Le Haye, 1834. 4 vols. 8vo.

DUGHLÁT, *The Tarikh-i-Rashidi of Mirza Muhammad Haidar.* A history of the Moghuls of Central Asia. Translated into English and edited by E. Denison Ross. London, 1895. 8vo.

ELLIOT, H. M., *The History of India As Told By Its Own Historians.* Edited by Professor Dowson. 1867.

ERMAN, *Travels in Siberia.* Translated by W. D. Cooley. London, 1848.

FABER, REV. E., *Chronological Handbook of the History of China.* Edited by P. Kranz. 1902. 8vo.

FA-HSIEN, *The Travels of* (399-414 A. D.), *or, Record of the Buddhistic Kingdoms.* A new and corrected translation by Herbert A. Giles. London, 1923. 16mo.

FRAZER, SIR J. G., *The Golden Bough.* A Study in Magic and Religion. 12 vols. 8vo.

——, *The Worship of Nature.* London, 1926. 2 vols. 8vo.

GILES, HERBERT A., *A Chinese Biographical Dictionary.* This Chinese "Who's Who" is a classic. It is filled with legendary and historic information written in a style that makes it certainly the most readable dictionary in our language. London-Shanghai, 1898. 4to.

——, *Confucianism and Its Rivals.* London, 1915. 8vo.

——, *A Glossary of References on Subjects Connected with the Far East*. London, 1900. 8vo.

——, *The Civilization of China*. Home University Library. 12mo.

——, *Dictionary*. Part III of this work gives a list of places mentioned by Marco Polo and identified by Yule.

——, *A History of Chinese Literature*. 600 B. C. to 1900 A. D. London, 1924. 8vo.

——, *Religions of Ancient China*. London, 1918. 8vo.

GILES, LIONEL, *An Alphabetical Index to the Chinese Encyclopædia*. Published by British Museum, 1911. 4to.

GILL, CAPT. WILLIAM, *The River of Golden Sand*. Introduction by Henry Yule. London, 1880. 2 vols. 8vo.

GOLUBORICH, *Biblioteca Bro-Bibliografica*. In Latin. A most important index of references related to church missions. Florence, 1919. 10 vols. 4to.

GRAY, J. H., *China*. A History of the Laws, Manners and Customs of the People. 1878. 2 vols.

GROENEVELDT, W. P., *Notes on the Archipelago and Malacca*. Compiled from Chinese Sources. Batavia, 1877. 8vo.

HAKLUYT, RICHARD, *Collection of the Early Voyages, Travels and Discoveries of the English Nation*. Vol. I contains text of Rubruck. London, 1809. 5 vols. 4to.

HAMILTON, A., *New Account of the East Indies*. London, 1744.

HAMMER-PURGSTALL, *Geschichte der Goldenen Horde*. Pesth, 1840.

HANNAH, IAN C., *Eastern Asia*. A history. London, 1911. 8vo.

HEDIN, SVEN, *Trans-Himalaya*. Discoveries and Adventures in Tibet. London, 1910-13. 3 vols. 8vo.

——, *Overland to India*. London, 1910. 2 vols. 8vo.

——, *My Life as an Explorer*. New York, 1925. 8vo.

——, *Southern Tibet*. Discoveries in former times compared with my own researches in 1907-8. Text, 9 vols; maps, 3 vols. 1917.

HIRTH, FRIEDRICH, *Chinesische Studien*. 1890. 4to.

——, *The Ancient History of China, to the End of the Chóu Dynasty*. 1923. 8vo.

HIRTH, FRIEDRICH, and ROCKHILL, W. W., *Chau Ju-Kua*. His work on the Chinese and Arab Trade in the 12th and 13th centuries, entitled *Chu-fan-chï*. Translated from the Chinese and annotated. In English. St. Petersburg, 1912. 4to.

Historie de Gentchiscan et de toute la dinastie des Mongous, tirée de l'Histoire Chinoise. Anthony Gaubil, Paris, 1739. This is a translation of the first part of Yüan Shi or Chinese History of the Mongol dynasty, in 210 chapters. The first 47 contain biographies of the 13 Mongol emperors.

HOWORTH, H. H., *History of the Mongols,* from the 9th to the 19th century. London, 1876. 4 vols. 8vo.

HUC, *Recollections of a Journey through Tartary, etc.* Condensed translation by Mrs. P. Sinnett. London, 1852.

HUNTINGTON, ELLSWORTH, *The Pulse of Asia.* A journey in Central Asia illustrating the geographic basis of history. Boston, 1907. 8vo.

IBN KHALDUN, *The Oriental Geography of Ibn Haukal.* An Arabian traveller of the 10th century. Translated by Sir William Ouseley. London, 1800. 4to.

JACKSON, A. V., *The Magi in Marco Polo,* and the cities in Persia from which they came to worship the Infant Christ. Journal American Oriental Society. Vol. XXVI, I.

——, *Persia Past and Present.* New York, 1906. 8vo.

Jamiut-Tavarikh (Collection of Annals), by Fadl'allah Rashid ed-Din. In Persian. Brosset. Gibbs Memorial Series, Leyden and London.

JENKINSON, ANTHONY, *Early Voyages and Travels to Russia and Persia.* Hakluyt Society. London, 1886. 2 vols. 8vo.

JOINVILLE, LE SIEUR DE, *Histoire de Saint Louis.* Paris, 1867. 8vo.

JORDANUS, FRIAR, *The Wonders of the East.* Translated from a Latin manuscript by Henry Yule. Hakluyt Society. London, 1863. 8vo

KIRCHER, ATHANASIUS, *China Illustrata.* Mentions Marco Polo and early church relations with the East. Amsterdam, 1667. 4to.

KOMROFF, MANUEL, *The Travels of Marco Polo.* New York, 1926. 8vo.

KOSLOW, GEN. P. K., *Mongolei, Amdo und die Tote Stadt Chara-Choto.* Expedition of the Russian Geographical Society, 1907-1909. The results of this expedition are also described by Yetts in *Discoveries of the Kozlov Expedition.* 1925. 8vo.

LAMB, HAROLD, *Genghis Khan, The Emperor of All Men.* The best and most readable biography on this conqueror. New York, 1927. 8vo.

LANDOR, A. H. S., *The Gems of the East, Sixteen Thousand Miles of Research Travel.* 1904. 2 vols. 8vo.

LI UNG BING, *Outlines of Chinese History.* Edited by Professor J. Whiteside. 1914. 8vo.

Literary and Historical Atlas of Asia, with a chapter on *Coinages of Asia* by J. Allan. Everyman's Library, London. 12mo.

LOEWE, H. M. J., *History of the Mongols,* in *Cambridge Mediæval History,* Vol. IV. Cambridge, 1923. 8vo.

LOWES, JOHN LIVINGSTONE, *The Dry Sea and the Carrenare.* Chicago, 1905. 8vo.

MAJOR, R. H., editor of *India in the Fifteenth Century,* taken from Latin, Persian, Russian and Italian sources. Hakluyt Society. London, 1859. 8vo.

MAUNDEVILE, SIR JOHN, *The Voiage and Travaile of.* Edited by J. O. Halliwell. London, 1883. 8vo.

——, *The Travels of.* The version of the Cotton manuscript in modern spelling, with three narratives from Hakluyt's *Navigations, Voyages and Discoveries.* London, 1923. 8vo.

MARCO POLO, *Voyages, Les Chercheurs de Routes.* Marco Polo, par G. Bonvalot. 1924. 8vo.

——, *Le Livre de Marco Polo.* Citoyen de Venise, Haut Fonctionnaire a la Cour de Koubilai-Khan, etc., etc. This work printed in China with the Chinese names in native characters on double paper Chinese style, but soiled by too much oil in printer's ink. Shanghai. 3 vols. 4to.

——, *Il Milione.* Testo di lingua del sec . . . illustrato dal Conte G. B. Baldelli Boni, Florence, 1827. Contains both the Cruscan and Ramusian texts. 4to.

MAYERS, W. F., *The Chinese Readers Manual.* A Handbook of Biographical, Historical, Mythological and General Literary Reference. A very good desk book for the student and scholar. Contains valuable chronological tables. Shanghai, 1924. 8vo.

MENDOZA, PADRE JUAN GONZALEZ DE, *The History of the Great and Mighty Kingdom of China and the Situation Thereof.* Translation by R. Parke and edited by Sir George T. Staunton. Hakluyt Society. London, 1855. 2 vols. 8vo.

MEYER, ERNEST H. F., *Geschichte der Botanik.* Königsberg, 1854-57. Contains a chapter on Marco Polo's records of plant life.

MONTGOMERY, JAMES A., *History of Yaballaha III Nestorian Pa-*

triarch and of His Vicar Bar Sauma. Mongol Ambassador to the Frankish Courts at the end of the 13th century. Translated from the Syriac. New York, 1927. 8vo.

MOSHEIM, L., *Historia Tartarorum Ecclesiastica.* Helmstadi, 1741.

MULLER, EUGÈNE, *Deux Voyages en Asie au 13° Siècle*, par Guillaume Rubruquis et Marco Polo. Paris, 1888. 18mo.

MURRAY, H., *Historical Account of Discoveries and Travels in Asia, from the Earliest Ages to the Present Time.* Vol. I contains accounts of Marco Polo and travels between India and China. 8vo.

NEWTON, ARTHUR PERCIVAL, *Travel and Travellers of the Middle Ages.* Contains chapters on "The Opening of the Land Routes to Cathay," by Eileen Power and "Prester John and the Empire of Ethiopia," by Professor Newton. London, 1926. 8vo.

OPPERT, G., *Der Presbyter Johannes in Sage und Geschichte.* Berlin, 1864.

PALAFOX, SEÑOR, *The History of the Conquest of China by the Tartars.* Translated from the Spanish. 1671. 8vo.

PALGRAVE, SIR FRANCIS, *The Merchant and the Friar.* An interesting volume of imaginary conversations between Marco Polo and Roger Bacon. London, 1837.

PARISIENSIS, MATTHAEIS, *Chronica Majora.* Edited by Henry R. Luard. London. 5 vols. 8vo.

PARKER, E. H., *A Thousand Years of the Tartars.* This volume gives an account of the nomad Tartars before the Conquests of Genghis Khan and a history of China before the arrival of Marco Polo. London, 1924. 8vo.

RANKING, J., *Historical Researches on the Wars and Sports of the Mongols and Romans*, in which elephants and wild beasts were employed or slain. 1826. 4to.

RAWLINSON, GEORGE, *Five Great Monarchies of the Ancient Eastern World.* London, 1879. 3 vols. 8vo.

RENAUDOT, EUSEBIUS, *Ancient Accounts of India and China by Two Mohammedan Travellers*, who went to those parts in the 9th century. Translated from the Arabic. London, 1733. 12mo.

RITTER, CARL, *Die Erdkunde von Asien.* Berlin, 1832.

ROCKHILL, W. WOODVILLE, *The Land of the Lamas.* New York, 1891. 8vo.

ROCKHILL, W. WOODVILLE, *Diary of a Journey Through Mongolia and Tibet in 1891 and 1892.* Washington, 1894. 8vo.

——, *The Life of the Buddha,* and the Early History of His Order. Translated from Tibetan Works. London, 1907. 8vo.

——, *The Journey of William of Rubruck to the Eastern Parts of the World, 1253-55, as narrated by himself, with two accounts of the Earlier Journey of John of Pian de Carpini.* Translated from the Latin. Contains many valuable and scholarly notes. Hakluyt Society. London, 1900. 8vo.

ROCKHILL, W. WOODVILLE, and HIRTH, FRIEDRICH, *Chau Ju-Kua.* His work on the Chinese and Arab Trade in the 12th and 13th centuries, entitled *Chu-fan-chi.* Translated from the Chinese and annotated. In English. St. Petersburg, 1912. 4to.

RUBRUK, *Der Bericht des Franziskaners Wilhelm von Rubruk über seine Reise in das Innere Asiens in den Jahren, 1253-55.* First complete translation into German, edited by H. Herbst. 1925. 8vo.

SCHILTBERGER, JOHANN, *The Bondage and Travels of, in Europe, Asia and Africa.* 1396-1427. Translated by J. Buchan Telfer. Hakluyt Society. London, 1879. 8vo.

STEIN, SIR AUREL, *Ruins of Desert Cathay.* London, 1912. 2 vols. 8vo.

——, *Sand-buried Ruins of Khotan.* London, 1903. 8vo.

——, *Ancient Khotan.* Oxford, 1907. 2 vols. 4to.

SYKES, MAJOR PERCY MOLESWORTH, *Ten Thousand Miles in Persia, or Eight Years in Irán.* London, 1902. 8vo.

TAYLOR, ISAAC, *The Alphabet.* An Account of the Origin and Development of Letters. London, 1883. 2 vols. 8vo.

TENNEY, C. D., *Geography of Asia.* Assisted by Hsueh Lung Hsun. Contains Chinese and English Vocabulary. 1898. 4to.

TYLOR, EDWARD B., *Primitive Culture.* Researches into the Development of Mythology, Philosophy, Religion, Language, Art and Custom. 2 vols. 8vo.

——, *Researches into the Early History of Mankind and Development of Civilization.* 8vo.

Tarikh-i-Rashidi, The, of Muhammad Haidar, by Dugulát. *A History of the Moghuls of Central Asia.* English version edited by N. Elias and translated by E. Denison Ross. London, 1895. 8vo.

TIMKOWSKI, *Travels.* Edited by Klaproth. London, 1827.

VARTHEMA, LUDOVICO DI, *The Travels of.* Translated by J. Winter Jones and edited by George Percy Badger. Hakluyt Society. London, 1864. 8vo.

VIGNE, G. T., *Travels in Kashmir, Etc.* London, 1842.

WRIGHT, THOMAS, *Early Travels in Palestine.* London, 1848. Contains text of Travels of Rabbi Benjamin of Tudela.

WYLIE, A., *Chinese Researches.* Contains chapters on Prester John, Israelites in China and Buddhist Relics. 1897. 8vo.

YETTS, W. PERCIVAL, *Discoveries of the Kozlov Expedition.* Giving an account of the objects excavated in 1924-5 from tombs in Northern Mongolia.

YULE, SIR HENRY, and CORDIER, HENRI, *Cathay and the Way Thither,* being a Collection of Mediæval Notices of China. New edition. Vol. I, Intercourse between China and the Western Nations before the Discovery of the Cape Route, 1915. Vol. II, Odoric of Pordenone, 1913. Vol. III, Missionary Friars, Rashíduddín, Pegolotti, Marignolli, 1914. Vol. IV, Ibn Batuta, Benedict Goës, 1916. Hakluyt Society. London. 4 vols. 8vo.

YULE, SIR HENRY, *The Book of Ser Marco Polo,* the Venetian, Concerning the Kingdoms and Marvels of the East. Third edition revised by Henri Cordier. The most complete and scholarly work on Marco Polo and his travels, containing a small encyclopædia in the form of notes on Mediæval Asia. London, 1921. 2 vols. Third vol. of notes and addenda, by Henri Cordier. London, 1920.

INDEX

Aaron, brother of Moses, 272
Abassi, Calif Emir-al-Mumenin al,
   244, 286 *et seq.*, 314
  benevolence of, 288-289
  character, 286
  friendliness toward Jews, 286
  household customs, 287
  in procession, 287 *et seq.*
  palace, 286, 287
  protection for, 287
  reception of pilgrims, 286-287
  revolt against, 314
Abchamas, King, 282
Abitaleb, Ali ben, 314
Abraham, 284
  house of, 278
Abulghazi, 33
Abydos, 264
Abyssinia, 315, 318
Acatron, 201
Acco, 271
Achelaus, 262
Acias (*see* Alans)
Acon, 206, 207
Acre (Acco), 271
Aden (Eden), 312
Africa, 200, 318
Agriculture, in the Nile delta, 315
Ahab, King, 271
  palace ruins, 272
Ahasuerus, King, 298
Ailah (Elim), 319
Aini, friars in, 204
Ain Japhata, 294
Ajalon, valley of, 273
Akbara, 285
Ala Kul Sea, 121
Alania, 81, 97
Alans, 22, 36, 77, 78, 86, 95, 97, 161,
  196, 197
  château of, 198
  country of the, 291
  Greek customs, 78
  murderous bands of, 96
  unconquered by Tartars, 197
Alayeddin Mohammed, 37 *note*

Albania, 97
Al-Boutidg, 317
Aleppo (Aram Zoba), 283
Alexander III, Pope, 257
Alexander the Great, 86, 97, 217, 262,
  263, 291, 317
  construction of Iron Gate, 198
  fortifications of, 199
  walls of, 104
Alexandria, 254, 316
  foreign trade of, 318
  hostelries in, 319
  lighthouse of, 317-318
  tomb of unknown king, 319
Algarve (*see* Portugal)
Algub, 283
Al-Khataab, Omar Ben, 274
Al-Khorkh, 292
Al-Kotsonaath, 294
Alma, 280
Al-Nil (*see* Nile River)
Alphabet, Chaldæan, 319
  Hebrew, 273
  Mongols acquired, 14, 117
Alsodo, 322
Al-Yemen, 295
Al-Zahara, sand storms in, 313
Amalfi, 260, 318
Amana River, 281
Amaria, 300
Ambassadors, 40
  at court of Mangu Khan, 187
  Christians from Damascus, 136
  gifts compulsory, 21
  Russian, 29
  suggested Mongol, 48
  treatment of, 20-21, 49, 135-136
  Vastacius's, 171
Amiri, 300
Ammon, worship of, 269
Ammoric, 136
Anatolica, 262
Anax, 207
Andalusia, 318
Andreas of Russia, Duke, 8

335